Journey to Obscurity

JOURNEY TO OBSCURITY

The Life of Octave Thanet

by

GEORGE McMICHAEL

UNIVERSITY OF NEBRASKA PRESS · LINCOLN

Arthur Davison Ficke's poem "My Princess," copyright 1922, copyright renewed 1950, is used with the permission of Mrs. Arthur Davison Ficke.

Publishers on the Plains

UNP

Copyright © 1965 by the University of Nebraska Press

All rights reserved

Library of Congress Catalog card number 64–19852

Manufactured in the United States of America

Contents

v

List of Illustrations

JOURNEY TO OBSCURITY

Introduction

Her real name was Alice French. A rich man's daughter, she used the fussy, Victorian-sounding name Octave Thanet while trying to describe life's common realities. Her treatment of nineteenth-century America was richly praised by the major critics: Howells once said she surpassed Mary Wilkins Freeman; Thomas Wentworth Higginson put her "at the head of American writers of fiction." For thirty years she was among the highest-paid authors in the United States. Her realism, her fictional representation of contemporary problems like the Pullman Strike and what she and her age called the "Negro Question" helped make her one of the most notable of what are now described as the local colorists. She was a woman who could have been equal to success and greatness, but the first was impermanent, the second came not at all. She has missed literary beatification by this age. Her name decorates neither monument nor park; her books are out of print; her short stories can only be searched out among bound volumes of old magazines; the art she practiced has been absorbed by regionalists and travel editors; and from a position of consequence among fiction writers of the last century, she has fallen to dutiful mention in literary histories as a member of a school and an influence on the course of American writing.

An example of the collapsed literary reputation, her fame transitory as her function was transitional, she shared her role with a number of the late nineteenth century's literary spinsters—the unique cluster that included the Misses Jewett, Wilkins (until she married at fifty), Murfree, and Woolson—an assortment of tempers and attitudes that will never be duplicated, for the world that created them and celebrated them has been pulled apart by its own paradoxes.

That Victorian world is now enjoying revival by a modern age attracted to the contradiction of *décolletage* and well-wrapped ankles. And it has remained a world best displayed in minor matters—not in presidents and parliaments but in the rages, the morals, and the manners of our grandparents, and in the origins, the achievements, and the failures of an Alice French.

I have tried to indicate what kind of person Alice French was, what she sprang from, how her ideas developed out of her family, her social group, and her own experiences. I have tried to show how she was like those around her and how unlike them, how she was like her own age and how unlike the one that followed. Some of her assumptions are obvious. She celebrated the Victorian eternals of honesty, loyalty, justice, courage, and common sense; but as with the rest of her age, doubt and panic undermined the solid ramparts of her morality—a lofty bulwark which came to her at birth, along with New England ancestors and a tendency to diabetes.

She was a blend of middle western and New England cultures, a combination that animated her writing but kept her from finding comfort in a world of drift and uncertainty. Her literary devices were a preamble for later writers, but she came to oppose change, social or literary: she defended conservative nineteenth-century free enterprise and all it embraced; she spoke and wrote against Prohibition, the naturalization of foreigners, even woman suffrage, as vigorously as she had once defended her realism or what she later joined with her friend Hamlin Garland in calling "Veritism."

Apostles of change get full treatment in biographies and histories; literary conservatives are rarely examined and little understood. But it is true that recently local colorists have figured to an increasing degree in biographies like this one, which discuss more life than literature. For the writers of local color, especially the literary women who were a large and effective part of the movement, are most valuable as indices to the taste and culture of their times and to the range of American culture. Alice French's heritage had origins old and elegant, and it culminated just before her birth. It is best to start there.

I. Monuments and Ancestors

In the United States, 1850 was a year not for retrospection but for apprehension and amazement. It was a time of expansion and contraction—of the Gold Rush to California and the abandonment of New England farm land, of the beginning of the railroads and the ending of the canals. Cholera came to the Middle West from Asia, and the first sparrows were imported from Europe to protect the shade trees of New York from caterpillars. Amelia Bloomer's full knee-length trousers for women were becoming popular, and so was chewing gum. In 1850, sophisticated New Yorkers, intrigued with the new possibilities of democracy, went to the theater to see *The New York Fireman and Bond Street Heiress*, the same year the slave trade was abolished in the District of Columbia. *Harper's Magazine* was founded in New York, and the Fox sisters held seances, popped their toe bones, and perplexed science. Zachary Taylor was President, the twelfth; the Civil War was still a decade away.

In March of 1850, George Henry French and his wife, Frances, were living in the right half of a double, brick house in Andover, Massachusetts, about a mile up Main Street from the center of the village. The house stood on Andover Hill, near the town's chief ornaments: across the way was the Andover Theological Seminary, and beside it, the buildings of Phillips Academy. In the midst of such manifest New England piety and learning, Alice French was born, on Tuesday, March 19, 1850.

She was born in the right-hand corner room on the second floor of the respectable three-story house which still stands and which like others in Andover was surrounded by green lawns, maple and walnut trees, and the tall, austere brick houses of the seminary professors. It was a large house with an immigrant servant to clean and cook—a proper establishment for a reputable family which would thrive in the world.

3

The parentage of the baby girl was as noteworthy to a nineteenth-century New England newly awakened to the glory of Pilgrims and ancestries as it would be one day to Alice French herself. The marriage of George French of Andover to Frances Wood Morton of Taunton joined two families whose forebears had come as pioneers to the infant colonies on the Massachusetts coast more than two centuries before. Later in life Alice French would find in this heritage an inspiration and guide for ethics and politics, a standard in retrospect that gave meaning and order to the confusing American experience, an ancestry she would memorialize in her fiction and in her membership in societies and sisterhoods which celebrated patriotism, New England, and distinguished genealogies.

William French of Essex, England, the first of the family to appear in America, arrived in 1635. With his wife, Elizabeth, and his four children, he had embarked in August, 1635, on the *Defence* out of London, with a group of dissenting notables including Thomas Shepard, soon to become pastor at New Towne (Cambridge), his brother Samuel Shepard, and, it is said, Thomas Hooker, escaping from the English Court of High Commission and charges of treasonous religious unorthodoxy. According to one tradition, Hooker (who later ruptured theocracy in New England by moving his congregation into the wilderness of Connecticut) baptized William French's youngest son, John, during the passage to the new world.[1]

The *Defence* landed at Boston after a voyage of slightly less than two months. Soon afterward, William French moved to Cambridge, where he became a tailor. By 1653, he had settled in Billerica, Massachusetts, and had become a church deacon, town selectman, examiner of children and servants in "reading, religion and the catechism," and the first representative from Billerica to the General Court (legislature) in Boston. In 1675 he was an officer in the war against the confederation of Indians led by Massasoit's son, King Phillip, and by 1681, when he died, William French had sired fourteen children by two wives, had reached the rank of captain of militia, and had left behind him a

[1] Hooker, "the sternest autocrat of them all," perhaps came as a servant to avoid having his name carried on the passenger list of the ship, in an attempt to side-step an order of the Privy Council that would have halted his passage. Later accounts of Hooker's passage to America differ. See James Savage, *A Genealogical Dictionary of the First Settlers of New England* (Boston, 1860), Vol. II, and the *Dictionary of American Biography*.

reputation as a leading citizen, author,[2] and Christianizer of savages, as well as an estate worth £300.

His descendants remained in New England, marrying Lathrops and Kittridges and continuing the martial reputation of their forebear. The rosters of soldiers in the American Revolution include five Frenches who honored their descendants by joining the force that was sent to occupy Bunker Hill but instead occupied Breed's Hill and there fought off an army of British regulars. Among the American casualties was one Eleazer French, whose arm was shot off by a British volley but who retired from the battle in good order, proudly carrying the severed limb in his other hand.

By 1800, William French's descendants had settled in Andover, where twenty-five years later Alice's father was born. When George French was twelve, his father and mother died. The following year he entered Andover's Phillips Academy. When he was sixteen, he apprenticed himself to a leather dealer in Boston; and after a five-year apprenticeship, he opened a shop of his own on Shoe and Leather Street in the center of Boston's leather and hides trade.

George French had a Yankee capacity for making money, and by the time he was twenty-three, he was a successful Boston leather merchant. Now a man with property and a good future, he began to look for a wife. According to family tradition, he fell in love with Frances Morton when he saw her picture in the window of a Boston photographer's shop, and within a year, on September 27, 1849, he married the twenty-year-old daughter of eminent Marcus Morton of Taunton.

The ancestry of Frances Morton was as distinguished as her husband's and provided their daughter not only with Morton family heirlooms but with a link to a "usable" past and an elevated social status that influenced the direction of her life and gave comforting sanction to her opinions. The Mortons, like the Frenches, were militant, literary, dutiful, and successful—qualities which later seemed to converge centripetally on Alice French and become her nature. The city records of Leyden, Holland, list the wedding of George Morton, "merchant from York in England," to Juliana Carpenter, "maid from

[2] A letter from William French to "a godly friend in England," describing an Indian converted to Christianity, was published in London in the early tract *Strength out of Weakness*, reprinted in the Massachusetts Historical Society *Collections*, 3d Series, IV, 149–196.

Bath in England," on July 23/August 2, 1612. The son of a well-to-do Roman Catholic gentleman at Harworth, George Morton had been impressed by the English Puritans and their zealous dissenting attacks on the "proud, Popish, presumptuous, profane, paultrie, pestilent and pernicious" Anglican clergy and that "masse of old and stinkinge workes," the established church.[3] He was attracted to the dissenting church in Scrooby, only a short distance from Harworth, and there was converted by William Brewster, the organizer of the Pilgrim Congregation, and became one of the members of the original Scrooby group before its flight to Holland.

After their marriage in Leyden, George Morton and his wife returned to England, where he apparently changed his name to Mourt, possibly to escape the wrath of his Roman Catholic family and the attention of the Anglican authorities. For a time he served as the chief Pilgrim agent in London, and there in 1622 received an account of the Pilgrims' adventures (largely the work of Governor Bradford and Edward Winslow) sent to London by the colonists. This earliest history of the Plymouth Colony George Morton published in London in 1622, under the name "Mourt" as *Relation Or Iournall of the beginning and proceedings of the English Plantation setled at Plimoth in New England, by certaine English Adventurers both Merchants and others*, a title so cumbersome it soon became known as *Mourt's Relation*. The book was designed to attract settlers to the English "Plantation" in New England, and it became famous for its descriptions of the Pilgrims' voyage on the *Mayflower*, their relations with the Indians, and the details of their first Thanksgiving.

In 1623, George Morton organized and joined the fourth company to migrate to Plymouth. The group left London on the *Little James* and the *Anne*, the latter carrying some sixty passengers, including George Morton; his wife and children; and his sister-in-law, the widowed Alice Carpenter Southworth, going to America to marry Governor Bradford, whose first wife, Dorothy May, had drowned, "falling from the deck of the *Mayflower*, into the sea."

George Morton lived less than one year in the new land when, "with much comfort and peace, he fell asleep in the Lord, in the month of June, Anno 1624."[4] On his death, Governor Bradford took the

[3] George F. Willison, *Saints and Strangers* (New York, 1945), pp. 29, 39.

[4] Nathaniel Morton, *New England's Memoriall*, ed. Howard J. Hall (New York, 1937), p. 48.

responsibility of raising the Morton children, now the Governor's nieces and nephews. The oldest, Nathaniel, became Bradford's secretary and a man his fellow colonists described as "very religiously tender and carefull in his observations of the Sabbath day and· of speaking the truth."[5] When he was thirty-five, Nathaniel became secretary of the Plymouth Colony, a position he held until he was seventy-two. Later he served as secretary of the council organized to conduct the war against King Phillip, the war in which William French was serving as an officer of militia from Billerica.

The bookish interests of George Morton were equally apparent in his son, for the best known of all Nathaniel's achievements was his *New Englands Memoriall* (1669), which was based on Governor Bradford's unpublished history of Plymouth Plantation and presented an account of the colony's development from 1620 to 1658, a description which served for almost two hundred years as the standard history of the settlement of New England. Like his father, Nathaniel Morton wrote in a plain style and with an evangelical fervor to commemorate good men and exhort backsliders, qualities and purposes which would be shared by his descendant Alice French two centuries later, for her mind and art were equally shaped by her locality and the sect in which she passed her life.

From the children of the original George Morton of the Scrooby Congregation, four generations of respected New England patriarchs descended to Alice French's maternal grandfather, Marcus Morton, the earliest ancestor she ever saw or knew and one of the most notable.[6] When he died, in 1864, he had fathered twelve children, among them, Lydia, the wife of the Episcopal Bishop of Iowa; Marcus Morton II,

[5] Willison, *Saints and Strangers*, p. 447.

[6] Marcus Morton was born one year after the American Revolution. When he was twenty-seven, he began one of the most unusual political careers in New England's history. First a clerk of the State Senate of Massachusetts, he then became Democratic representative from Massachusetts to the Fifteenth and Sixteenth Congresses. Four years later he was lieutenant-governor of Massachusetts and in the same year (1825) became a justice of the Massachusetts Supreme Court. Three years later he began his notable marathon as a perennial candidate for the office of Governor of Massachusetts: from 1828 to 1843 he ran sixteen times, winning only twice. In 1839 he defeated the Unitarian preacher and incumbent, Edward Everett, in an election he won by a single vote; in 1842 he was elected over John Davis. At the age of sixty-four he acquired further distinction by refusing to run for the Vice-Presidency of the United States on the Free-Soil ticket with Van Buren.

also a justice of the Massachusetts Supreme Court; and Frances Wood Morton, the wife of George French.

In addition to Mortons and Frenches, there were other honored New England names in the family ancestry—Danforth, Endicott, and Mayhew. Many of them belonged to people who were humble in their origins and in their lives but who became aristocrats in the recollections of their descendants and provided names for the affluent heroes in the fiction of Alice French. In the splendor of her genealogy there was even one of the first company of Pilgrims to land at Plymouth from the first *Mayflower*—a Degory Priest, hatter of London.

II. The Dove's Nest

The Massachusetts town in which Alice French was born was self-conscious, Protestant, learned, and penitent. The 1850 census of Andover reported a population of seven thousand in its three parishes, and the 1847 *Gazetteer of Massachusetts* proclaimed that its female academy possessed "a valuable philosophical apparatus and a cabinet of minerals." Over the years since the town's original site had been purchased from the Indians for £6 and a coat,[1] Andover had acquired all the historical sanctity necessary to a well-bred New England village. In 1692 it had suffered from the witchcraft delusion—sufficiently to interest antiquarians without exciting sentimentalists. Of eight Andoverians who admitted baptism by the devil in riotous, midnight meetings, three were eventually hanged and one died in prison. George Washington had visited Andover, first as a Revolutionary War general, later, in 1789, as first President of the new republic, when he addressed the Phillips Academy student body from horseback.

Andover of the 1850's was full of respectable men and women and proper boys and girls. Their stock was overwhelmingly English. Some immigrant Irish had arrived, but they made good servants and knew their station, and few Middle Europeans had come with gross habits and *Sozialismus*. Middle-class economy was more evident than poverty, and gentility most apparent of all. Some industry was visible, but nothing like that in Lowell or Lawrence, and what little there was remained largely on the other side of the Boston and Maine Rail Road tracks. Even the principal exception, Pike's Soap Works, adjacent to the Theological Seminary, demonstrated the unique state of grace of a town where cleanliness was literally next to godliness.

Andover's major product was the educated mind—secular and divine, and most prominent in creating this commodity was the

[1] Federal Writers' Project, *Massachusetts* (Boston, 1937), p. 492.

9

Andover Theological Seminary, across the street from the Frenches. The seminary had set a tone of Calvinistic rectitude for the villagers since it was established early in the nineteenth century to counteract the outbreak of Unitarian heresy at Harvard, and it had succeeded in making Andover the town Oliver Wendell Holmes called "the very dove's nest of Puritan faith." Because of the seminary, religiosity permeated the lives of village children as well as adults. Proper little boys did climb trees and walk fences, but they also played preacher and addressed make-believe congregations, expounding the theologies of their parents. Little girls fervidly studied the canons of Congregationalism, hearing lectures on purification and immortality; and they displayed their knowledge in ecclesiastical quiz games, worried at the doctrine of original sin, and took part in rigid observances of churchly propriety. But while the seminary's orthodoxy was spread around the world by zealous missionaries, its Congregational doctrines failed to cross the street and penetrate George French's red brick house and its Episcopalian inhabitants.

A second and even more celebrated instrument of righteousness came to Andover two years after Alice was born. There were precedents for such an advent; the village already had some literary monuments: Anne Bradstreet, the "Tenth Muse Lately Sprung Up in America" had lived close by on a farm near the Merrimac River; Elizabeth Stuart Phelps, the daughter of the formidable theologian Moses Stuart, had just written *The Sunny Side*; and in 1832 a seminary student named Samuel Francis Smith had composed the anthem "America" in half an hour. But in 1852 all this mattered little compared to the arrival of the most famous woman in the world, Harriet Beecher Stowe.

Calvin Stowe, Harriet's husband, had been appointed Professor of Sacred Literature at the seminary, and shortly afterward, his wife arrived at the dour town with its "long street of houses with closed doors and window blinds."[2] Soon the Stowes were living near the Frenches in a building close to the seminary grounds, a stone structure that had been the school's gymnasium, only recently converted from a shop producing the seminary's second most popular product—coffins. While living in her stone house, Harriet Stowe wrote *Dred*, a novel that later was compared, and unfavorably, to one written years afterward by the daughter of the Frenches living across the way.

Authorship was only one of many of the duties of Harriet Stowe, for

[2] Forrest Wilson, *Crusader in Crinoline* (New York, 1941), p. 405.

"thin and dry as a pinch of snuff," as she described herself, she was everywhere, directing charities, raising funds for the female academy, holding levees, planning trips to the beach at Salem for a chowder, and discussing "that most hideous blot and foul disgrace—slavery." Andoverians soon were calling her ugly old stone house "Uncle Tom's Cabin," and to the Andover children, the woman in it became the "goddess from Olympus." Such an audacious newcomer had seldom been seen in Andover, and soon Harriet Stowe's enterprise brought criticism of her elaborate decoration of what she had christened her "Stone Cabin," and ugly rumours spread that she had been seen in a Boston theater and leaned toward Anglo-Catholicism.

Shortly after Harriet Stowe moved into her new home and began to write her *Key to Uncle Tom's Cabin*, the Frenches moved off Andover Hill into a 140-year-old white frame Manse on School Street, opposite the South Congregationalist Church. The Manse was larger than the house on the hill and only two blocks along School Street from the home of Frances French's brother, Marcus Morton II. The family no longer lived close by the Theological Seminary, but for George French, the Manse was only a short walk past the parsonage of his Episcopal Church and down Brook Street to the Boston and Maine passenger station for the twenty-three-mile trip to Boston and his leather firm.

George French had come a long way from his apprenticeship. He was now one of the new and acquisitive patricians—the rich business-men and merchants who lacked the education or the inclination to enter the New England vocational trinity of the law, medicine, and the church—and thus he was unlike his dissenting New England ancestors in more things than his return to Anglican theologies. Yet the French family still observed New England traditions, particularly the homely ones like Saturday night baked beans and brown bread with cider vinegar and black New Orleans molasses, followed by Sunday morning breakfasts of codfish cakes. A modern and more cosmopolitan fashion was late dinner after the more formal custom of the bigger cities. Each day when Alice's father returned from Boston, the evening meal was served in the dining room, still the chief room of the house. Sometimes Alice's august grandfather, Marcus Morton I, or her uncle, Marcus Morton II, came to sit at her mother's right, at elegant meals from which Alice was sent early to bed.

The house on School Street had spacious rooms with high ceilings and a front hall decorated with substantial furniture, some of it brought to the marriage by Frances, some of it saved by George French from his parents' home. Upstairs there were rooms for the growing family; by 1853 three children had been born: Alice, now three years old; Morton, who was one year younger than Alice and had been born while the family still lived on Andover Hill; and in the nursery the new baby, Charlotte. The following spring, Charlotte died, but her place was filled a year later by a baby boy named Nathaniel after his mother's illustrious Pilgrim ancestor, Nathaniel Morton of Plymouth.

In 1855, the Andover census of the house on School Street listed George and Frances (entered on the roll as "Fanny"), Alice, four-year-old Morton, and Nathaniel; as well as two maids, the Slane girls, and the man servant, Timothy Callahan, all immigrants from Ireland.

In that same year, sometime after Alice was five, her father began to display symptoms of tuberculosis. When his ailment was first diagnosed, George French considered moving to Missouri. In the middle of the ninteenth century, life in the West was thought to be a strong anodyne for consumption, and business had once taken George French to the Mississippi at St. Louis. But an alternative soon appeared. Frances' sister, Lydia, was the wife of the Reverend Henry Washington Lee, once Episcopal Minister of Rochester, New York, and since 1854 the first Episcopal Bishop of the new state of Iowa. In October, 1855, Bishop Lee had toured the East to solicit funds for his new diocese, and the Frenches and Mortons in Andover heard of the virtues of Iowa and the town of Davenport, the seat of the diocese.

The enticements of Iowa which the Bishop described were complemented by the flow of propaganda directed eastward from Iowa in the 1850's and designed to promote migration of settlers and capital, just as the Pilgrim tracts of the seventeenth century had sought converts to godliness and prosperity. In the year of the Bishop's visit, *Iowa as It Is in 1855: A Gazetteer for Citizens and a Hand-Book for Emmigrants* appeared in New England, and the next year, the *Iowa Handbook for 1856* offered work for laborers, land for farmers, and addressed itself to the moneyed with:

> A word to Capitalists—Here as elsewhere, it "takes money to make money," but not so much of it. Eastern men . . . can make 50% more money here, with the same investment, than they can in the East. . . . There is scarce a river, town or city in the state where buildings are not rented . . . for from one third to one half their original cost per annum.

These were impressive "words," even when discounted 50 per cent by wise readers; and in the spring of 1856, George French decided to move his family west to Davenport, Iowa.

The business on Shoe and Leather Street was sold—and for a good price. The family withdrew from Christ Episcopal Church, said goodbyes to friends and relatives, made last visits to Charlotte's grave, and in May gathered at the Andover station of the Boston and Maine to begin the journey west. Their trunks—including a large, round-topped trunk holding Alice's childhood possessions—were piled on the station platform, and the children gathered around their parents to await the train that would take them to Boston on the first portion of the long trip. It was not an easy undertaking. George and Frances French were leaving behind deep roots in the barren New England soil, on a migration that would take them across half a continent; they were seeking a new American Canaan as their dissenting ancestors had, but now the journey was less arduous, for the new railroads went all the way to the Mississippi River, and the family was not leaving persecution for starvation. George French was going west with thirty thousand dollars in sound Massachusetts money.

III. Davenport and Andover

The whole nation was moving west. The lowly were leaving the eastern seaboard to seek the New Jerusalem; the mighty were deserting plantation lands that no longer supported ruinous farming and large families. Others were wanderers—by now wandering was an American characteristic.

If George French had taken his family west only a few years before, the trip would have been a long ordeal by wagon across New England, then by boat down Lakes Champlain and George to the Erie Canal and westward to the Great Lakes and Chicago, and from there, farther west by wagon on corduroy roads and double-track trails over the prairie to the Mississippi River. But by 1856 the journey that had required three weeks took less than four days by train.

What had been harrowing was now only uncomfortable and squalid. One of the many Englishmen who suffered barbarisms in America for the benefit of English readers had complained of the trains:

> There is no room to deposit any small articles under one's feet, and even if there was, they would be spit on to a certainty; indeed, even in the event of dropping money on the floor no decent person would venture to pick it up unless he put on an old glove.[1]

For such indecencies, Alice and her mother dressed in the protective muffling of the day's traveling gentlewoman—high-necked dresses with bell-shaped skirts under long linen dusters worn to shield them against the dirt and filth of a railroad trip.

The coaches they rode in had rigid, uncomfortable seats. Some coaches had reclining chairs, but ladies did not recline in public nor did they enter the new sleeping cars. Heat came from wood stoves, and when it was dark, candles provided light—it was dim but candles were

[1] Quoted in August Mencken, *The Railroad Passenger Car* (Baltimore, 1957), p. 115.

better than oil lamps that would set the coaches on fire when the train lurched off the rails, an event so common that some railroad tickets stipulated that passengers could be required to help shove derailed cars and engines back on the track. Yet in spite of dirt and dim lights, most of the terror of migration west by train had disappeared. New "T" rails were replacing the deadly iron straps that often came loose and curled up through the floor of the flimsy cars to skewer an occasional passenger and pin him to the roof, and an exploding boiler on a locomotive was much less dangerous than a boiler explosion on river boats the Frenches might have taken.

The journey west really began at Boston. From there the family traveled to Worcester, where a dray took them across town to the Western Rail Road and its line to Albany. Such a transfer was repeated in town after town as the Frenches progressed from Buffalo to Cleveland to Toledo and to Chicago, for the individual lines were composed of a variety of rail gauges, and coaches could not be shifted. Arrival in Chicago meant the trip was almost over; George French's objective was the new mercantile and industrial frontier just developing on the Mississippi. The government's official frontier line, indicating two to six inhabitants per square mile, had passed through Davenport in 1830, and even the line of settlement that moved slowly behind it had long since passed beyond the river. Davenport was only eight hours from Chicago, and for five dollars each the Frenches could ride west on the Rock Island Rail Road over the newest line in the state, a route opened only two years before when the mayor of Chicago and the city council had ridden a flag- and evergreen-bedecked train to Rock Island to the accompaniment of bands and exploding cannon.

Alice first saw Davenport from the levee on the Illinois shore, where the family stood waiting for the ferry to take them across the Mississippi to Iowa. Earlier in the month they could have ridden the train over the first bridge to cross the Mississippi. That engineering marvel had been finished in April, but after only three weeks, the steamboat *Effie Afton*—directed, some said, by St. Louis money—struck one of the piers of the bridge, setting it on fire. Had it been winter, the family would have ridden over one of the roadways laid out across the ice of the frozen river, but by May the ice was out, and the only way across was on the steam ferry.[2]

At Davenport the ferry landed at the foot of Brady Street, on the

[2] At 18 3/4¢ for a footman or a mule.

levee. There the family was greeted by Bishop Lee and his wife, the children's Aunt Lydia. The new arrivals, mother and father and the children, could see the town rising on the bluffs before them—blocks of houses, churches, mills, and shanties, with the burnt criss-crossed members of the wooden bridge stretching across the river to their right, and the sawdust burners of the lumber mills shooting sparks into the sky along the Iowa shore. Davenport was a farming and river town like others on the Mississippi, and in 1856 it was a mixture of earnest pretension and sordid reality. It boasted thirteen hundred houses and two miles of macadamized streets. Though it had no sewage system, the town was on the new telegraph line that stretched all the way to the Atlantic. Reminders of frontier days were mixed with signs of migrant eastern gentility. While the 1855 census of Davenport males recorded more laborers and carpenters than anything else, it also listed three architects, five booksellers, sixteen clergymen, four professors (one of moral and mental philosophy), as well as six "gentlemen" and five "loafers."

The two newspapers, the Whig *Gazette* and the *Democrat*, were less devoted to the news than to politicking and blatant endorsement of advertisers. The advertisements themselves were unlike anything seen in Andover—a curious mixture of Victorian rectitude and frontier exuberance, describing derringers, ladies' dresses, church services, and female pills that carried a solemn warning of their power to cause abortion.

The town was swollen with opportunities for a businessman with money, for good money was scarce. Silver and Mexican dollars were at a premium, and smaller coins were so rare that Mexican dollars were cut into eight pieces, or bits, worth twelve and one-half cents each. No national currency existed—individual banks printed their own, and inflated or "wildcat" currency issued by disreputable banks was purposely circulated as far away as possible to make redemption difficult. The problem was especially severe in Davenport. Issuing paper money was illegal in Iowa; thus Davenport banks offered a bonus of 10 to 25 per cent for such respected currency as George French had brought from Massachusetts.

Fortunately, the city had escaped the checkerboard standardization imposed on villages laid out by the railroads. It was not unlike New England—rawer perhaps, with less shade. Dusty streets were common in Andover, but here there was more dust—and more mud in the spring. The unwary easily got mired when crossing streets that the spring rains and churning wagon wheels had turned into sloughs of deep mud. Alice's uncle, a giant 280-pound man, had once sunk so deep into the mud at Second and Brady that a team of passers-by assembled a human chain to deliver their bishop from the morass and the ridicule of thinner townspeople. And there were other signs of civic rawness. Scavenging pigs ran wild in Davenport streets. Two especially wild animals inhabited a den under the board sidewalks of Second Street and periodically burst forth, scattering groups of startled pedestrians. And even more destructive than pigs were the farmers who annually drove to town and scoured their plow blades by setting the sharp points in the middle of the sandy streets and plowing up and down the roadway by the hour.[3] Worse still than the bad streets was the shortage of decent houses. It was the same in every swelling western community, but fortunately for the Frenches, the Bishop and his wife had found them a gray frame house on the south-west corner of Ripley and Sixth, on rising ground overlooking the river. The house was less elegant than its counterpart in Andover, but it was noble for a time and place where flowers in a bay window were a sign of quality and money.

Wealth was only one of George French's assets. He had all the profitable qualities traditionally assigned to the New England Yankee: he was quick, intelligent, shrewd, and honest; and once his family was established, he looked into a proper business. He had been fortunate enough to arrive in a decade when the population of Iowa was quadrupling from migrants flooding through Davenport on their way to the rich lands of the Iowa interior. And prairie farmers had begun to pour grains, pork, beef, hemp, hides, and even tobacco through Davenport for trans-shipment down the river or eastward over the railroad that began at Rock Island.

Blessed with opportunity, wealth, and the industrious and meticulous habits which seemed to embody all precepts of Poor Richard, George French joined with a John Cannon and formed the Cannon and French Lumber Company. Lumber mills were flourishing in the river towns of the Upper Mississippi. In the past, finished lumber had been shipped all the way from Cincinnati—the wood from trees in the Alleghenies. The product was expensive but necessary, for there was no wood on the

[3] On April 7, 1861, the Davenport *Democrat* reported that the practice had been going on for twenty years.

prairie and farmers needed fences, corn cribs, barns, and houses. Sod huts were no solution—weeds grew out of the walls and the roofs continually leaked. Livestock had to be penned, yet barbed wire fences were thirty years in the future. Osage orange hedge had been used as fencing, but it took four years to grow, and hard winters killed it. Some farmers had even tried ditches three feet wide and two and a half deep, but more cattle were trapped than protected, and the ditch walls collapsed in the winter. The only solution was wood, and it poured out of the Davenport mills, making the farmers happy and the mill owners rich.

The source of it all was a huge forest extending west from Lake Huron into Minnesota, four hundred miles on a side and bisected by the Mississippi. Down that river came long rafts of logs, as much as fifty-four acres a day passed the bridge, logs cut in the northern forests and floated to Davenport and other river-town mills with their efficient new circular saws and their immigrant German mill hands working twelve hours a day, six days a week.

By 1858, the Cannon and French mill had eighty-four employees and was the second largest mill in town. Alice's father had become a man of consequence. He was a Whig turned Republican in a town that had been Democratic until the Kansas-Nebraska Act opened the way for slavery in Kansas and made Republicans out of antislavery westerners. As a solid member of the Davenport oligarchy, George French became treasurer of the school board and of the Episcopal Church.

New as it was, Davenport had an oligarchy—Republicans and businessmen, many of whose views, like their furniture, were made in New England. George French could detest slavery—nothing less was expected from an Andoverian—but he had little faith in social leveling, and for members of his family there was less mixing in a cultural melting pot than there might have been in Hannibal downriver. Alice French was never exposed to the frustrations of village life that led sons and daughters of other middle western settlers to create a literary genre out of their descriptions of the agonies of life in the rural West. And she was not the daughter of a Populist farmer and thus not moved to social protest, as her contemporaries, the prairie realists, were. On the contrary, she enjoyed a social and economic status and an ancestry of Puritan patriarchs that prescribed her mature viewpoints and animated her writing. Westerners like Howells, and Twain, and Garland created literary successes out of the anguish and longing that drove them east to get on in the world. Alice French never had to escape from deprivation or seek a usable past. If her contemporaries achieved greater art with their protests, it was partly because their distance from their origins had given them greater detachment, if not greater skill.

Not all the French family was content with the West even if it brought them prosperity. To Frances French, the land seemed to have the qualities of the American "waste and howling wilderness" that had overawed the first of her Pilgrim ancestors. Shortly after her family was settled in Iowa she wrote home to her friend Lizzie Barrows in Massachusetts:

> Between you and me dear Lizzie, I am heartily tired of the West. I have been bothered to death since I came. How I wish someone I did not love very much would die and leave me a legacy. How quickly would I leave this country behind me. My little ones are playing in the mud which is . . . very deep. Of course, they make terrible work of their clothes. . . . I intend to send them to school. . . . It is high time they were learning something.[4]

In 1858, a third son, George, was born. Two years before, another girl had been born, the couple's fifth child, but a year later the second to die. Deaths of children were common to American families everywhere, but tragedy could be short-lived, and westerners were less concerned with the eternal than were New Englanders. Fewer Davenport children were named for biblical characters, and theology was not disputed in the country and in the town by learned farmers and mechanics. What remained of the traditional New England pastimes was mostly secular—bees, socials, and sleighing parties during the long winters when whole families, packed in sleds full of clean straw, drove fifteen or twenty miles on the heights above the river. Girls learned cooking and housekeeping, boys went hunting, although Alice often accompanied her father and brothers on shooting expeditions where the peak of marksmanship was to "bark" squirrels by shooting into the tree bark under a squirrel's throat, killing without breaking the skin.

In summers she went rowing on the river and horseback riding on the prairie. In the winter she joined in skating races on the frozen Mississippi and refought the Battle of Buena Vista with children on

---

[4] Frances French to Mrs. William Barrows, Reading, Massachusetts, March 2, 1857, quoted in Ruth Tucker, "'Octave Thanet' A Biography of Alice French," MS, Newberry Library, Chicago, p. 1.

the bluffs along the river. Later in life she recalled that her greatest wish was to be so masterful at "one old cat" that she would always be chosen as a team member, even over boys. Childhood fights between Alice and her younger brothers followed a rigid code which permitted fighting only with fists. If Alice bit or scratched, her brothers were allowed to pull her hair.

As she grew older, Alice escaped many of the restraints imposed on little girls in New England. She was living in a masculine world, in a western town where hardships and savages had been the rule only a few years before and where virtue was less palpable than in Andover. Like her brothers and the other children, she was often entertained with tales of Indians and savage wars. The famous Black Hawk had camped at Davenport; and not long before the arrival of the Frenches, roving bands of Indians had come again to the river town, where they spent their days and nights drinking whiskey and frightening the townspeople. Some Indians remained in the area in the late 1850's, but they were mostly half-breeds or partially civilized caricatures of their predecessors. It wasn't until the Civil War that large numbers of Indians appeared again in Davenport, and they were federal prisoners.

In the town itself, the great majority of the population was white— native-born or European. There were a few Negroes on the streets, many of them deck hands on the river boats, but Mississippi River towns were dangerous for freedmen: wandering slave catchers often made little effort to determine the status of the black men they caught and shipped downriver.

While it was a masculine world, girls still played with dolls, though for Alice their attraction was unconventional, for she mutilated the expensive dolls her parents failed to protect and decapitated her paper dolls and nailed their heads to the wall. Her favorite was a knight named Conrad, whose many versions were created out of folded paper. In the midst of high ceremony, she would dress him in armor she had made out of tinfoil and then cut off his head with a pair of sharp scissors and pin it with spears to the wall. In fragments of autobiographical sketches she wrote in her sixties, she recalled, "Conrad belonged to the time when I believed every word of Abbott's 'Napoleon' and devoured Macauley's 'History of England.'" And "there was some thrill in that kind of game. . . . I mourned him long and well. In fact, after Conrad died, I was like the King of England who 'never smiled again.' I played with dolls no more."

Alice French and her brothers (left to right) Morton, George, and Nathaniel

If her energy was deflected into phantasies that cloaked less acceptable impulses, her hostilities to males like Conrad never weakened her attachment to her father, and in her adulthood she never abandoned the dogma of male superiority. Furthermore, it was easy to see Alice's acts as rising less from hostility than from her reading of the lurid popular fiction of the day. The whole family read Robert Bonner's story-paper, the *New York Ledger*, which in the 1850's and 60's was the special province of Mrs. E. D. E. N. Southworth and Sylvanus Cobb, whose novels ran on week after week, one exciting incident and episode wandering disconnectedly into another. The waxy heroines of the novels suffered from chlorosis and high purpose and were a composite of middle-class mores. Heroes were antiseptically pure. Villains were clearly wicked and that was that. The chief problem was virtue's protection. The question was never what to do—all decent people knew that—the problem was how to do it.

The magazine's greeting card sentiments and moralizing romances engaged a vast section of literate America before and after the Civil War and gratified the enormous longing for excitement and romantic adventure that Sir Walter Scott had first satisfied in America's reading public. At the Frenches', when each copy of the magazine arrived, Alice read it avidly, taking it to the table during meals and sitting on it to preserve ownership until the most recent chapter of the latest serial was finished. She suffered anguish and terror with the heroes and heroines of the *Ledger* while it serialized Mrs. Southworth's *The Doom of Deville*, and later *In the Depths* and its sequel, *Self-Raised: Or Out of the Depths*. All the novels were committed to the most pious rectitude. The hero of one, when confronted with a choice of starving or spending money he had found on the road, announced sanctimoniously: "I am sure George Washington would not approve of my taking what don't belong to me for that or any other purpose. And neither would Patrick Henry nor John Hancock."[5]

The alarms and excursions of Mrs. Southworth's novels, like those of Sylvanus Cobb, filled with their mechanical people run by mottoes, stimulated Alice's private daydreams. She was plump and had light brown hair, but the autobiographical fragments that remain among her private papers describe the early heroine of her dreams as dark, languid, and lovely, and with a fashionable neurasthenia—"an adorable beauty what with her long black hair, her pale, classical features and her dark, sad eyes. Why in the world she was unhappy, I

[5] Quoted in Mary Noel, *Villains Galore* (New York, 1954), p. 162.

do not know for she had everything my heart could desire for her."
But even this reverie was out of place in the practical world of duty,
enterprise, and thrift; and a half-century later, in a speech on her
literary apprenticeship, before an audience in Indianapolis, she
described the doubts and fears her daydreams caused:

> I cannot remember an age when I was not telling stories to myself. I told
> them to myself alone for many years; since with the queer secretiveness of
> childhood, I hid my innocent romancing as if it had been wrong. I knew
> it wasn't wrong; but I dreaded lest someone should make fun of it; and I
> loved it so that ridicule would have torn my heart.

By the time Alice was ten, a third daughter had been born to the
family. Named Lydia Lee for the Bishop's wife, she was the Frenches'
third daughter to die in less than ten years—a common enough ratio in
nineteenth-century America. Two years later, in 1862, a fourth
daughter, Frances Morton, was born and survived, but she was never
as close to Alice as her brothers were, or her father, whose personality
dominated the family and drew admiration from the townspeople.

As the family grew and prospered, Davenport itself grew and
continued to shape all their attitudes and interests. And some of the
changes were rapid and unappreciated. Wonderful fires were disasters
to the grownups but roaring spectacles for the children. One great fire
on Brady, three blocks from the Frenches' home, almost burned down
the Roman Catholic Church. Such conflagrations were so common that
an early Davenport ordinance required every householder to have two
water pails for fire fighting, and not long afterward, the town bought
its first fire engines, the *Pilot* and the *Witch*, ten thousand dollars'
worth of gleaming metal and paint that were the joy of the town
children. Alice took trips to the stores, where she wandered with her
mother and one of the help among shelves and racks holding bright
bolts of cloth, men's round-toed shoes that fit either foot, and boys'
boots with bright copper toecaps. Great hogsheads of brown sugar
from St. Louis stood in rooms redolent with the smell of rope, chewing
tobacco, and penny cigars. Usually a barrel of whiskey—free drinks for
the customers—had a tin cup dangling from a chain nailed to the side.
Guns and ammunition were for sale; some men still went armed on the
streets.

The town was full of transplanted New Englanders who had helped
establish a school system years before. George French had the Yankee

passion for self-improvement and formal education, and by 1859, when he was serving as treasurer of the school board, Alice was enrolled in the school at Seventh and Perry, five blocks from her home. The stone schoolhouse had rooms above ground for three departments and living quarters for the principal in the basement. Classrooms were heated by wood-burning stoves that made islands of warmth in large chilly rooms and caused teachers to seat far from the stove those scholars sewn up for the winter in their underwear or pungent from the asafetida bags hung around their necks to ward off illness. In the grammar school, Alice studied Mitchell's geography, Ray's arithmetic, and the ubiquitous *McGuffey's Reader*. Her school days began with devotional exercises; most lessons had a religious tenor, emphasizing that virtue lay in the church, the school, and the family—in about that order. Reading selections presented the same Victorian morality that floated on the surface of popular novels and animated the cant of the day. It was meant to mold bright hearts and a sense of duty, but its relevance was often so specious that it could flourish only in the schoolroom and in the success stories of Ragged Dick or Mark the Match Boy. The poor and honest profited financially, while wicked boys were whipped, starved, and drowned. In fact, wrongdoing was punished with such a Calvinistic certainty that suffering and financial ruin came almost to signify an undiscovered sinfulness. McGuffey ideals were generally ignored by the adult world that preached them; nevertheless, they were absorbed by many who were not daily brought up against their fallibility, if only because of the pertinacity with which a wishful society kept insisting they were true.

Political philosophy in the McGuffey books was conservative and Hamiltonian. Students of the *Eclectic First Reader* learned that in the divinely ordered universe some men were rightfully up and others down. Alice's teachers led their students in chanting out stories and essays expressing doubts about the common man and whether republican America could survive universal suffrage. Such political assumptions were more popular in towns than on farms, and they stuck well in the minds of upper-class children everywhere. Thirty years later they were apparent in Alice's stories of odious foreigners, muddled workers, and social experimenters who erred in upsetting the natural order of society. And they appeared in her writing bathed in a relentless didacticism which overrode her artistry and helped bring her literary eclipse, for one day the world began to lose its abiding faith in hard work and trust in the rich and the inevitable triumph of right over wrong.

By 1863, when Alice was thirteen, a high school had opened at Sixth and Main, in an old church building purchased from the Baptists. Alice attended school there until a final decision was made about a proper eastern education. In high school Alice learned rhetoric, moral philosophy, and some rudimentary science, and she had bookish studies supplemented by Socratic discussions with her father. He had not worked out a philosophy; that had been done for him, but he knew what he believed in. His mind moved around a series of fixed points that lent his conclusions a solidity and consistency that often appeared as probity. He put a high value on law, order, and the existence of classes. He had the standard sentiments about thrift and duty. He assumed the inequality of men and the necessity of obedience. It was the late nineteenth century's "Universe of Discourse," and it led to the aristocratic conclusions successful men enjoyed in every era.

From her father Alice took her belief in the obligations of capital and its perquisites, and the virtues of a society based on conservative traditions. She heard the ideas of revolutionary change and the schemes of the western "levelers" assaulted with such vigor that what Emerson had called the "rank-rabble party, the Jacksonism of the country," became as unattractive to the daughter as it ever was to her father.

Furthermore, Alice was growing up in a highly unusual intellectual environment, partially compounded of a Yankee intellectuality and an immigrant Jewish and German idealism seldom identified by cultural historians drawn largely to the third element in the mixture, frontier practicality and bumptiousness. Davenport had acquired its first printer by out-bidding a neighboring village for his services, for he was not only a civic monument; he could be counted on to advertise his town. Civic pride also demanded a library association and a theater —called an "Opera House" to enhance its value and pacify moralists. The Opera House in Davenport presented Ole Bull, Teresa Paradi, *The Drunkard, East Lynne, Uncle Tom's Cabin, Our American Cousin*, as well as *Othello, Hamlet*, and *Macbeth*, and it shamed competing cities that lacked such signs of municipal high-mindedness.

For less refined audiences, touring freak shows came to Davenport, sometimes as part of a floating circus traveling from town to town up and down the Mississippi and its tributaries—in 1857, Davenport newspapers reported that the large crowds drawn to the latest circus largely went to gaze upon its prime attraction, Julia Pastrana—"half-human, half-beast." "Panoramas," which were moving pictures of painted landscapes or narratives, many over a mile long, were unrolled from tall scrolls before awe-struck audiences and portrayed such things as *Paradise Lost*, or Ireland, or the Overland Route to the Pacific. Between these extravaganzas, eastern lecturers came to western audiences and their money. Davenport and the Frenches listened to Horace Greeley, Henry Ward Beecher, Wendell Phillips, and Emerson.[6] Geologists came, military heroes, authorities and illuminati of all ranks and forms. Characteristically, some of the reasons for bringing in lecturers were immediate and practical ones: in May, 1855, the *Gazette* had emphasized the "economic advantages which might result to the town if outside talent was brought to the city," the point being that Horace Greeley had lectured in Dubuque the year before and had then praised the city in his New York *Tribune*.

Davenport's German immigrants imported their own lecturers and had Middle European fests and massed exercises. The Germans were exiles from the mid-nineteenth-century revolutions in the German states, and having suffered from oppression themselves, were liberal, antislavery, and anti-temperance, dismaying qualities to New Englanders repelled by the foreigners' affinity for socialism[7] and their "love of lager, sour-kraut and Bolognas [and] free and easy habits of Sunday

[6] Emerson lectured several times in Davenport between 1855 and the 1870's. Sponsors paid more to hear Wendell Phillips ($110) than Emerson ($75) because, as the December 31, 1855, *Gazette* announced, "Those who assert that Mr. Emerson is an orator are simply mistaken. That he writes and reasons well no one can doubt, but he is *no* orator. In that respect we are much disappointed." In Rock Island, where Emerson was advertised as the "Celebrated Metaphysician," the skating rink was closed to swell the crowd at the lecture. In Davenport, where he was simply the "Essayist and Poet," Emerson's audience was so small that he returned $50 of his $75 fee. The *Gazette* commented, "His lecture, like Laocoön, should have been ascribed 'To Those Who Think.'" The reason for his many return engagements was noted by Emerson himself, "In every one of these expanding towns is a knot of loving New Englanders who cherish the Lyceum out of love to the Charles and the Merrimac and the Connecticut rivers. . . ." See Hubert Hoeltje, "Ralph Waldo Emerson in Iowa," *Iowa Journal of History and Politics*, XXV (April 1927), 237–276; William Charvat, "Chronological List of Emerson's American Lecture Engagements," *BNYPL*, LXIV (December 1960), 663; and Emerson's *Journals*, December 31, 1855.

[7] In 1882, thirty years after it was organized, the local *Sozialistischer Turnverein* abandoned socialism to become the *Davenport Turnverein*.

afternoon."[8] Objections to loud music on the Sabbath, when the German Shooting Society collected its members for the trip to the range by marching a brass band up and down the streets, resulted in an agreement that German parades on Sundays were not to cross Brady Street, the boundary line between the "English" and "German" sections of the town. The immigrants' ideas of trade unionism and their arch-liberalism disturbed Alice's father, yet he left Alice and her brothers with his own high regard for German virtues. As a member of the city's school board, he urged German instruction in the public schools. In 1866, he enrolled Alice's younger brother, twelve-year-old Nathaniel, in the local Frei Deutsche Schule and years later sent two sons to study in Heidelberg.

But it was the river more than the cosmopolitan population and its varied entertainments that gave the city the unique characteristics Alice French was to use in her short stories. The first steamboat had passed Davenport on its way up the river in 1823. When traffic was at its peak before the Civil War, yearly steamboat arrivals numbered in the thousands. Nevertheless, the first landing in the spring was always a municipal event. Townspeople abandoned schools and businesses and gathered on the levee when news spread that the season's first steamboat was coming to Davenport. Sometimes the giant Gothic ship displayed a bright gilded ball or a star hanging between her chimneys; and great panoramas, some of buffalo hunts or St. Anthony's Falls, were painted on the paddle boxes. Alice and the rest of the children would hear five blasts on the whistle, two long and three short, from the middle of the river. Both paddle wheels on the steamboat would stop as the boat drifted toward the shore and the echoes of the whistle broke and rolled through the town and the hills and along the bluffs. Then, just as she seemed about to drift onto the levee, the engine bells would sound and both wheels would spin in reverse, churning up the water as the bow gently touched the shore.

The waterfront was not peaceful, nor was it idyllic as New England could be. The river at Davenport was a graveyard of steamboats that had foundered, colliding with natural hazards or the new railroad bridge that the rivermen called the "invention of Satan and the Rock Island Railroad." Catastrophes were so common that ferryboatmen and skiff owners grew highly efficient at rescuing passengers from the

[8] The August 16, 1862, Davenport *Daily Democrat and News*, quoted in Joseph E. Schick, *The Early Theater in Iowa* (Chicago, 1939), p. 89.

wrecks. When Alice was eleven, the steamboat *Grey Eagle* crashed against a bridge pier and sank in seven minutes, yet all the passengers and crew were saved except seven—and one of those was a mad man chained to the lower deck. Boiler explosions were almost as common as crashes and often more memorable. The packet *Lansing* blew up not far from Davenport and hurled, it was said (and believed by children and grownups alike), the body of the clerk across the river into Iowa and the pilot well inland beyond the Illinois shore.

The boats brought rivermen to the town, many of whom lived in Davenport. In his own estimation, the Upper-Mississippi riverman was a cut above any other boatman, including Erie Canal men, the "packet rats" of the clipper ships, and certainly those who steamed on the river below its juncture with the Ohio. To Alice and the other children of the town, only the stage drivers could compare with the rivermen, and sometimes parents exploited such awe. In Andover, wicked boys and girls were chastised with examples summoned up from "Sinners in the Hands of an Angry God." In Davenport, children were frightened into obedience with tales of rivermen as combinations of Mike Fink and murderers from the Natchez Trace. Punishment and fear were more theological in New England than on the Mississippi. Where pious New Englanders might shun the devil when he was abroad, prudent Davenporters locked themselves in their homes on nights when a river gang was in town, drunk on homemade whiskey.

Every town on the Mississippi had districts especially devoted to the rivermen and their broad appetites. Davenport had its saloons and dancehalls, the latter often only façades for whorehouses that one time or another boasted inmates who were English, or German, or New Orleans French, or high-yellow girls from Cuba and Jamaica. Davenport bawdy houses like Black Hill's Den on Brady Street or Rachel's Place located conveniently on the levee for rivermen who were in a hurry, or Meyer's Dance House at Second and Fillmore, where gentlemen were "taken in and done for," were famous along the Mississippi.

It was axiomatic on the river that attempts at reform were continual, especially when profits were down. Sometimes when faced with uprisings from respectable citizens, the more inspired entrepreneurs of sin appeared in Davenport with floating resorts that could tour up and down the river, anchoring near the most willing market. When threatened by law and order, the entertainers had only to cast off their moorings and float across the steamboat channel, the dividing line between states, and accept the hospitality of another government and more appreciative customers. Such mobile amusement came to Davenport often, usually housed on two or more flatboats fastened together and covered with low one-story deckhouses and towed by a steamboat. Then at night the river would echo to the shouts and screams of the customers and the ladies of diversion. But though it was noisy and continual, proper children were unaware of such earthy activities, the endless variety of murder, thievery, and venery that occurred along the river and on it. The daughter of George Henry French was aware of the color of the scene, the life of her family and friends, and of the experiences her father described to the family in the evenings, but not of the boisterous and unwashed inhabitants of the town; and when she came to write, the river became a locale, not a deterministic force giving rise to fundamental and therefore questionable and perhaps even tasteless human problems.

Greater and more popular issues like slavery occupied serious, thoughtful young gentlewomen. Davenport, like other towns on the river, had Southern ties, but it was fiercely Abolitionist. That attitude rose partly out of a series of events that made slavery a personal issue for adults as well as their children. John Emerson, an assistant surgeon in the United States Army, had kept a Negro slave named Dred Scott with him while stationed at the military post on Rock Island. Emerson had died in Davenport, and Scott's subsequent treatment by the Supreme Court and Chief Justice Taney touched off bitter local reaction. Furthermore, John Brown had used the city as a station in his underground movement of slaves north into Canada; and Barclay Coppoc, one of Brown's men who became a fugitive after the attack on Harpers Ferry, fled to Davenport, where he was hidden above Eli Adam's bookstore on Brady Street, a few blocks from the Frenches. When Brown was hanged, December 2, 1859, many Davenporters wore crepe for mourning, and the Germans draped their theater in black. To the idealistic and the bellicose, he was a "noble assassin," and long after his execution Alice remembered the day her father gathered his family to pray for "the soul of Thy servant, John Brown, who will today sacrifice his life because of his efforts to succor the poor and needy and undo the wrong committed by our forefathers."

The coming of the Civil War that was marked by such turbulence also brought prosperity to George French. His earlier partnership had been dissolved; a new associate, named John Davies, was taken in and the lumber business reorganized and expanded. It all went well, and because business success conveyed a sort of civic sanctity in Davenport as elsewhere, and because he had been elected treasurer of the city school board four times,[9] George French's Republican friends urged him to become the Republican candidate for mayor in Davenport's 1861 election. Early that spring he accepted nomination and began campaigning on his record as a successful businessman and public servant. And he took his stand on national issues, for the political ferment of 1861 would permit no election to concern itself only with local problems. Eleven-year-old Alice listened to her father and his political supporters and absorbed Republican arguments and local conservative dogma. George French's political opposition, strong and vocal, attacked him for his business dealings and his temerity; on election day, April 6, 1861, the *Democrat* urged: "Vote for David Higgins. . . . Voters of this city should support him over George H. French. He is a better financier. . . . He is not an office seeker." But on April 8 the newspapers announced George French's victory, 907 to 779; he had carried every city ward except the Fifth, where the Irish lived. Nevertheless, the *Democrat* charged that the election was invalid because voters had been imported from Illinois by Republicans—the only faction wealthy enough to provide for transportation. Two days later George French took the oath of office, although celebrations were smothered by news of secession in the South and the likelihood of armed rebellion. The issues were simple for everyone, and doubts that remained were swept aside by the attack on Fort Sumter; it was now that most costly of all disruptions—a civil war.

When news came that war had finally begun, Davenport reacted with river-town vigor; wild shouting broke out in the streets and along the levee. The students of Episcopal Griswold College climbed the cupola on top of the square college building and hoisted the Union flag. On April 16, four days after Fort Sumter was attacked, President Lincoln called upon Iowa to supply one volunteer regiment. The request was wired to Davenport—still the only Iowa town on the telegraph line—where Alice's father received the news and presided the next day over a meeting of state officials summoned to plan Iowa's contribution to the war. Part of their job was obstructed by the confusion that sprouted everywhere and the terrifying rumors that sped

[9] Ultimately he was elected twelve times.

through the frenzied town. Word came that a steamer flying the Confederate flag was going to run past Davenport from Galena on its way through the blockade to Memphis. Townspeople crowded on the levee, where the local militia was assembled to man guns commanding the river, but the fugitive steamer never appeared.

Soon the Mississippi was completely blocked, and traffic was at a standstill. By July, twenty thousand rivermen were out of work—an economic crisis for them. For others, for meat packers, iron makers, speculators, and industrialists, the war was a bonanza. Davenport was to be the marshaling center for the state's contribution to the war. Military camps were to be built to house the troops while they trained for the fighting. On August 10, 1861, the *Democrat* announced that the firm of French and Davies had won the contract to build Camp McClellan, the first of five military posts around the city.

Soon thousands of soldiers were moving into the camps, living in white tents arranged in company streets and drilling in fields quickly churned into a "jelly of mud." Alice and her brothers went with their parents to weekly dress parades and watched when cavalry mounts raised clouds of dust as they were driven twice daily to the levee to be watered. Reviews and displays, mock battles, and drills continued for two months after the hostilities began, and then a great parade was held to honor the departure of the first troops to leave the city for the battlefront.

City dignitaries, including Mayor French and his family, were invited to join the reviewing party on the portico of the Burtis House; and when the parade began, all the Frenches were present except Nathaniel, who had disappeared shortly before the family had left home. But for Alice, thoughts of the absent six-year-old quickly fled before the sight of all the patriots marching in close ranks through the crowded streets. The soldiers' uniforms were a variety of colors and styles, and their weapons were as mixed as their dress. Some carried old-fashioned muskets from the War of 1812, hurriedly adapted to use a primer cap instead of an awkward flintlock. But the bayonets flashed and the flags stood out bravely, and though war might be cruel, it was exciting. As the last rank went by—Iowa men who would eventually fight at Shiloh, Corinth, and Atlanta—the spectators below the reviewing stand began to laugh, and the mystery of the missing Nathaniel was solved. Behind the last of the troops, Alice's brother solemnly marched on his way to war. He had taken his father's talk of the northern crusade to heart, and he paraded with the soldiers, hoping to join them on their voyage downriver. He was too young even to be a drummer boy; but when the Scott County troops of the volunteer three-month regiment returned in August for mustering out and reorganization, they invited Nathaniel to their banquet, and he sat with his heroes as an honorary member of the company.

In April, 1862, Alice's father was again elected mayor, in spite of a Democratic trend indicating that Davenport, like the rest of the North, was voting its protest for the humiliations the Union Army had suffered in the first year of the war. George French became an aide to the governor, sitting on advisory boards directing the state's war effort, while Alice and her mother scraped lint for bandages for the Sanitary Commission and knitted rough wool socks for the troops. They attended bazaars to raise money for the families of the soldiers, and socials where young ladies spurred on hesitant beaus by singing, "I Am Bound To Be a Soldier's Wife or Die an Old Maid."

In the summer and fall of 1863, the federal government built a prison camp on Rock Island for captured Confederates, and from the heights on the Iowa shore, Davenporters could see the north end of the island, where a twelve-acre compound crowded twelve thousand prisoners into facilities built for ten thousand. There, in most obvious display, was misery raked up by the war. They were Rebels, of course, and cruel to their black brothers, but with her mother, Alice helped collect food and clothing to be distributed at the camp where almost two thousand prisoners died before the surrender at Appomattox brought relief.

The coming of the war had ended Davenport's Conversation Society, and the showboats had ceased to come—the last of them had boasted a monkey circus and a balloon ascension—but the Scott County New England Society continued to meet; and the troops at Camp McClellan established a Lyceum in 1862 to promote soldierly interest in "debates, declamations and exercises of a literary nature," naming their organization the "Soldier's Hope Society." Lecturers still appeared at the Opera House and Metropolitan Hall. Clara Barton came to plead for funds for hospitals and to describe her experiences as the "Angel of the Battlefield." Louis Agassiz came to speak on Davenport's glacial history, and others lectured on phrenology, American politics, and modern British poets, or presented scientific demonstrations that sometimes ended with the Confederate flag disappearing in a blaze of liquid phosphorus, to the accompaniment of hisses and cheers from the audience.

It all ended when Alice was fifteen. On April 11, 1865, less than a month after her birthday, the *Gazette* printed in large, black type:

GRAND GALA DAY
Rejoicing over Lee's Surrender
Davenport Wild With Enthusiasm
IMMENSE PROCESSION
Stirring Speeches—Brilliant Illumination
and General Glorification.

The celebrations in Davenport were more frenzied than they had been four years earlier, and after even the most somber assessments of the cost of the war, it was apparent that great benefit had come to a few. Alice's father was richer than ever. Contracts for the materials used in building Camp McClellan had been followed by contracts for other military posts and for the construction of quarters and prisons on Rock Island. In addition, George French had joined in establishing the nation's first national bank, a device promoted by a federal government hoping to buttress a faltering war economy. The bank's rate of repayment on the original investment was large—10 per cent within the first six months. In 1865, with the war over, Alice's father, now free from his other duties, became president of the bank.

Alice was fifteen, a tall girl with light brown hair, bright blue eyes, and some new interests. Her appetite for the romantic fiction of Mrs. Southworth and Sylvanus Cobb had been replaced by an interest in Sir Walter Scott's novels, the novels Twain in *Life on the Mississippi* accused of setting "the world in love with dreams and fantoms . . . with decayed and degraded systems of government . . . and sham chivalries of a brainless and worthless long vanished society." Alice later lived among southerners who suffered from some of the derangements Twain reviled, but for Alice, as for innumerable readers in the nineteenth century, Scott's romances carried her far beyond the limits of her narrow world and into renaissance and medieval realms filled with ideals and adventures and packed with the details of European history. Early in the war, Davenport's subscription library had withered, and Alice had turned to the library of the Bishop, her uncle. By the time she was fifteen, she was spending hours in the Episcopal rectory, reading theology and sixteenth-century history, Foxe's *Book of Martyrs*, Latimer, Cranmer, and church histories. In an unpublished manuscript which she marked "Personal Recollections," she later recalled,

> I discovered the Parker and Camden Society reprints. I found Stow and Holinshed, Strype, and Foxe. I wonder how many clergymen have read Latimer's and Cranmer's and Ridley's sermons . . . ?
>
> They are not the easiest reading in the world, but the dogged adventurer who plods through them is richly repaid by their first hand pictures of the dawn of our industrial era in the time of Henry Tudor, who did a great many things besides divorce his wives.[10]

Theological abstractions were less interesting to Alice than the events of sixteenth-century politics and the phenomena accompanying the rise of the Protestant middle class, though she was caught by the same clear and homely style of Latimer's sermons that had attracted the London crowds more than three hundred years earlier, and she sat for hours reading the Bishop's copy of John Foxe's roll of Christian martyrdoms, with its grisly illustrations and pious dark stories of persecution and agony. The acts and monuments of martyrdom, like the sermons and edifying diaries of early America, fostered strong moral attitudes in their readers. They had helped her Protestant ancestors persevere in their faith, but to Alice, the miseries of the 1500's had a special relevance to the problems which aroused her father and confronted the middle class that was emerging in the western cities.

Church literature was rich fare for a fifteen-year-old girl with a limited formal education in a Mississippi River town, and once the war ended, George French and his wife faced the problem of their daughter's deficient schooling. Some conservative Americans felt that higher education for women was indulged in by "unsexed things" or "men-women," eccentrics and nonconformists, but Alice's father had a New Englander's faith in education even beyond the pious knowledge of the scriptures needed "to defeat the old deluder Satan," and George French was well aware of his daughter's talents, for she was shrewd and quick to speak out.

Her uncle's Griswold College was only for men. Years before, a female seminary had risen in Davenport, but that had expired for lack

[10] Alice French, "Personal Recollections," MS, Newberry Library.

of students. Iowa College, once the town's prized educational ornament, had moved inland to Grinnell after its reverent board found
"the atmosphere of a river town was not favorable to a Christian
college." A university had opened at Iowa City in 1856 and in 1858 had
become the first state university to accept women. It had enrolled
six hundred "ladies and gentlemen" by 1867, but even so, critics of
such coeducation vigorously denounced it as a threat to the home and
as a producer of "strong-minded" women and "unmanly" men.

Suitably, in 1861, a philanthropic brewer named Matthew Vassar
had endowed a college for women in Poughkeepsie, New York. He
had announced to his trustees that "woman, having received from her
Creator the same intellectual constitution as man, has the same right to
intellectual culture and development," and he set out to establish an
institution offering a Preparatory Program and a Collegiate Course
which would give young ladies an education equal to that available to
young men at Yale and Harvard. With the end of the Civil War, the
school had opened with 353 students and a faculty of 30, and it promptly was classed as "what bids fair to be the best educational institution
for the Muslin Sex in America." [11] To fill its dormitories, the college
had advertised its opening with colored prints of its buildings and
grounds reproduced in newspapers and magazines circulated through
the West. The pictures and the elegant descriptions made daughters of
many emigrants from New England and New York long to enjoy the
refined blessings of the East and to undergo the dangerous stimulation
of their womanly intellect. To Alice, going to Vassar required a long
journey, but it was an incomparable distinction and well worth the
$350 annual fee. And when she was sixteen, she left Davenport for
Poughkeepsie to enroll in the Preparatory Department of the new
Female College. [12]

Alice and her mother arrived in Poughkeepsie in September of 1866
and were driven through the college grounds in a horse-drawn hack.
Vassar had a Main Building, which was fashioned after the Tuileries,
an Observatory containing a telescope that was pronounced "the
third best in the United States," a Gate-House, and a "building for

[11] Frank Luther Mott, *History of American Magazines* (New York, 1930), II,
82.

[12] The following year the New York State Legislature officially changed the
name to Vassar College. Feminists, and notably Sarah Josepha Hale, editor of
Godey's Lady's Book, had found any suggestion of femininity demeaning when
applied to higher learning, if not to popular journalism.

Gynestic or Riding School." Four hundred feet away from Main was the Boiler and Gas House, Vassar being "the first institution in the world to be heated by a central plant in a separate building."

Alice's teachers in Davenport had judged her "a fine pupil, good in everything except penmanship," and they had prepared her to demonstrate the competence in "spelling, reading, writing, arithmetic, geography, English grammar, and the history of the United States" that college regulations required entering students to possess—in addition to a "shawl, a warm sack and a breakfast cape."

Eleven departments offered instruction varying from mental philosophy to music and hygiene. Life was rigorous and designed to suit a school that was founded to be "an honor to the state and a blessing to the world." Even Vassar's buildings were constructed to symbolize the feminine virtues of "solidity and chastity," for it was an age that wanted to believe that its buildings and its art expressed morality and shaped ideals. Here too, instruction had the religious cast thought best capable of inculcating the students with Christian goodness. The girls rose at 6:00. Morning prayers lasted until breakfast at 7:00. "Silent Time" with more prayer and meditation continued until 9:00. Classes met for six hours, and more "Silent Time" followed from 6:30 until 8:00. But solid and chaste as it was, Vassar had little appeal for Alice. She found life restricted and her fellow students pretentious. All letters home were censored by the Lady Principal. All students were examined at the entrance to the dining hall to see if they had taken the required two baths a week. And Alice squabbled with the girls most conscious of their status. Once in a dormitory discussion of breeding and ancestry, after listening to others brag about their families, Alice was asked about her father's profession. Comfortable in the grandeur of her New England ancestors, she announced, "He's a carpenter," a statement which shocked her high-born audience and one which she often recounted in her old age to describe her fellow students and explain her actions, for at the end of her first term at Vassar, Alice went home to Davenport and refused to return to Poughkeepsie.

The next September, 1867, she enrolled at Abbot Academy in Andover and became one of the sixteen girls in the senior class. Abbot was situated just up School Street from the house in which she had been born, and across the street was the home of her uncle Marcus Morton II and his five children, her cousins. Where Vassar had been new, Abbot was old. Vassar was full of the daughters of the war rich, while Abbot was full of the daughters of seminary professors used to the slender means of academic life on Andover Hill. Vassar had a non-sectarian dedication to what Matthew Vassar called "things, *Interlectural and Material the Best*." Abbot announced that with Phillips Academy and the Theological Seminary, it was "the support and ornament of virtue's cause."

Little had changed in Andover since 1856. In spite of the war, the town remained gently above the gilded preoccupations now engrossing the nation. The influence of the great Moses Stuart still prevailed at the seminary where he had once been a professor, and the Calvinistic rigidity of the faculty had weakened only a little since Emerson had shocked them with his anti-Christian, blaspheming observation that Bronson Alcott's was the greatest mind since Plato. Literary-minded townspeople now supported a Chaucer Club, with a judiciously bowdlerized text. Unitarianism was being talked about with less suspicion, but the atmosphere of rectitude persisted in the village and the female academy.

When she arrived at Abbot, Alice was assigned a roommate, Octavia Putnam of Bath, Maine, and a dormitory room twelve feet. square in the southwest corner on the second floor of Smith Hall. The room had a large double bed—the scholars slept together—a Victorian bureau with a small mirror,[13] a sink, towel rack, table, and two chairs.[14] Life was strict and spartan, although hot and cold running water had been added to the bathrooms two years before.

Now she had friends: her roommate, Octavia, the three Means sisters, Anna Dawes, and cousins Kate Roberts and Lizzie and Hattie Davis; and Alice could visit her uncle Marcus Morton and his wife and their five children in the house across the street. Phillips Academy boys sometimes serenaded under the windows of the dormitories or hid in the Abbot coal cellar, but Abbot girls could not go to parties if Phillips boys were invited, and even at chapel there was little chance to do more than study "Phillipians" through the holes the young ladies secretly cut in their fans. Bold girls sometimes tied blue Phillips neckties to their window blinds, but few Academy girls waltzed, or fluttered in Bar Harbor, or read French stories or yellow

[13] She never forgot the small mirror. Forty years later she donated a full length plate glass mirror to be placed at the head of the second-floor stairs.
[14] The school catalog announced "window-curtains and valances extra."

Alice French at about 17, as a student at Abbot Academy

novels, and it was reported proudly that one Andover young lady cried for twenty-six hours after being "furtively kissed" by a "daring boy"—a moral cataclysm that aroused an unprecedented furor and the pious observation that at least the culprit was not a native of Andover.[15]

Abbot Academy offered its 163 students "Superior Instruction in English Branches, Latin, Modern Languages, and Music." Alice studied the Latin of Caesar, Virgil, Livy, and Horace; the sciences; [16] politics; metaphysics; more ecclesiastical history; and the arguments for Christianity in Bishop Butler's *Analogy of Religion, Natural and Revealed*. With all the other girls she was drilled in military tactics, marching and wheeling right and left in the tedious mass exercises that became popular following the Civil War. Such exertions were easy for a western girl who had played baseball, walked fences, and hunted and fished with her father and brothers. Students made edifying excursions to the factories of Lowell (the philosophy class went to see the Pacific Mills at Lawrence), to Mount Auburn Cemetery, and to the historical sites of Boston. They took pensive strolls under the arches of the seminary elms and went to Indian Ridge for hepaticas, or walked to the cemetery to collect pretty fungi to make bracelets of. For their individual salvation, Abbot girls were washed in Andover Congregationalism while they sat in the school's pews in the Congregational Church or gathered in the dormitories to listen to earnest talks by Headmistress Philena McKeen and her sister, Phebe, the First Assistant Teacher. Harriet Stowe's daughters went to Abbot at this time, and their theologian father, Calvin Stowe, lectured the students on biblical history. Abbot girls often went to the seminary to hear sermons preached by its famous professors. Alice and her cousins would help swell the chapel crowds that spilled out into the aisles—there were no fire laws in Andover then—especially on days when tall, gaunt Edwards Park repeated his "Judas Sermon" or the famous emotional "Peter Sermon" during which, cynics noted, tears always filled the preacher's eyes and always at the same moment. The sermons engaged the whole town for a week, but in spite of the omnipresence of Andover's special orthodoxy and the failure of transcendentalism to rise from Concord to

[15] Elizabeth Stuart Phelps Ward, *Chapters from a Life* (Boston, 1896), pp. 27–28.

[16] Abbot boasted a "cabinet for illustrating Conchology" and "expensive models for illustrating Anatomy," but had no microscope until 1871.

Andover, the tenets of Congregationalism had only indirect influence on Alice. Her father, the family's arbiter in such things, had even broken with the Anglican church of his brother-in-law, Bishop Lee, and had joined in forming the first Unitarian church in Davenport.

Of greater importance to Alice was Abbot's emphasis on writing. Smith Hall students concentrated on English. Seniors studied "General Literature" and the English literature from the time of Queen Elizabeth contained in *Chamber's Encyclopaedia of English Literature*. Smith Hall students devoted every Saturday to what the school catalog listed as "miscellaneous literary exercises adapted to promote general intelligence and to establish habits of investigation." The regimen had produced a number of literary alumnae: Elizabeth Stuart Phelps the younger had gone to Abbot; Sarah Lord Hall, the author of *Child Life in New England*, had graduated two years before Alice entered; and the author of *Kismet*, Julia Fletcher, had been a member of the class of 1867.

Beyond developing Alice's taste for plain style and her knowledge of literature, Abbot Academy's major function was to nourish her middle-class inclinations and to shield her from other ideas at an age when she was likely to be moved by them. The school's reflection of a stable and ordered society shaped her virtues and heightened her delusions, and it provided a continuity in her life and a sense of rooted security which other westerners like Garland or Dreiser could never find.

By the end of the school year in July, 1868, Alice was on the honor roll, sharing with another senior the pleasure of reading commencement essays. Just before the ceremonies were to begin, while making last minute revisions of her speech, Alice spilled a bottle of ink down the front of her ruffled, white muslin graduation dress. Fortunately, the whole of the graduating class was at hand to be directed in washing out the ink and ironing the dress dry just in time for the ritual to begin. Dressed in white muslin still warm from the iron, Alice read her essay, "Blowing Bubbles," before townsmen, parents, and her own mother and father, all assembled in the old South Church.

Alice was eighteen when she graduated, but she felt her youth was over and what had taken its place was worrisome. The Sunday following the close of school, 1868, she confided in a letter to her schoolmate Anna Dawes:

I'm sorry and I'm glad and I'm a little frightened. The world is so large and woman's future is so uncertain. Life is getting to look remarkably queer and earnest.

I haven't been to church this morning. Staid at home and got on charmingly with such a nice novel. A first class one. I always make a distinction and read only first class novels on Sunday. I mean to, at least, in the future.[17]

[17] Alice French to Anna C. Dawes, July 4, 1868, quoted in Tucker, "'Octave Thanet,'" pp. 33–34.

Here, as elsewhere, quoted passages are given exactly as they appeared in the original; misspellings and grammatical errors have not been corrected.

IV. Innocence and Might

When Alice French returned to Davenport in 1868, the family was living in a larger house on the east side of Rock Island Street, near Fifth. Her father had retired as president of the First National Bank and was devoting his time to the lumber business. Her mother was reconciled to the West and Davenport society.

Eighteen-year-old Alice confronted a problem common to well-educated daughters of the rich, a problem her diploma from Abbot had not resolved: What should one do in life? In the West, maidens were expected to marry. Marriage was a cultural necessity, and it was easy in a land where men outnumbered women. But Alice had been in New England, where the war had stocked farms and villages with surplus ladies who cheered each other in spinsterhood. Celibacy was a sanctuary for females with delicate sensibilities, or it was a weapon for vigorous "New Women" who were armed with college degrees and their own ideas. Thirty-five years before, Mrs. Trollope, in her *Domestic Manners of the Americans*, had observed that American females revealed their insignificance as soon as they married. Now, girls from academies and colleges felt they had abilities as well as duties. Fewer of them were delicate blooms. Fewer lapsed into marriages that were sexual and social martyrdoms.

In Davenport an unwed maiden of respectable family who cherished her virtue could teach school at twenty dollars a month, more often only fifteen, or she could live with her parents and do good by visiting sickrooms, succoring the poor, or by giving herself to His Service and His Glory. In an age of feminine letters she might join what Hawthorne had called that " d——d mob of scribbling women "—if there was time. The house on Rock Island Street absorbed the days of both mother and daughter; and since immigrant German help and native-born girls, even the decent ones, lacked the New England devotion to service, Alice learned to cook and to serve as hostess at parties and "at homes."

She went to socials given by her childhood friends in town or in the country at Jane Allen's or west of the city, where Celestine Fejervary lived in a replica of a Hungarian castle built by her father after he had fled to Davenport from the Hungarian Revolt of 1853. Alice went calling or hunting, or to skating parties and sleigh rides, once with a man identified by her hopeful mother only as "not young" but "not married." Alice recorded one week's activity in a letter to an Abbot schoolmate: "I feel rather knocked up, having killed a snake, shot a bird, fired a revolver—a charming powder mark on my hand remains as what an old lady called a 'momentum'—walked incalculable distances, waded in the Mississippi and finally gone to a party to end up the week."[1]

George French yielded to his daughter's appetite for finery and sent her on shopping trips to Chicago for high fashions unavailable in Davenport. In her new clothes and escorted usually by her father, she went to the Opera House or Turner's Hall for Shakespeare and lectures, or she rode through the countryside in the family carriage. The social customs of the day required a punctilious adherence to the tradition of "calling," and Alice and her mother went about the city in a brougham, making calls or leaving cards. It was a very genteel life, and Alice had no need to break away from an impoverished family to hunt riches in the West or fame in the literary salons of Boston and New York, even if such things had been possible for a young lady of condition.

In the 1870's, Alice's reading grew more discriminating. The *New York Ledger* had been supplanted by the respected *Galaxy*, which also carried serials, sometimes as many as two or three in each issue. Henry James was appearing in the *Galaxy* by 1875, and Alice read his stories as well as Justin McCarthy's *Lady Judith*. Later she read Tolstoy and Turgenev, whose *Fathers and Sons* introduced her to the ideas and actions of the Nihilists, the American counterparts of which she attempted to portray in 1905 in her most ambitious novel, *The Man of the Hour*. Unlike Turgenev's fictional peasants, Alice French's local-color poor whites and laborers were never shown as more attractive than their masters, and she never moved, as Howells did, from Turgenev to become a follower of Henry George and Edward Bellamy. Yet she preferred Turgenev to Tolstoy: "a greater artist, a better man."[2]

[1] Quoted in Tucker, "'Octave Thanet,'" p. 36.
[2] *Ibid.*, pp. 32, 36.

She read Gogol, Pushkin, and Dostoievski and came to disagree with Dostoievski's social pronouncements and assigned his "premature" death to a reckless pursuit of impractical ideals. She read Trollope, Gautier ("I tried to catch the trick of Gautier's wonderful jugglery of sound"), and Balzac, George Eliot, and Thackeray. In 1893, when the *Book Buyer* queried her on her literary tastes, she listed Montaigne, Scott, Charles Lamb, and Thackeray as her favorite authors, *Henry Esmond* as her favorite book; her favorite literary character was Colonel Newcome, another mustachioed and benevolent father who rewarded children out of trouser pockets that were heavy with silver and gold.

Henry James was disgusting: "The futility of his characters revolts me." A decade later, in the *Californian* of January, 1881, she published a sketch, "The American Imitation of England," which concluded that there were some good things in England for America to imitate: society, gentlemanliness, and the Civil Service; but not Henry James—"a smart young American who lives in London, and is making a fortune ridiculing his own country." It was a lack of will in James's characters even more than ridicule of Americans which bothered her; after 1890 she was similarly irked at literary naturalists whose fictional characters were unable to control their own fate.

In spite of Alice's belief in free will, her reading had left matters of the spirit unresolved. Her experiences with the Misses McKeen of Abbot had failed to calm religious doubt, and the winter after her return to Davenport from Andover, she was still groping for some kind of faith. Her parents had helped form the new Unitarian Church in Davenport, with a suitable Bostonian, Mr. Seaver, as the minister, but this concession to the inroads of the new rationalism was little help to Alice. She turned instead to the German philosophers and began reading Hegel, Schopenhauer, and their expositors, but she found no satisfactory answer to her questions about the existence of God. She had never been at ease with moral ambiguities. Around 1870 she wrote to her school friend from Abbot, Anna Dawes of Pittsfield, Massachusetts:

> Unfortunately, I never get a near view of any religion, but the beauty vanishes. You know how I used to sit in the seat of the scornful at Abbot. Well, it's just as bad ... here. I have a really dreadful state of mind toward all philanthropists and liberalists, whose liberality is nicely arranged to fit their own peculiar cases. ... Alas, my dear, I was never meant to

be a religious sort, one of the "pious" girls. I am sorry for it, yet there are so many other things. One has so many duties, even if one is not a philanthropist, to perform for her fellow-men, that her duty to God is rather lost sight of.

One of the "duties" was work in the missions of the factory sections of Davenport, which she described to Anna Dawes:

> You would be annoyed at my docility. I go nobody knows what distance to the Mission School . . . and teach a harum-scarum group of boys who are really very interesting and then tramp back again. *Mais qu'est ce qu'importe?* I should spend my Sunday afternoons in much worse manner if I did not spend them that way.[3]

At Abbot she had composed a sentimental short story, which her classmates had praised, and now in Davenport she began to rework it, for there was a market at hand. The Davenport *Gazette* carried fiction in the manner of eminent newspapers in the East, and the editor of the Republican *Gazette* was a friend of Alice's father and knew the virtues of local authors. Three years after she had written it in Andover, Alice submitted "Hugo's Waiting" to the *Gazette*. The story appeared under the name "Frances Essex" in February, 1871. It was her first published work.[4]

Shortly before its appearance, Alice wrote to Anna Dawes with news of her success:

> I also send that little story I read so long ago to you. . . . Do you remember it? Mr. Sanders wanted something for this Saturday's *Gazette*, so I furbished up that. It is very stupid, I know, but it is written for the popular taste, which is also stupid.[5]

There was no payment; publication and local fame were all the *Gazette* could offer, and even the fame was limited to those who knew the real name of the author. The "Frances Essex" was an amalgam of names, each with a circumspect two syllables, the first name taken from her mother and the second from Andover's Essex County.

"Hugo's Waiting" described the mutually puzzling ways of the rich and the poor. The hero, a crippled, simple-minded fiddler named

[3] Alice French to Anna C. Dawes, quoted in Tucker, "'Octave Thanet,'" pp. 32, 36.

[4] The manuscript remained among her papers after her death. Her mother had written on it "This is Alice's first published story."

[5] Alice French to Anna Dawes, February 4, 1871, quoted in Tucker, "'Octave Thanet,'" pp. 40–41.

Hugo, played his instrument on a city street corner. At the end of each day he returned to a Dickensian hovel he shared with Guido—dark, sinister, and foreign-born—who took all Hugo's earnings and offered in return floggings and a bed of rags. One day a beautiful young girl with bright golden hair and much money capriciously gave Hugo a large bank note and announced that she would return. Months passed while Hugo stood on the street corner, waiting. Summer ended, the leaves fell, and then snow. Hugo, in his threadbare overcoat, grew tubercular. One day he entered a church, for what reason he hardly knew, and saw a somber black procession bearing a coffin. Inside was the body of the lovely blonde girl; she had at last returned. Hugo waited until the funeral service ended and then plodded through the rain in the wake of the procession to the cemetery. Waiting out of sight until the mourners left, he threw himself on the new mound of earth. The next morning his body was found stretched over the grave. A smile was on his face.

Such sentiment and adoration were traditional at a time when the fictional dead were mourned at length and graves were embraced with vigor. Alice had mastered the stereotypes of popular fiction, and she had also read the novel *Hedged In,* by another Abbot alumna, Elizabeth Stuart Phelps, which had appeared in 1870 and had similarly told of an orphan who played the tambourine on the streets and was brutally treated by cruel guardians. Still, Alice's characters, if worn and derivative, were drawn from "life." Hugo was created to resemble one of the unfortunates at the mission school, and the story's golden-haired heroine was a wan, idealized replica of the author. Like other beginners, Alice had put too much in too little space, yet she was following a literary tradition, however Gothic, and she displayed an idea of form. Unlike her later work, her first story had little dialogue and no hint of the dialect upon which she came to rely and which enlivened, and eventually blighted, some of her mature work.

The publication of "Hugo's Waiting" was exciting enough, but two events occurred in 1871 which were more celebrated. One was the birth in July of Robert, the family's last child. Twenty-one years younger than Alice, he provided a focus for her interests that mission work and "Hugo's Waiting" left unfulfilled. The other was the coming of Bronson Alcott to Davenport and the Frenches'.

The year 1871 started in a traditional way. On New Year's Day the family went to hear Mr. Seaver preach at the Unitarian meeting at the Burtis House.[6] As one of their New Year resolutions, the family members began recording the year by entering their activities in a family diary, and on January 2, 1871, George French noted that the family "kept a holiday," and that he, in company with the mayor, made fifty social calls, while "Alice and wife had sixty-five calls in afternoon." Alice's brother, sixteen-year-old Nat, also "made round," in the words of his father, who wrote soberly in the diary, "It was premature for Nat to make calls."

Later that same day, the Reverend Mr. Seaver called to introduce Bronson Alcott, and Alice's father recorded: "Wife invited him to stop with us during his stay here. He proposes to give parlor 'conversations.' Will give one at our house tomorrow."[7] Alcott was a prize guest, for his reputation had grown since the lean years when his *Conversations on the Gospels* had ended up as trunk linings, and he had not yet become a sad remnant of Transcendentalism. *Little Women* had appeared in 1868, three years before, the same year as his own *Tablets*; and while Carlyle had judged him a "terrible old bore," westerners loved him as much for his daughter Louisa May as for the gospel according to Concord, which he spread among transplanted Yankees. A half-century later, Alice recalled,

> I remember him distinctly, a long, lean, large-framed man with a gentle clean-shaven face, graying hair, worn rather long, and a benignant eye. He had a kind of tolerant wisdom; and he brought out of many disillusions a humorous clarity.... His conversations were delightful. They were held at our house and a number of our friends and his made up purse of such generous proportions that he was vastly pleased.[8]

The man Emerson had called the "greatest mind since Plato" stayed with the Frenches for a week, holding his "conversations" and touring the countryside with the family. On January 3, Alice's mother noted with relief in the diary that Mrs. Bates, the dressmaker, had offered to take Alice's new black dress to her own home to work on it—out of the way of Mr. Alcott. With the dressmaker gone, Alice

[6] During their early years in Davenport, the Unitarians lacked a church building and held their services in the Burtis House. One of the group's leaders was George French, who, upon leaving his brother-in-law's Episcopal Church, had become a charter member and one of seven persons filing articles of incorporation for the Unitarian Church.

[7] The French family diary, MS, Newberry Library.

[8] Alice French to Hubert Hoeltje, March 31, 1926, Newberry Library.

took "the lion (*id est* Mr. Alcott) out in the morning. Mrs. Van entertained him with frontier stories which he seemed to enjoy. He is like Goldsmith's pastor. Fain would he gladly learn and gladly teach." After Mrs. Van's, Alice took Alcott to meet her uncle, Bishop Lee. The Bishop had received his LL.D. from the University of Cambridge in 1867, and he felt himself a match for Alcott. The two men conversed on philosophy and theology and, with Alice, examined her aunt's newest household innovation, an egg beater, a device that must have interested the former "Yankee Pedlar." In the afternoon Alice took Alcott on a tour of the city's bookstores: "He seemed pleased" at their number, but when Alcott and Alice "tried to find some of Thoreau's books, only found however that no one bought him."

That evening, Alcott gave his first "conversation." The topic was "New England Authors," and after the paying guests filled the Frenches' large living room, sitting on borrowed chairs, Alcott catechized them and presented aphoristic observations of his fellow New Englanders:

> Most of us, authors and all, are only very slightly removed from European associations. Thoreau, with his intensity of democratic feeling, was perhaps the only one truly American, but perhaps it would be best to have only one Thoreau in the world, constituted as it is at present.[9]

Alcott's listeners were only slightly familiar with Thoreau, but they knew Emerson. Alcott delighted in describing him and other famous New Englanders:

> ... a man with a certain feminine grace, a gentleness which one expects in a woman and is the strength of genius. He is a tall, slender man with a remarkable head, of which phrenology can make nothing, since he contradicts all its theories. . . . Emerson's church consists of one member— himself. He waits for the world to agree with him. . . . Emerson lives in a plain house—but then Concord is a plain town, too. Running through it is a river which flows both ways, it is said, after the manner of its leading genius. Concord has recently been enlarged by the annexation of Boston. . . . Hawthorne was [my] next-door neighbor, but was in [my] house only twice. The first time the stove was too hot, the second time the clock ticked too loud.

[9] Iowa City *Daily Press*, December 27, 1872, quoted in Hubert Hoeltje, "Some Iowa Lectures and Conversations of Bronson Alcott," *Iowa Journal of History and Politics*, XXIX (July 1931), 375–401. Alcott's remarks about Emerson and Hawthorne are from the same source.

Such declarations made the "conversations" a success, and Alice marked it in the diary: "Everybody showed their cultivation by praising it.... [Though] one poor woman tried to get a few little naps behind the drapes." When the audiences were gone, the family sat listening to Alcott as he talked into the night, theorizing about knowledge, and learning, and the education of children. Alice's mother asked so many questions about Alcott's daughter Louisa May that he announced, "I believe you are more interested in my daughter than you are in me." And Frances French replied, "Indeed I am."

On the second day of Alcott's visit, Alice's mother served him fried buffalo steaks, raising the problem of Alcott's vegetarianism. To pragmatic Alice, the ensuing debate about the evils of killing the buffalo was needless. The buffalo was already dead; lamentations were wasted. Alcott's principles, however, caused his hostess little trouble, and Alice later recalled: "mother, by christening each soup from its predominant vegetable and never mentioning its evil companion, rather smuggled meat past his scruples," and Alcott himself submerged his standards enough to eat oysters and eggs and drink milk, "even if it were stolen from the calf." [10]

The last "conversation" (on the "Pagan Philosophers") drew such a crowd that even more chairs had to be borrowed to seat all the guests who had paid the fee of fifty cents for ladies, seventy-five cents for gentlemen. The profits were heartening to Alcott, even though he had performed twice for nothing: on the fourth day of his visit Alice had taken him to the orphans' home, where he addressed the children and ate a meal that was "well meaning if not very good," and later he spoke to the Sunday School of the Unitarian Church. Still, he was vastly pleased by the money his "conversations" earned him and announced to the Frenches, "This will please Mrs. Alcott.... She will be surprised too. She didn't expect so much, she is contented with little; she knows I am not worth much." [11] The next day, with his linen washed and mended for him by Alice's mother, Alcott left for Chicago.

Without the guest, the family returned to its normal life. Mrs. Bates returned for final fittings of Alice's dress; a man came to install a new

[10] Hoeltje, "Some Iowa Lectures," p. 377.

[11] Alcott's 1871 tour lasted four months and earned him over $800. He returned to Davenport in 1872 and 1874, sponsored by the Unitarians, but he made few converts: the newspapers reported that his "ideal church" would appear "when cockle shells turn silver bells, and jewels grow on ilka tree" (Hoeltje, "Some Iowa Lectures," pp. 377, 379).

cloth on the billiard table; and Frances French and her daughter returned to their social duties and visited the sick and the poor. To comfortable nineteenth-century Americans, the poor were not a class but a condition. Every town had its paupers, driven by filth and despair into drunkenness, theft, and evangelism. Ladies of good family called on them, for it was thought beneficial to visit the "good poor," if they were servile and if their parade of woes displayed some moral lessons. Shortly after Alcott left Davenport, Frances French noted in the family diary that her two daughters had gone "out calling on a poor woman," and after returning, Alice added her own comment to her mother's entry: "Saw case of poverty. Woman three children and husband in jail. Fannie gave a slate to the family."

When Elizabeth Cady Stanton came to Davenport to plead for woman suffrage, Alice went with a Mr. Lewis to hear her. The irrepressible editor of the militant feminist publication *Revolution* was convinced that voting women would bring a new era of good government and decency; and she spoke out for all women, whether whores, divorcees, or wives of laborers. In the minds of many women, the suffrage movement was identified with trade unionism, indecency, and social turmoil. The *Revolution* for April 16, 1868 had announced, "Capital is absorbing more than its share of the profits of trade. Labor is defrauded of its just dues. The rich are becoming richer and the poor poorer every day." Alice, who had the education, determination, and talents which in another time and place might have led her to embrace woman's cause, viewed the suffrage movement and its advocates with distaste. Her world had prepared her for a journey through life in which she discovered only what she already knew, and after the turn of the century she actively fought against the vote for women in debates and lectures during referendums over woman suffrage in Iowa. Most of Elizabeth Stanton's Davenport audience had no patience with such "strong minded women" as she was, but Alice's mother agreed with her and stoutly maintained that women had natural rights with the rest of humanity, though the laws of the 1870's recognized a married woman's responsibilities more than her rights.

Custom and the law favored obedient and early marriage. Alice would have qualified for neither. She was strong-willed and passing beyond the marriageable age, something that caused more anguish in her parents than in Alice. In the January following Alcott's visit, Frances French entered in the family diary that a Mr. Swits asked Alice to accompany him to a party, although unfortunately he called the next day to beg off: "he was too busy." In February, Alice's mother noted hopefully in the diary that a Captain Adams of the army garrison on Rock Island "took Ally out to ride. He is quite attentive to her," and two months later, Frances French observed that Alice went to a "Calico Party" with a Mr. Hobson. But when a ball was held at the Opera House and even Morton, who was at the university in Iowa City, came home to attend, Alice was escorted by her father. At the last minute she refused to go, and her mother offered reasons in the diary, "she had a headache, but I think the want of a new dress was the chief reason." But not everyone else had found a husband. Alice's friend Celestine Fejervary and the Bishop's daughter, Cousin Carrie Lee, were still unwed, though Jane Allen had married and seemed interested only in her new husband.

On March 19, 1871, when Alice was twenty-one, the family followed its birthday custom and gathered at breakfast to present gifts. Frances French gave her daughter a "toilette set," and George French gave her a writing desk with a felt cover, and an inkwell, and a wicker basket for letters. Alice was beginning to show an interest in a literary career—such a thing was possible for a determined girl—although for her family her concerns were overshadowed by an abrupt change in her father's position, a change which raised him to an eminence that nineteenth-century America esteemed as an embodiment of success and righteous power.

George French's political ambitions had altered in the decade following his terms as mayor of Davenport. In the spring of 1871 he ran for alderman of Davenport's Fifth Ward, the only ward he had failed to carry when he was first elected mayor in 1861. The Fifth Ward rejected him a second time. In the family diary he announced his defeat "by Baldwin of the Gas Co. . . . too much Democracy—and too many Irish for me to succeed." Yet the Whiggism and the managerial talents which had failed to endear him to the Irish now brought him the offer of the presidency of a railroad.

In 1864, George French had led a group of Davenport merchants to press for the construction of a canal from the Mississippi River to Chicago. The coming of the railroads had not always been fortunate for westerners. Monopolistic rail lines charged crippling rates to farmers, who had little alternative but to submit. Many efforts had been made to break what was essentially a protectionist franchise set up by government land grants. One of the plans was the canal to Chicago that would circumvent the railroads east of Davenport and permit shipment of bulky western products by water across Illinois to the Great Lakes and from there to eastern markets and the Atlantic coast.[12] That the canal would make Davenport an important transportation center was not lost on the local businessmen; and with work begun on what eventually was to be the Hennepin Canal, another group assembled three years later to discuss linking Davenport with the farm lands to the north and west to supply the canal with traffic. In 1868, with the help of a 2 per cent tax voted by the county, the Davenport and St. Paul Rail Road Company was incorporated. From the beginning it lost money because it lacked power to extend its lines into Davenport itself and to connect with the railroad bridge over the Mississippi River. By 1870 the railroad had only reached Jackson County, forty miles away, in an uneconomical route that wandered snakelike from town to town in an attempt to capture local support and financial assistance along the way.

Because of the line's troubles, its supporters approached George French following his defeat at the polls and requested that he take control of the railroad. On October 10, 1871, after disposing of his lumber mill, he became the railroad's president, an appointment that was acclaimed by his associates, but not by his wife, who commented in the family diary, "Husband accepted the office of President of the Davenport and St. Paul Railroad and enters on his duties today. I don't like it much—as it will take him away from home so much of the time."

George French had been chosen to improve the finances of the road, which had international aspects, for much of the stock had been purchased by German investors attracted to American railroad securities in the prosperous years preceding 1873. Hope for the railroad's success lasted only two years when, on September 18, 1873, the economic collapse precipitated by the fall of Jay Cooke and Company in the East struck all the railroads. In the midst of over-expanded credit,

[12] The struggle for the Hennepin Canal was a long one. The first sections were not completed until the 1890's, after a lengthy battle with the railroads, particularly the Rock Island, whose tracks paralleled the canal. The railroad tried to obstruct construction of the canal by raising the freight rates of the canal's supporters; but chicanery was unnecessary, for when the canal was completed its locks were so short that no steamboat could pass through them. By the twentieth century traffic on the canal was almost nonexistent.

three million unemployed, wild speculation, stock-watering, and the inflation that remained as an aftermath of the war, railroads failed all over the country, and one of them was George French's Davenport and St. Paul.

The next year, 1874, with the line in receivership and in debt for $3,450,000, its president decided to travel to Europe to meet the Frankfort investors and plead for more capital. Promise of assistance came from an unexpected source. George French was a rich man, a civic leader, and a man of significance beyond the Fifth Ward of Davenport and the borders of Iowa, and he had come to know a short, vain Scotsman named Andrew Carnegie, who had once come to Davenport from Pittsburgh and had met George French and his family. In the 1870's, Carnegie was famous not for his riches but for his salesmanship and his ability to cultivate the friendship of railroad presidents and get their orders for his structural iron. When Carnegie heard of George French's mission to Europe, he offered to meet with the German bankers and support the cause of the Davenport and St. Paul when he himself went to Berlin that same year.

A trip to Europe had other attractions for the Frenches. In June, 1871, Morton had left the university at Iowa City for three years of study in Heidelberg. Two years later his younger brother, Nathaniel, had joined him. Thus, a trip to Germany meant that George French could visit his sons. And he agreed to take Alice and three of her New England cousins with him.

On March 11, 1874, twenty-four-year-old Alice, her father, and her cousins Kate Roberts of Andover and Lizzie and Hattie Davis of North Andover sailed on the Cunard Line's *S.S. Abyssinia* from New York, bound for Liverpool. It took only eight days for the steamer to carry its one thousand passengers across the Atlantic, and by March 19, they were in England.

On board ship, Alice's father had written to his wife:

> Alice is in good spirits. She is a little disposed to put on style, but I think this trip will have a chance to tone her down and thus do her good. B—— was down to see her off. Poor fellow, he has no chance.[13]

From Liverpool, they went on to France and from there to Frankfort on the Main, where George French had made arrangements to have preliminary talks with the stockholders and a family reunion with his

[13] George H. French to Frances M. French, March, 1874, Newberry Library.

two sons. Then to Heidelberg, Alice noting that Nathaniel was "nice as a new pin" and admiring her brothers' student uniforms and Morton's full beard. At Heidelberg her brothers took Alice on tours of the city, showing her the gabled houses and the Heidelberger Schloss. She rode up to the castle above the city on a donkey, with a man walking behind guiding the animal by the tail. With her guidebook in hand, she visited the tower and the enormous century-old tun in the cellar, the chapel and the monk's hole at the castle, and had lunch at an inn in the forest. And she met a baron.

From Heidelberg and Frankfort the group set out on a tour. It was the era of touring innocents abroad, and Alice and her New England cousins were almost representative types of the "American Girl" who moved "pertly and bravely" through foreign capitals, "stepping forth in innocence and might," like the American maidens soon to be celebrated in social novels. They went to Florence and from there to Venice, where Alice bought coral earrings for her younger sister and a shell thimble case and a pair of mosaic sleeve links for her mother. The travelers visited Geneva, where Alice heard her first nightingale, and they went to Vevey across the lake, staying at one of the many hotels. In Vevey in the spring, Americans were numerous; it could be said, indeed, that Vevey assumed at this period some of the characteristics of an American watering-place. There was a flitting hither and thither of young girls, a rustling of muslin flounces, a rattle of dance music in the morning hours, a sound of high-pitched voices at all times. It was like a scene awaiting a novelist who, with the proper, not to say delicate touch, would record or even duplicate it.

To Alice, Geneva with its nightingales had been the "ultimate in romance." But Rome in 1874 was even more exciting. She climbed the Spanish Steps near the Via Gregoriana, where Henry James came to live and observe the American girls who were flocking to Europe. George French, wearing his Victorian mutton-chop whiskers, directed his charges through a brief hour in the Protestant Cemetery in Rome, in visiting the Forum, which was then being excavated, and in touring palaces designed by Bernini. Some of the art seemed naked, even the modern art, for the nineteenth-century "Girl" had begun to lose her clothes in painting and sculpture if not yet in literature. Alice and her cousins saw the Colosseum, though not by moonlight; and they were stunned by a tragedy, for Cousin Hattie grew ill "of the prevalent fever" and died in Rome, one more "lonely flower cropt in its bloom."

After arrangements for Hattie's burial were completed, the travelers quickly left Rome as if to escape the numbing fact of Hattie's death and went to Ireland and then to London.[14] In London they sought out Fitzroy Square, where Alice's favorite, Colonel Newcome, had lived. They saw Queen Victoria riding in a coach in Hyde Park, and suddenly the Baron appeared, "up for the sights." Alice's father commented, "Either the Baron is very much interested in Alice, or he is very fond of the sights!"

Next the travelers recrossed the channel and went to Paris, where Alice tried her Abbot Academy French in Parisian shops and bought her first Paris gown and a fur jacket. Then the group returned to Frankfort, toward the end of June, 1874. In Frankfort there was more bad news. In spite of Carnegie, no help was forthcoming from bankers frightened by defaulting American businesses, so the travelers prepared to return to America in the early summer.

On the last day of the tour George French entered his final reflection in his diary—it was not about his failure to save the railroad: "If Alice could find a good husband, I would not object, but she has not confided in me."

[14] It is obviously unlikely that Hattie Davis was the original of Daisy Miller, but the parallels are noteworthy.

V. Troublers in Zion

In the 1870's, a European tour was a rarity for middle western young ladies, even for daughters of the gentry, so when Alice returned to Davenport, she was questioned by friends and strangers at teas, parties, and meetings of the literary society, and by callers whose fathers' incomes had not allowed such extravagances. She told her listeners of London and the Queen, of visits to Paris and Heidelberg, and of her two handsomely bearded brothers, of the Alps and the Colosseum, of Hattie Davis' tragic death in Rome, and of the Baron— especially the Baron, for he was a unique subject for gossip at afternoon socials in well-upholstered Iowa parlors.

She had kept a journal of the trip; it was something to show friends and perhaps it would be worth writing up someday, but not for several years; other matters were intervening now. Her youngest brother, Robert, now three years old, came more to be Alice's responsibility. And soon after returning from Europe, George French began to build a new home for the family. That meant conferences to hold and plans to make. The women were busy constantly, only pausing briefly at Christmas when the family had its traditional gathering at the Bishop's. Alice and her mother had to select colors and materials and buy new furniture in Chicago at the store of the father's friend, Marshall Field, and what furniture they could use again had to be refinished before it could be put in the new house. Crewelwork, pyramidal whatnot shelves, and bowls of wax fruit were going out of style, and upholstery was not the rage it had been twenty years before. Dark red or green plush, and fringes and tassels on chairs, tablecloths, curtains, and even around piano legs, were passing out of favor, to be replaced by ebonized or gilt furniture and filmy curtains and gloomy William Morris wallpaper in green or brown. There was money enough for the new house and its furnishings. George French had managed to reorganize the railroad with largely the same board of directors and without financial assistance from Europe,[1] and not long after the holidays, the family moved into the new house on East Eleventh Street in Davenport.

When moving and decorating were out of the way, Alice set out to write. In spite of the work at the mission school, discussions to prepare for the literary society, and a full social schedule, she managed to complete a short story early in 1875, the first she had finished since "Hugo's Waiting" four years before. It was a children's story, entitled "A Friend of a Dog." She submitted it to the new *Wide Awake* magazine, which had been advertising its issues in western newspapers and should, she thought, be interested in new fiction. But "A Friend of a Dog" quickly came back—with regrets but also with the encouraging suggestion by the magazine's editor, Ella Farnum Pratt, that "A. French" submit anything else he might have on hand. Things were hopeful after all.

Not long after Christmas, Alice's uncle, the Bishop, fell down a flight of stairs and died abruptly from complications of his injuries. Perhaps it was an omen—a great many more lustrous bulwarks of propriety were collapsing in the middle of the 1870's. The Panic of 1873 had not only bankrupted her father's railroad, it had closed banks by the hundreds; businesses went under; mills were shut down; and the farmers of the Northwest were faced with a unique destruction which made it appear that Nature herself intended to continue the troubles begun by the fall of Jay Cooke and Company. Soon after the panic, overwhelming invasions of grasshoppers appeared in the Middle West, returning each season until 1877. Every year the insects descended on Iowa, Minnesota, and the Dakotas in sky-blackening clouds, drifting onto the railroad tracks in layers thick enough to stall locomotives. Crops in the fields vanished as the farmers stood watching helplessly, and when the fields were bare, the locusts ate the wooden handles of implements left standing in the open.

During this economic calamity, what Daniel Webster had termed the "contagion of democracy" started to spread. In 1871, farmers near Davenport began organizing as Patrons of Husbandry and called

---

[1] The reorganization was not a success, and in 1879 the line was sold to the Chicago, Milwaukee and St. Paul Railroad for one million dollars, the stockholders getting about thirty-five cents on the dollar. Afterward, George French, who had become receiver for the railroad's creditors, again became a director of the First National Bank.

themselves Grangers, united against the railroads and angry at big business. By 1874 there were twenty-four Granges in Scott County. Before the 1870's, labor demonstrations had been local and short-lived, a display of bad manners to some, to others, including Alice, a study in folly. Her peers assumed that to the everlasting credit of God, nine-teenth-century capitalism was a work of Providence and demonstrated common sense. Ideals had to be considered in light of practicality; the matter of the buffalo steaks and Bronson Alcott had multiple applications. Middle-class dogma proclaimed that unionism was unprofitable: strikes didn't work.

By the late 1870's, labor troubles were a common topic of conversation, and middle-class America felt uncomfortable. The Knights of Labor had not yet appeared in Davenport. The organization had grown out of America's faith in decency and self-improvement, and it barred from membership all who were gamblers, physicians, or liquor dealers. Yet elsewhere the Knights of Labor were frightening well-to-do citizens by marking mysterious signs in public places to indicate meeting calls and by making loud noises that too often sounded like social protest. Craft unions had come to Davenport, and there was some cause for discomfort for George French in that, for not long after returning from Europe he resigned from his position with the railroad and a year later became president of the new Eagle Manufacturing Company, producer of agricultural implements. The company, or at least its president, was sensitive to the threat of unionism, although there had been little agitation among Davenport laborers. Even the local streetcar workers, who were on the job fifteen hours a day, seven days a week, gave only moral support to the new Eight-Hour Leagues that were springing up everywhere and versifying their demands for:

> Eight hours for work,
> Eight hours for rest,
> Eight hours for what we will.[2]

In 1876, the Centennial celebrations stimulated hopes that the difficult years might be over. The war had been won, the depression was easing, and the Centennial Exhibition at Philadelphia, with Alexander Graham Bell's new telephone on display, seemed to suggest that infinite progress lay before the Republic. The art and architecture

[2] Richard Ely, *The Labor Movement in America* (Boston, 1886), pp. 72–73.

of the exhibition did not then seem to be the sterile rehash that epito-
mized to later ages all the limitations of what came to be called the
Gilded, the Tragic, the Dreadful, or the Genteel Age. Business had
come to dominate the imagination of the time. The Business Man
who built a factory built a temple. He was no longer "the wicked
baron, bad of heart and bloody of hand"; he was now the central
figure in the life of the people, but with him had come a frantic materialism that created wealth and bitterness. Herman Melville's poem
"Clarel" was published in the Centennial year, 1876, and expressed
the possibilities good men dreaded.

> "'Twill come, 'twill come!
> One demagogue can trouble much:
> How of a hundred thousand such?"

The serenity of the period in which Alice matured had begun to
dissolve with the depression of 1873. The class system, which had
existed all along, became more openly recognized. The workers
charged capital with bloodsucking; the upper classes retorted with
praise of self-reliance—their kind.[3] The lines were drawn by 1874
with the Fall River strike of cotton-mill workers. Then came the
coal strike of 1875. Both were broken but were followed by the railroad
strike of 1877, the first violent national eruption of working class
anger in America. To Alice, who followed developments closely, the
strikes duplicated all the follies of all the lower-class protests she had
read of in English history.

In the summer of 1877, the Davenport newspapers had been discussing the Turkish-Russian War, the rebellion of the Nez Perce
Indians in the West, and a Cuban revolt against the Spanish, but they
took little notice of the first signs of social unrest among lower-class
Americans. On July 7, a demonstration in Chicago urged authorities
to collect delinquent taxes from the rich and begin public works to
avert starvation and suffering among the unemployed. The vigor of
the demonstration indicated the attitude of the population over much
of the industrial North, and later in July, 1877, when four eastern

[3] In 1874 the homeless of New York City were permitted to sleep in police
stations, but only in the face of complaints by conservatives who felt that the
benches of the police stations were sapping the independence and self-reliance
of the impoverished. Sleeping on the streets built character; sleeping in police
stations, according to the *Nation*, was "thoroughly communistic."

railroads announced a wage cut of 10 per cent (the second in five years), the railroad workers struck. They were soon joined by the unemployed, by farmers who hated the railroads, and by mill hands and miners wanting revenge for their defeats in 1874 and 1875. The railroad strike began near Baltimore and spread to West Virginia. By the time it got to Pittsburgh, the newspapers were calling it revolution: the July 22 New York *World* reported, "Pittsburgh sacked. The City Completely in the Power of a Howling Mob!" President Hayes's Cabinet discussed the possibility of declaring Pennsylvania in a state of insurrection; and preachers and politicians quickly convinced each other that the lower classes had gone mad, that the strike was an attempt to establish another French Commune.

Alice read of the riots and watched them creeping west. On July 17, the papers reported that federal troops under a General French[4] were being brought up, with artillery pieces, to help break the strike, the first such happening since the administration of Andrew Jackson. On July 21 soldiers fired on demonstrators in Baltimore, killing fifteen. On July 22 besieged militiamen fought their way out of a Pittsburgh roundhouse, firing a Gatling gun into the crowd. In the violence, numbers of troops deserted and joined the strikers, a good sign to revolutionaries, but to comfortable people everywhere it seemed as though greedy railroad workers had set off a cataclysm. By July 24 the strike had come to Chicago, but it was no longer a railroad strike only. It had grown into a general strike of all the dissatisfied, a protest by the unemployed, the underpaid, the angry, and the deranged. Chicago's mayor, thinking the violence to be the work of drink-crazed men, closed all the saloons. Rioters promptly occupied a brewery, and the strike gained momentum. Even so, protest in Chicago was relatively peaceful at first, in spite of what the newspapers reported, and it never became what the New York *Times* claimed when announcing "City in Possession of Communists."

While the uproar grew, Alice was in Davenport, compiling data on the riots and assembling notes on the mobs collected in Chicago. On July 25, a crowd of fifteen hundred gathered at the Halsted Street viaduct. The next day, more than ten thousand were thronged there when they were set upon by an assortment of police, federal cavalry, and solid citizens excited by the opportunity to carry a gun and

[4] He was not related to Alice's family. On July 25, 1877, the New York *Times* announced that he had been recalled and charged with drunkenness.

emboldened by announcements that life insurance companies would not annul policies of those who helped suppress the riots. The peak came on July 26 in Chicago. Twelve persons were killed, scores were injured—the rioters broke before gun fire and cavalry charging with drawn sabers. By July 27 the rioting had ended and the railroads were running again. Absolutely nothing had been won by the strike.

In Moline, across the river from Davenport, the workers at the John Deere plant struck that same month; and on the day the cavalry attacked the Halsted Street crowd in Chicago, rumors sped through Davenport, Moline, and Rock Island that the strikers were going to burn down the Deere plant, but nothing came of the threats. Alice was fascinated and appalled. Defeat for the strikers was clear proof of all she had learned about organized labor. The brutality and violence of strikes were not even justified by success.

At the end of July, as the strike was collapsing, Alice began a story based on the recent events in Davenport and Chicago. Mixing descriptions of battles between strikers and federal troops at the Halsted Street viaduct, and portraits of rampaging mobs of rioters and of life and laborers in Davenport and Moline, she produced her first notable short story, one that always remained among her favorites.

The story dealt with the fate of a communist in Moline and Chicago during the violence of 1877. The story's heroine was a Countess named Von Arno, aide to the owner of the Seleigman plow factory situated in "M——." [5] The Countess, a woman of fortitude, owned a small share of the business and was its most valuable asset. Her altruistic dream

[5] Moline, Illinois, the site of famous plow factories. The reference here is to George French's Eagle Plow Company or to the John Deere plant, which had been established in Moline in 1847. Alice often similarly identified Davenport as "D——," but even without such clues her northern manufacturing towns, whether given such names as "Fairport" or "Xerxes," are easily identifiable as Davenport and the nearby river towns.

Her use of "D——" for Davenport, a partial step toward realism, was her solution to a problem that later faced literary naturalists and realists. Small towns generally had to be given fictional names (a custom which still prevails) often because the fictional events set in actual villages were too controvertible by observable evidence and thus were not "realistic." On the other hand, New York, Chicago, New Orleans, and San Francisco could be identified as such. Their inhabitants were numerous and anonymous; and furthermore, from the 1880's on, the city presented a rich and alluring image of wickedness to the popular mind. Since each big city suggested unique debauchery and degradation, each deserved to be identified.

was that one day the firm would be Seleigman and Von Arno, with the "yellow eagle" of the company's plows in every country in Europe, not for profit but because then "we can perhaps persuade the workmen to buy stock in the concern, and have a few gleams of sense about profits and wages."

One day the Countess was visited by Martha Bailey, who had come to beg a job at the plow factory for her husband. The Countess, however, had doubts about his loyalty—he was a union man:

> If we were to take your husband on, and the union were to order a strike, even though he were perfectly satisfied with his own wages, wouldn't he strike himself and do all he could to make the others strike? . . . Naturally we don't want to risk one; so we have no union-men.

Shortly afterward, the Countess called at Bailey's shanty on the bank of the Mississippi River. There, while the "gleaming eyes of a great rat" peered through a hole in the ceiling, the Countess lectured William Bailey on his antagonism to the middle class. To Bailey's charge that his hard life was the fault of society which "grinds a poor man to powder so as to make a rich man richer," the Countess countered with the argument from "human nature" that the vogue of Herbert Spencer had made popular:

> A man will work better for himself than he will for somebody else. And you can't get him to work unless he is guaranteed the fruits of his labor. Capital is brain, labor is muscle. . . . You can't alter human nature . . . restraints of morality . . . are bound up inseparably with the rights of property. . . . Marx, Lasalle, and Bradlaugh,[6] clever as they are, can't prevent the survival of the fittest.

The Countess then offered Bailey twenty dollars a week if he would peacefully make plowshares and not strike at the first opportunity. He refused.

Months later, the Countess, visiting Chicago during the dangerous days of the 1877 strike, saw Bailey once more. In the midst of rumored threats by radicals to burn Chicago a second time, the Countess bravely rode out in her coach on an inspection tour. She was soon surrounded

---

[6] The reference, to Karl Marx, Ferdinand Lassalle, and Charles Bradlaugh, yoked together an economic "radical," a Jewish social agitator, and an atheist who advocated contraception—a nice touch, and some clue to the breadth of Alice's reading in contemporary politics and sociology as well as an indication of the knowledge assumed for the readers of *Lippincott's*.

by strikers shouting, "Bread or blood," and by a solemn parade of Poles, Bohemians, Norwegians, and Germans, but only a "sprinkling of Irish and Americans," all led by William Bailey. The Countess then fled to the Halsted Street Police Station and there witnessed the battle of the viaduct between the strikers and the police and federal cavalry. When the riot was finally suppressed, Bailey was arrested as one of the ring-leaders, and as he was brought in to the station house, his wife Martha was carried in on a shutter, killed by a wild shot during the fight. With such a coincidence for its climax, the story ended with the angry husband raging at capitalism and the Countess noting paradoxically: "He is not half a bad fellow . . . but for all that he has murdered his wife."

While the story distorted problems of labor and management, it was an attempt at serious social and economic commentary, and it was unusually topical, especially for literary ladies of the 1870's.[7] Alice had presented a moral drama of the triumph of middle-class ideals, yet she had avoided the grossest banalities of contemporary feminine writing. The sins she presented were more intricate than simple drunkenness, tobacco smoking, blaspheming, gambling, and bastardy, and she avoided the timeworn devices of rediscovered birthmarks, forged letters, and sneering villains who get their comeuppance, to the pleasure of all. Instead, she described laborers and rich men, strikers, communists, and radicals who lived in slums and shanties. And she was sensible enough to acknowledge the slight virtues of her villain, a noteworthy concession at a time when society, literate society at any rate, was predominantly opposed to organized labor and saw little that was praiseworthy in its advocates.

The story showed a new kind of insight into a different kind of world from that which filled the pages of genteel magazines. Alice was working in two literary traditions, romanticism and the emerging realism, and her philosophical assumptions were similarly old and new, a union of traditionalism and the new thought that was imbedded in the works of the English philosopher Herbert Spencer. His theories had appeared in the first years of the decade in works on biology and sociology which suggested that science had finally taken sides in the class struggle. Alice studied Spencer as she had previously studied

---

[7] John Hay's *The Breadwinners*, the first novel to use the 1877 strike as a background, did not appear until 1884, six years after the publication of Alice's story.

Cranmer and Latimer, and in him she found confirmation of her beliefs in the natural superiority of the middle class. Translating Darwin's theories of adaptability, Spencer and the Social-Darwinists convinced intelligent people in the 1870's and 80's that the universe was on the side of Republicanism, property, conservatism, and the respectability of respectability. Henry Ward Beecher announced to Spencer, "To you, sir, I owe my intellectual being"; Carnegie called himself Spencer's disciple and celebrated the great "truth of evolution" he had discovered: "All is well since all grows better."[8] Such buoyant optimism captured even Walt Whitman, and the phrase that provided answers and excused excesses was "survival of the fittest." Like her contemporaries, Alice did not pause to question whether possession of wealth and the triumphant pursuit of what William James had called the "bitch-goddess success" really signified "fitness." To a later age it would seem a most questionable assumption in the light of the survival abilities of Fisk, Gould, Cooke, and Astor. To Henry Adams, the evolution from Washington to Grant was enough by itself to upset Darwin, but to most of Alice's peers, the simple truth of "survival of the fittest"—as it had been translated—was as obvious as the sun and moon. Notwithstanding Ecclesiastes, the race was to the swift, the battle to the strong, bread to the wise, and riches to men of understanding.

Spencer confirmed Alice's inclination to believe the worst about the poor—that, as Spencer suggested, they were poor because they were "negligent, shiftless, inefficient, silly and imprudent." She never felt that such characteristics were as much the result of poverty as its cause. Political rights were judged illusory, a special folly when pursued by women. Nor did Social-Darwinists feel that a state which protected its citizens from physical abuse had any responsibility to protect them from economic abuse.

To middle-class America of the 1870's, Spencer did not reveal such truths so much as he ratified them. The audience that could afford and understand his books had already accepted protestantism, individualism, and the self-assertiveness that had come down to them from Calvin, Luther, Locke, and Hobbes, although most men were unaware of the sources of their ideas. Spencer gave his world and generations of writers a new dogma to replace the Christian world view, a new

[8] Andrew Carnegie, *Autobiography of Andrew Carnegie* (Boston, 1920), pp. 332, 336, 339.

Heavenly City revealed through science rather than scripture. Fore-ordination was now biological, though nonetheless appealing to the rich and other visible saints. And for those who wanted to, socialism could now be refuted with a scientific absolutism as potent as anything Alice's Puritan ancestors had used against the antinomian taint.

Spencer stirred more popular response in America than did any previous philosopher. Thomas Carlyle called him "the most unending ass in Christendom," but by the close of the century, almost a half-million copies of his books had been sold. Hamlin Garland studied Spencer in borrowed books. Jack London read him, and so did Theodore Dreiser while working in Pittsburgh as a reporter. In the memoirs of numerous Americans who matured in the 1860's and 70's, the coming of Spencer to their consciousness is reported as pivotal in their lives—a revelation, an epiphany.

Spencer had proclaimed that evil and immorality must disappear; man must become perfect. Yet he seemed to inspire pessimistic deter-minism in his readers as much as optimism and faith in unlimited progress. Spencer clarified Alice's ideas about society and her trust in success, but he also confirmed her doubts about immigrants and the poor and demonstrated that communism and socialism were foreign and unnatural, quite unlike the native phalanxes, Brook Farm, and the common storehouse at Jamestown. And in Alice's fiction, individualism, goodness, and business enterprise came to be identified with the native-born, while her foreigners were disloyal, idealistic, and vicious.

Her story of the 1877 strike also contained the first instance of her attention to the language of the people she portrayed. As she used the symbol of her father's Eagle plows in the pursuit of realism, she used the words she heard in the speech of people she had met in her father's house and had seen in his mills. In notebooks she listed long examples of bizarre and archaic words and phrases to be later mortised into her sentences, a habit revived with particular success in the stories based on her experiences in Arkansas ten years later. Finally, and typically, she introduced the figure of the masterful woman—in this case the Countess—a character embodying the author's personal ideas set forth to present a neat lesson and to settle confusion caused by men.

When the last page was written—there were thirty-one, some cautiously rewritten in painstaking longhand ten or twelve times [9]—

9 In her old age, she acknowledged that the painful necessity of revising her early manuscripts had at least made her handwriting legible.

she chose a title, "Communists and Capitalists," to suggest conflict and timeliness, and then she appended the subtitle "A Sketch from Life" as a claim to realism.

She needed a new pseudonym. The "Frances Essex" she had used for "Hugo's Waiting" would not avoid the bias that she was convinced male editors had against literary women. Later in life she reported that part of her pen name had come to her during a trip to Massachusetts when her railroad car passed through the railyards in Cleveland, Ohio, and she saw chalked on the side of a bright red freight car the name "Thanet." The next choice was a deceptively masculine first name, and for that she took "Octave," the nickname of Octavia Putnam, her roommate at Abbot.[10]

Magazines of the 1870's had almost doubled in number since the Civil War, and they favored honest riches, so there was a ready market for her story. First she tried *Scribner's Monthly*. Signing the letter accompanying the manuscript "A. French" in the most manly way possible, she sent "Communists and Capitalists" by "Octave Thanet" to New York and the editor, Josiah Gilbert Holland.

The story was rejected. It was timely, exciting, imbued with melodrama, but *Scribner's* was not interested. As soon as the manuscript returned, Alice took it from its envelope, erased the editorial marks and sent it off again, this time to *Lippincott's Magazine* in Philadelphia. Three weeks later, a large oblong yellow envelope arrived in Davenport, addressed to "A. French" and with "*Lippincott's*" running across the top in white letters. Inside was a letter of acceptance from the editor John Foster Kirk, and a check for forty-two dollars. She never forgot the moment—or the money:

I think it simply went into the bank with the other money I received that

[10] There are varying stories about the origin of Alice French's pen name, particularly Thanet, which she pronounced with a hard final *t*. One was that she saw the name on a boxcar during a visit to the South, not Cleveland. Another was that "Thanet" was marked on a boxcar that the neighborhood children in Davenport played on. The latter, while homely, is unlikely, considering the quality of the neighborhoods she inhabited and their distance from any railroad tracks. It is more likely that she had merely come across references to the Isle of Thanet in British history, although in an interview published in the Chicago *Tribune* of August 16, 1926, she reported having seen "Thanet" on a red freight car in Cleveland and added, "I have never seen the name before nor have I seen it since." In any event, she seemed unwilling, in interviews, to stick to one story, and of them all, the one just recounted has a plurality of citations, if not a majority.

year. It was not a vast sum, under $200, the first year's earnings of my own, but it gave me so much more happiness than any other money received before or since that I shall never forget it.

For a beginner, forty-two dollars was not bad. Twain was getting two cents a word from the *Galaxy*, and in the 1880's, Howells got as much as five thousand dollars for a serial; but after the Civil War most short stories sold for less than one hundred dollars, and in 1878, *Lippincott's*, *Scribner's*, and the *Atlantic* were paying no more than ten dollars a page to established contributors and only half that to newcomers. "Communists and Capitalists; A Sketch from Life," not quite eight and a half printed pages in the October, 1878, *Lippincott's*, got the beginner's rate, calculated exactly.

VI. In League with Riches

Five months after the appearance of "Communists and Capitalists," Alice's third published short story, "One of the Congregation," appeared in E. F. Merriam's *Sunday Afternoon,* a quality magazine whose editor, the Reverend Washington Gladden, had undertaken to fill the Sunday reading of the family with stories of "sound moral tendency." [1] But well before the story appeared, Alice had begun writing her first essays on the social and economic problems of the times.

One consequence of the 1873 depression was what newspapers called the "tramp evil." Thousands of farmers, mill hands, unemployed clerks, and laborers swarmed over the land, looking for jobs and handouts and frightening good citizens with their prevalence and their cabalistic sign language. Sometimes the tramps massed in armies and raided the countryside. In 1877, during the ferment of the railroad strikes, newspapers reported that hobo bands were ransacking rural homes in New England, forcing householders to flee to protection in nearby towns. Alice read of similar uprisings in the Middle West— trains in Illinois had to carry special guards to protect against pillaging mobs, and for a short while, tramps had actually taken over the town of Durant, Iowa. She saw the hobo rabble that periodically invaded Davenport in the ten years following 1875. The tramps usually came by train, as many as four hundred at a time riding in, under, and on top of box cars, in hordes like the locusts that were then descending on Minnesota and the Dakotas. In Rock Island and Moline, when news came of an approaching trainload of tramps, church and fire bells were rung to warn the citizenry. In Davenport it was common to see hundreds of tramps lounging around the city, scratching their backs on the lamp posts or sleeping in the streets. Rock Island police customarily drove hobo bands across the Mississippi River bridge into Davenport, and there the police herded them into the public market

[1] Washington Gladden, *Recollections* (Boston, 1909), p. 272.

and watched them through the night before escorting them westward to the city limits the next morning. It was not the plight of the vagrants but their disgusting presence that irritated citizens, and as early as 1876, state legislatures began passing anti-tramp laws designed not to eliminate the causes of the "tramp evil" so much as to remove the tramps themselves. Experts were divided between those who wished for the problem to be relieved and those who wished to see it suppressed. History supported all theories. Rich businessmen pointed out that tramps, like the poor, were always present: their relief was senseless and their appetites inexhaustible. The tender-hearted, and in some cases the very hardhearted, insisted that tramps were less sinister than a society which would produce them and then beggar them. Laborers turned to trade unionism. Impoverished farmers organized against banks, middlemen, and the railroads. Each faction offered its own relief as the solution to all public maladies. The rich won the philosophical debate—they owned the magazines. The poor—and their demagogues—triumphed in oratory and in songs like the anti-monopoly protests of the last quarter of the century:

> For Vanderbilt and Company 'tis indeed a gilded age
> But poverty increases, 'tis thus that tramps are made.

Conditions aroused apprehension among the middle class and among plutocrats fearful of revolution and expropriation, and their fears were reflected by editors of popular magazines, who began to fill their publications with political and social essays and economic fiction that was meant to deal common sensibly with social turbulence.

Alice French had some historical perspective on social upheavals which she had acquired in the Bishop's library. The world's ills and popular interest in social problems made her views timely, and in May, 1879, *Lippincott's* carried her fourth published piece, "The Tramp in Four Centuries." The essay had some of the dramatic quality of a short story, for she quoted from four letters; the first, written in the sixteenth century by one of Edward VI's commissioners of enclosure, described the distress brought by land enclosures: "The countrie is filled with ydle knaves and begars." The second letter, written in the seventeenth century, cited the prevalence of highwaymen infesting the roads and "Ye multitood of begars and criples and misrubble poor folk." The others described how elimination of wool production in Ireland and introduction of agricultural machinery in later centuries displaced the peasantry and reduced them to poverty. Each letter described suffering workers and carried the suggestion that four hundred years of English history served only to demonstrate that such problems were permanent and the natural result of social and industrial progress.

Alice concluded that superficial remedies did more harm than good, and among superficial remedies, she put all attempts at legislation that ignored what she held to be a fundamental economic truth—social and economic distress would only right itself by itself; misery, then, was the ransom the lower class must pay for the progress of all. Nor did the essay avoid a conventional nineteenth-century conclusion that the source of wealth somehow lay in moral and natural superiority. Survival of the fittest was not mere theory; it was an incontestable truth that satisfied good men and women who could believe in both permanence and progress. Alice's faith in such a contradiction was not complacency in the face of suffering as much as it was a sign that her utterances rose from the passions of the community in which she passed her life, that, like her Puritan ancestors, she was shaped by the hand of her sect and her locality. She was a member of the gentry, even if it was in Iowa, and she accepted its regnant codes and delusions, including the fiscal Calvinism of the Gilded Age and its doctrine of the holy stewardship of business. Society, which must "excrete" its idle, its imbecilic, and its sick, must permit men to lay up riches for the greater glory of God. The Episcopal Bishop of Massachusetts himself pronounced, "In the long run, it is only to the man of morality that wealth comes. . . . Godliness is in league with riches."

The dispassion with which Alice French could look upon the poor appeared in her sociological essays long before it animated her local-color stories of the 1880's and 90's. Her written statements were never as impudent as those of Bishop Lawrence, but her constant faith in similar principles, her pedagogical urge, and her distance from the people she described led her from true realism into a didactic local-color fiction cluttered with the same machinery of social argument that had appeared in her early essays. Although her mature short stories were laden with grim realistic details that were often bloody and shocking, they seldom failed to show that good men prospered and that fate was governed by comprehensible and acceptable moral laws. It was a romantic faith, but to Alice it was ineluctably relevant to the real world.

Not all writing of the 1870's and 80's celebrated the virtues of middle-class America. The most popular social document of the age, Henry George's *Progress and Poverty*, was written during the same upheavals of 1877 that had moved Alice to write her first notable short story. But while the last quarter of the nineteenth century made best sellers out of *Progress and Poverty* and such other attacks on orthodoxy as *Looking Backward* and *Robert Elsmere*, the public that read Edward Bellamy and Mrs. Humphry Ward and Henry George also read books by Robert Louis Stevenson and A. Conan Doyle, and in greater numbers. Even the emerging realism came well mixed with romance in such successes as *The Hoosier Schoolmaster*, which sold ten thousand copies in its first six months and seemed so wholly American that it was translated into French [2] by the famous critic Madame Blanc for the *Revue des Deux Mondes*, the apex of French literary judgment which had restricted its attention to recent American writers to the pirating of Henry James.

The appearance of "The Tramp in Four Centuries" aroused interest in "Octave Thanet" and brought congratulations for her practical, common sense views. Andrew Carnegie, whose friendship with the Frenches had continued since the unsuccessful trip to Germany, knew the identity of "Octave Thanet" and wrote to Alice, praising her for her insight into social and economic matters and suggesting that they exchange copies of everything they wrote. Carnegie considered himself something of an essayist. When he was sixteen, his letters were being published in the New York *Tribune*, and by the 1870's he was formulating the theories he presented in his "Gospel of Wealth" and in *Triumphant Democracy* (1885). To Carnegie, capitalism offered a solution to the problem of the poor. The laws of accumulation and distribution should be left free; then the individual millionaire would act as trustee for the dispossessed, and a better—because wiser—trustee than any community or government. It was as aristocratic an ideal as anything current in Europe, and it was a natural corollary to the industrial expansion that followed the Civil War in America, for the idea of the millionaire had come to be a part of the wholesome and reasonable tradition of rugged individualism. The faithful in acquisitive society embraced a new trinity: the stewardship of wealth, the efficiency of laissez faire, and the survival of the fittest.

[2] As *Le Maitre d'Ecole de Flat Creek*.

When Carnegie sent his congratulations for her writing, Alice replied, thanking him for his praise and accepting his offer to exchange works:

> The exchange business will be delightful if you will only be more liberal than your word and send every scrap and shred you write about the tariff and the currency. On my part I will faithfully promise not to send anything of which such writings of yours may be inspiration.

Carnegie had complimented her for what he called her "advanced opinions," and she concluded her letter with her views on the woman suffrage movement and a description of her outdoor activities. She knew Carnegie liked active gentlewomen:

> I fear I couldn't pass my examination before the Woman's Club, especially after I had confessed my lurking admiration for Mr. Parkman's late articles in the North American. . . .[3]
>
> In default of riding I tried lawn tennis last summer and this winter I have been reviving my skating. My experience is a most awful surprise. I used to be more at home on skates than on my feet but now my left foot appears to not belong to me at all; and I never have the least idea what is to become of me when I start out on a stroke . . . luckily the ice is strong. If you ever please us so much as to make us a visit we shall be ashamed to show you your book, its dainty appearance is fast leaving it beneath a run of borrowers. Yesterday it went to a literary club. Wouldn't you have been amused to have listened to their comments? Give my love to your mother, please. I should like to play a game of whist with her. Goodbye; not in form, but really I wish you a *happy* New Year.
>
> Very truly yours,
ALICE FRENCH.
>
> P. S. Excuse paper; I am going through an interregnum of stamping. Your monogram is very pretty I think. I was once beguiled into silver, but soon repented.
>
> A. F.[4]

---

[3] Francis Parkman had written a series of articles for the *North American Review*. The last article, "The Woman Question" (*North American Review*, CCLXXV [October 1879], 303–332), had appeared two months before and opposed woman suffrage because, among other reasons, women with their "rounder outlines" were built for things other than the vote.

[4] Alice French to Andrew Carnegie, December 31, 1879, Andrew Carnegie Papers, Library of Congress.

Four months after the appearance of "The Tramp in Four Centuries," *Sunday Afternoon's*[5] editor, Washington Gladden, accepted another essay, "Latimer as a Social Reformer," and the same fall, *Sunday Afternoon* accepted her fourth short story. It was her first to follow closely the local-color tradition of the identifiable locale in short fiction. She had often taken the excursion steamers up the river from Davenport toward St. Anthony's Falls and passed through Lake Pepin on the Mississippi between Wisconsin and Minnesota. In this picturesque site she had set an account of the adventures of newlyweds confronting the conflict between science and religion.

In the last quarter of the century Darwinian theories, with the help of Spencer and Huxley, were having their greatest effect on traditional theologies. Ministers were abandoning their flocks and vice versa; believers began to doubt and doubters were confirmed in their ways. Alice's own family had turned from the Bishop's Anglicanism to Davenport's Unitarian church. And Alice had heard the arguments for agnosticism advanced by another of her father's friends, the Peoria, Illinois, lawyer Robert Ingersoll. Ingersoll's unorthodoxies had shocked General Lew Wallace into devout Christianity and the writing of *Ben-Hur*; but Ingersoll was a strong Republican and exemplified enterprise and diligence, and his antiscriptural views did not seem too secular in the polite respectability of the French home. Furthermore, Alice was reading the philosophy of Arthur Schopenhauer, who had similarly been moved by the strife and poverty of industrial workers and the unrest and misery that seemed to fill the world. She read *The World as Will and Idea*, and the story she sent to Washington Gladden, "Schopenhauer on Lake Pepin," reflected Schopenhauer's faith in the necessity of strife and misery.

The story began on a steamboat traveling up the Mississippi. A rhapsodic description of the scenery along the shore preceded the appearance of the heroine, Ethel Berkely, and her husband, Captain John Berkely of the United States Army. Twenty-six-year-old Ethel, another idealized self-portrait, was a beauty of "the English type which New England had preserved or possibly revived; there were the fair broad brow, the pale gold hair, the mildly Roman profile, the exquisite coloring and the charming figure of English loveliness." And like the author, Ethel Berkely was clever and "played a strong

[5] The name was changed to *Good Company* in October, 1879.

game of whist, never hesitating to sacrifice her own hand to her partner's."

At a steamboat landing on the shore òf Lake Pepin, the Berkelys briefly left the boat and met a recluse who yearned to talk of his life. His parents had been German; his mother had been decent, but his father had married above his station and was only a foreman in a foundry, though "he wasn't even that long, for he fell first into socialism and then into drink."[6] To rise above his father, the hermit had become a Methodist preacher, yet he was a failure in spite of the fact that he was successful as an orator, kept up with popular thought, and periodically "refuted Robert Ingersoll." The poor depressed him: "They were stumbling blocks. They gave me an awful sense of the burden of life. There wasn't anything sentimental or poetic about their suffering . . . and the worst of their poverty in many cases seemed to be its apparent necessity." In his despondency he had turned first to Kant and Hegel and finally to Schopenhauer. As a result, he had left his church—spurning even the congratulations of the Unitarian minister. Because of his apostasy his family starved; his wife and son died of diphtheria, and he was forced to give his daughter to relatives.

To the hermit's catalog of woe, Ethel replied that man had made progress from the ape, and there was a way out—good works. Finally, with arguments strewn with references to Fichte, Schelling, and Hegel, Ethel converted the hermit, and the Berkelys departed. But it was not until years later that they learned the result of their afternoon on Lake Pepin when they read the former preacher's name in a death list of those killed by a pestilence in Mississippi, where he had gone as a volunteer to nurse the sick.

The story suggested that it was dangerous to flout society's rules, that men who followed ideals impractically would suffer, and it reflected the rise of the social gospel that was bringing the establishment of settlement houses and the social Christianity of General Booth and the Salvation Army's "slum brigades." The story's ending was abrupt;

[6] To suggest that socialism was the first step toward drink and debauchery was not as ludicrous to the popular mind of the 1880's (and certainly not to the pious readers of *Sunday Afternoon* and *Good Company*) as it is today—or was until recently. Socialism in the United States was largely a Middle-European importation, nurtured in beer halls and the sinister places hospitable to immigrants and paupers with strange tastes and alien habits.

its author was more interested in her protagonist's conversion than in his elevation. Otherwise she observed current literary conventions, especially the local-color blend of realism and romance that would dominate short fiction until the end of the century.[7] The story had an exotic locale, an interesting and odd character speaking out in a setting that reflected his personality, and all of it was seen through the reportorial and normalizing eye of a middle-class observer with the patronizing viewpoint that became a staple of local-color short fiction.

In 1879, Alice sold three short stories and two essays. The year 1880 was even more profitable, beginning in January, when the *Western* in St. Louis published "My Lorelei: A Heidelberg Romance." The story had come out of her diary of the 1874 European tour and exhibited her feelings for her father and her habit of identifying herself with her heroines. The heroine of "My Lorelei," a visitor in Heidelberg as Alice had been, deeply loved her husband, who, like George French, had traveled to Frankfort on business. The heroine, in a platonic Victorian way (and with unself-conscious verve) also declared her love for a maiden named Undine, although the relationship abruptly ended when Undine was killed in Heidelberg castle by a mad cretin from the nearby forest.

As in "Schopenhauer on Lake Pepin," Alice was content to present conflict in "My Lorelei" and to leave its resolution to an abrupt and cleansing event which had little relation to the moral dilemma she had tried to create. The story was ample evidence that she had yet to develop her talents much beyond a reportorial capacity to present events and scenes. It was a limit that bound most local colorists to superficiality and a dependence on dialect, strange characters, and unusual scenes.

The same indifference to structure was apparent in May, 1880, when San Francisco's new *Californian* carried Alice's "The First Xerxes Loan Collection," which fictionalized her experiences in helping organize an

[7] The term "local color" began to appear prominently in American literary criticism in the 1860's, having been taken from French literary terminology of the first decades of the century. While the vogue of local color in the United States grew out of the popularity of the stories of Bret Harte in the late 1860's, the production of local-color fiction did not become a flood until the 1880's and 1890's, when it provided editors of an increasing number of magazines with a means of satisfying a vast audience hungry as always for morality and entertainment and now awakened to a new national spirit and an interest in its own legends, customs, and people.

art museum in Davenport (Xerxes). She reserved her serious labors for nonfiction, for she was discovering that her appetite for success could be fed more by essays than by short stories. Her fiction could only command the attention of editors of second-quality journals; her sociological studies appeared in the nation's famous magazines.

In April, 1880, *Lippincott's* printed the first of a two-part essay on laborers, "The English Workingman and the Commercial Crises," which examined the problems of labor in nineteenth-century England as a means of arriving at principles applicable to the difficulties then confronting industrialized America. The essay was a long and learned demonstration of her wide reading and her assumptions about the central problem of capitalism—"the condition of labor." Once again, she turned to the life of the workingman in the sixteenth century to find parallels to the upheavals following the introduction of finance capitalism in the United States after 1865. With footnoting not likely to be tolerated in a popular magazine today, she refuted the theories of Cobbett, Godwin, and Owen and offered the Spencerian postulate that artificial support of the poor was bad because they would overbreed and clog evolution.

Like her fellow Social Darwinists, Alice felt that letting the weak go under would produce a better race—a principle sufficiently evident among farm animals. Attempts at collective protection by the poor only frustrated that farseeing benevolence of evolution. And that was not all. Unions, for example, produced "clan" loyalty and thus brought the "clan's despotic morality," with the result that skilled workmen had "an aggressive infidelity in the place of religion." To Alice, industrial harmony was a matter of morality, loyalty, and understanding. Men were contentious not because they were poor—there had always been the poor—they were contentious because they persisted in their ignorance.

She repeated the same theories elsewhere. After the appearance of "The English Workingman," *Good Company* published "Jails" in December, 1880, and "Charity" in February. The thesis was familiar— destitution was the result of idleness and intemperance: indiscriminate charity discouraged honest labor, and for every beggar in real want, twenty were imposters. Alice was trying to be realistic by reaffirming the myths of hard good sense which dominated her world. She had written to her Abbot schoolmate Anna C. Dawes: "There is disposition to give pity to the poor as indiscriminately as once we gave alms, and our pity is sometimes more mischievous than our gifts;

for our gifts often lifted the souls of the givers even if they harmed the recipients."

In May, 1881, Merriam and *Good Company* published "Creeds," and Alice sent copies of the essay to Carnegie as she had promised. Largely as a result of their exchange of essays, Alice had entered his mind when he began to make plans for the summer of 1881. Carnegie, who had risen from bobbin boy in a cotton factory, had promised himself that he would some day hire a coach-and-four and "drive a party of my dearest friends from Brighton to Inverness," and in an elegant manner that would redress some of the deprivations of his impoverished childhood. One month before Alice's thirty-first birthday, she received a St. Valentine's day message from Carnegie. He invited her to report to the Windsor Hotel in New York on May 31, 1881, prepared to embark with ten others on a three-month coaching tour of Great Britain. She telegraphed her reply: "Will I go to Paradise for three months on a coach? Agent of Providence, I will." At the end of May she met with Carnegie and his other guests[8] (he dubbed them the "All-coaching Eleven") at the hotel on Fifth Avenue, where Carnegie announced that they would embark for Liverpool the next day on the *Bothnia*, "Cunard Line, of course."

Carnegie was forty-five, fourteen years older than Alice. He was dapper, vain, and cocksure; and in spite of the fact that he was just five feet four inches high and weighed only 130 pounds, he was one of the most eligible bachelors in the world. He had promised his mother that he would never marry while she lived, but he was looking for a wife, and at the time of the trip he had been courting a New York girl, Louise Whitfield, for more than a year. Louise Whitfield had been invited to join the coaching tour, and Carnegie had even obliged his mother to present a personal invitation, but when she requested Louise's presence on the trip, Margaret Carnegie announced to the girl's mother, "If she were a daughter of mine, she wouldna go," at which Louise was sent off to the Catskills for the summer,[9] and Alice was left as the only eligible female on the tour.

The group left New York on June 1, 1881, and ten days later caught sight of Great Britain. In his diary of the trip, Carnegie recorded

[8] The group included Carnegie's mother, Margaret, his business associates and friends G. F. McCandless, Henry Phipps, Jr., Benjamin Vandevort, Alexander King and his wife, Aggie, David McCargo and his wife, as well as Carnegie's niece Jennie Johns, and Alice French.

[9] Perhaps it was a wise maneuver. Carnegie married Louise Whitfield in 1887.

hearing the noise of the "booming of great guns at regular intervals," as the ship approached the English coast, and he observed that it was Britain's reply to "Watch der Rhine," adding, "I hope [the English] will pattern after the Germans in many particulars. Music included."[10]

Eleven days from New York, the travelers docked at Liverpool, where a special railway car waited to take them to London. The group remained in London for six days, making daily excursions through the city and meeting at breakfast and dinner to exchange experiences. Through Carnegie's influence with a cabinet minister, Alice was admitted to the gallery of the House of Commons, where she heard the Quaker John Bright speaking on temperance. Traveling through London in a parade of hansom cabs, the pilgrims visited the Tabard Inn and went to Stafford House, where their tour was conducted by the Marquis himself. Finally they went to Albert Hall and heard a performance of the *Messiah* which seemed superior to any they had heard in America, though all agreed the *Messiah* conducted by the elder Mr. Damrosch came close.

Six days after arriving, the travelers left London to begin their tour to Scotland. At Brighton their coach was waiting, a magnified stagecoach pulled by four handsome horses, three brown and one white. Inside was room for four passengers, and on the top, exposed to the weather, were seats for fourteen. The coach was new and was painted a glistening black with red trim; it had red velvet cushions and a coachman and a footman dressed in blue and silver livery.

The coach carried supplies for seven days. Each passenger was allowed to carry a handbag and a "strap package"; large trunks were forwarded to the destination for the following Sunday so that once each week the entourage could appear at dinner in formal dress. Two luncheon baskets had been purchased in London, and Carnegie appointed Alice to see them properly filled with food at each inn before the day's journey began. In his account of the tour, *American Four-in-Hand in Britain* (1883), Carnegie, the apostle of Spencer and Social Darwinism, explained that it had been "a process of natural selection that she who had proven her genius for making salads . . . during the voyage should be unanimously appointed to fill the important position of stewardess and given full control of the hampers."

On June 17 the group prepared to leave Brighton on the first leg of the journey. When all passengers were ready to depart, they were

[10] Trip Diary, Andrew Carnegie Papers, Library of Congress.

Andrew Carnegie's coaching party in England. Alice is seated fifth from the left on the coach.

photographed in their places on the coach: Alice, who was dressed in proper black traveling clothes with a feminine bowler set above her full round face, sat on top of the coach and looked at Carnegie posing in the driver's seat, wielding a long black whip and stretching his short legs and size five shoes to the footrest.

Once the trip began, Carnegie left most of the driving to the coachman, but everything else he directed as closely as he did the management of his mills. When the coach stopped for the night at an inn, one of the party was chosen to examine the available rooms and assign them to the travelers, while another appointee supervised the unloading of the coach and the unpacking of two American flags, which were then brought to the main room of the inn and placed on the mantel. In the mornings Alice rose early and filled the luncheon hampers; then the travelers breakfasted together, collected the flags from the mantel, and rode off before an audience of local rustics who had collected to see a coach full of foreigners.

A day's journey averaged thirty-two miles of riding and walking, for when the horses were pulling up a steep grade the passengers alighted and walked beside the coach. When it rained, four rode inside and the rest sat outside in the weather, protected by umbrellas, waterproofs, and woolen underwear. In all but the worst weather Alice preferred to ride on the top of the coach, for she could then see over the hedges into the neat English gardens and their owners' houses.

Near Windsor, when the coach took Alice through her first real English lane, she carefully noted it in her diary. Then Carnegie took the reins, and with his mother seated beside him—a position she coveted when single women were near—he drove through the royal forest to the door of Windsor Castle. Queen Victoria was absent, but the next day the group attended church in St. George's Chapel inside the castle walls, and Alice saw the Prince of Wales and Gladstone come in the door together. The Prince flustered all the ladies as he strode up the aisle, and Carnegie, who liked to rank swells, was pleased to record that Gladstone followed "at a respectful distance and took his seat several pews behind."

At Stoke Poges, Carnegie led the "All-coaching Eleven" into the country churchyard and read Gray's *Elegy* to them. They visited the manor house of Stoke Poges, where Charles I had been confined (it was for sale), and at Reading they played lawn tennis in the twilight, the ladies moving decorously in their long skirts—haste and overhead shots were bad manners. The next morning they visited Oxford. Thirteen years earlier, in 1868, Carnegie had promised himself that he would quit the degrading pursuit of money within two years and settle in the university town where he could "get a thorough education." Now he led his guests through some of the college buildings, commenting on their noble Victorian Gothic style. Then, shortly after noon, he led all the travelers to see the University Museum, except for Alice, who went instead to see the memorial to Latimer and Ridley.

On the way to Banbury from Oxford the travelers passed Blenheim Palace, which a grateful English Parliament had built to honor Marlborough's victory in the War of the Spanish Succession. The sight of such ducal opulence angered Carnegie—he had not yet occupied his own Scottish castle—and he lectured his "All-coaching Eleven" on nations that reward warriors, whom he called "successful murderers of their fellows," rather than statesmen and men of letters. And at the battlefield of Edgehill in the Cotswolds, where the roundheads had fought the cavaliers two hundred years before, another democratic urge led Carnegie to halt the coach and address his audience on the virtues of the Puritan cause.

Luncheon time once found the travelers at Kenilworth Castle, where picnic parties were never admitted, but the keeper was so impressed with the elaborate coach and the American pilgrims that he permitted them to enter, and Alice spread lunch under a hawthorne tree—the very tree, they assured one another, where Queen Elizabeth confronted Amy Robsart, the unfortunate wife of Robert Dudley, the Queen's lover.

Near the end of June the travelers entered Shakespeare country; stopped in Stratford-on-Avon; visited Charlecote House, built by Sir Thomas Lucy; and drove through Charlecote Park seeing hundreds of deer—descendants, they were told, of those that attracted the young poacher William Shakespeare. At Coventry, vestiges of George Eliot were a greater attraction to Alice than the folklore about Lady Godiva that interested the rest of the travelers. Alice visited the room where Mary Anne Evans (who had also chosen a masculine pen name) first went to school, and guided by the town's ex-mayor, Alice was introduced to the man who had been the novelist's teacher. Alice recorded each incident in her diary. The lives of the two women had certain parallels: Mary Anne Evans' father had taken her about the manufacturing center of Coventry, and she, too, had observed much about people and the way they lived. And, like Alice, she was interested in provincial towns, and goodness—how it was acquired and how lost.

From Coventry the group rode through the industrial Midlands, passing bleak, grim houses, smoking chimneys, coal pits, rolling mills, dirty children, and hard-bitten men. In her journal Alice noted the evidence of the drunken husbands, the dead children, the daughters who went wrong, and the constant sight of women overburdened with their children and no sign of diminishing fertility. After seeing one woman with nineteen children, Alice wrote in her diary, "Poor thing! I suppose when she got up to eleven or twelve the ordinary British number she thought she was done! Fancy her sensations over the nineteenth!"

At Wolverhampton, Carnegie saw a free library and once again lectured his mobile audience, this time on the wisdom of such institutions—he had just begun endowing libraries himself. At Chatsworth, on July 4, news of the shooting of President Garfield caused Carnegie to cancel plans for an Independence Day celebration. Instead, each traveler signed a telegram, which Carnegie dispatched to Secretary of State Blaine, offering the group's congratulations at the news (mistaken, it turned out) that Garfield would recover.

In the Lake District, Alice went boating and stayed in Keswick at a hostel advertising "PATRONS: ROYALTY AND AMERICAN PRESIDENTS." And on July 15 the coach crossed the border into Scotland, where it halted while Alice stood with all the others and, much to the joy of their host, gave three cheers for Scotland. In Gretna Green, Alice visited the blacksmith's, where so many hurried weddings had taken place, and saw Carnegie stop a small boy to give him money and a calling card and to advise him to "learn Burns and Scott and become a mechanic and I will give you a place."

At Carnegie's birthplace, Dunfermline, where he had endowed a free library and built municipal baths, the travelers were met by five bands and a mile-long procession of Odd Fellows, foresters, gardeners, weavers, dyers, foundrymen, and masons, who cheered Carnegie through the streets to the Abbey, where the coach stopped while all its passengers stood up to salute the Stars and Stripes that flew from the tower.

After three days of celebrations Carnegie and his guests left Dunfermline, passed through Birnam Wood, and the Pass of Killiecrankie, and finally arrived at Inverness, seven weeks and a day and 831 miles after leaving Brighton. At Inverness they abandoned the glorious coach-and-four—sent by train back to London—and journeyed by omnibus and canal boat to Oban and then to Glasgow. There the party disbanded, and Alice left for Paisley and a visit with Carnegie's mother before returning by train to Liverpool, where the journey had begun. She had seen half of Britain from a vantage point on top of a coach driven by a world-famous millionaire. Her life could never be the same. On August 12 she sailed on the *Algeria* for New York.

VII. I Write from Experience

Alice landed in New York as she had when she returned from Europe with her father in 1874, but the world had changed in seven years; authority seemed impotent and society disordered. In 1881 laborers in the United States struck 23,000 times, and the Federation of Labor Unions of the U.S.A. and Canada was founded, forcing capitalists into unaccustomed subtleties: George Pullman began to build a model factory town near Chicago, which he named after himself and provided with everything but saloons. In April, 1881, the Postmaster-General uncovered the scandalous "star route" frauds in mail delivery contracts and a conspiracy of high government officials, among them the United States senator from Arkansas. In Europe, Czar Alexander II was killed by a nihilist bomb. In America, the Standard Oil Company was being organized as a trust under John D. Rockefeller. The art of selling gold bricks was introduced to New York City by a westerner; Mrs. Eddy had become the faculty of her own Massachusetts Metaphysical College; and a future friend of Alice's, Theodore Roosevelt, had graduated from Harvard and decided to run for the New York state legislature.

Although some of these events would shape the course of the world, they hardly ruffled the surface of Alice's life as she prepared to return from New York to Davenport. She was making the trip alone. Decent women traveled alone on the railroads now; the Pullman car had become so respectable that lady passengers could take off their clothes to sleep, and spinsters over twenty-five could ignore the rules of chaperonage—it was assumed that they had left behind what books of etiquette called the "wild grace of a giddy girlhood." The thirty-one-year-old woman who boarded the train in New York for the trip to Chicago and Davenport was tall and handsome—now getting a little stout—with blonde hair and blue eyes. And while she had brought no gowns from Paris on this trip, she was modishly dressed in the current fashion of the pannier and extended bustle, even if these made a long train trip uncomfortable.

When she arrived in Davenport, her father met her at the Rock Island depot, where her luggage, including her journal of the coaching trip, was loaded on the family carriage and driven to the big house on East Eleventh. There she was greeted by her mother and her sister and brothers, among them Robert, who had turned ten the month before, and Nat, who had completed his service as law clerk to the famous Robert Ingersoll in Peoria and was now a practicing attorney in Davenport.[1] Copies of the *Atlantic* were waiting for Alice, too. The family had saved them during the summer while the magazine carried her longest sociological essay, "The Indoor Pauper."[2]

Alice had encountered the orphans' home in Davenport long before the day she took Bronson Alcott there for the edification of the inmates. She had read of the reforms in the Massachusetts state prisons and asylums in the 1840's, largely the work of Dorothea Dix, who also had taught a Sunday school class to ruffians and wrote sentimental fiction. On visits to Andover and Boston, Alice had journeyed around eastern Massachusetts, calling at almshouses and asylums, and in the previous winter, 1880, she had gone to Chicago for a tour of the Cook County Alms House, west of the city. The scene there had been disturbing, but nothing compared to the shocking things she had seen the following spring when she visited an asylum in southern Illinois.

When she arrived, the gate to the institution was opened by a lunatic bound in chains that forced him to hobble and skip as he moved. The yard beyond was crowded with other chained inmates, some shuffling about, one sitting with his chains locked to a post. Inside the building Alice saw a room of unrestrained lunatics screaming and fighting; a legless man wiggled over the floor on his back, propelling himself with his hands. In another room, feeble-minded mothers aim-

---

[1] After leaving Heidelberg, Nat had gone to the Harvard Law School. After graduation he became Ingersoll's clerk; and when Ingersoll left Illinois for Washington, D.C., Nat returned to Davenport to practice. In 1882 he became city attorney, and the year after that, judge of the circuit court.

[2] Sharing issues of the *Atlantic* with Charles Egbert Craddock's (Mary Noailles Murfree) "Over on t'Other Mounting" and the later chapters of Henry James's serial *Portrait of a Lady*.

lessly paced the floor, carrying their illegitimate children in their arms.

From such scenes and from data she found in various state reports, she had compiled her exposé of insane asylums and poorhouses and had submitted it to the *Atlantic*. In the 1870's, the *Atlantic* under Howells had become bolder and more broadly national. Contributors were no longer so consistently from New England, although the attitudes apparent in the magazine tended to remain, as Alice's and Howells' had, Bostonian and genteel. In the 1880's, the *Atlantic* was still the most august literary journal in America; and when the new editor, Thomas Bailey Aldrich, accepted "The Indoor Pauper" (Howells had resigned as editor earlier in the year), Alice could assure herself that her work was now literature even if it was nonfiction.

Her essay began with the grim suggestion that pauperism in 1881 was not the menace in the United States that it was in Europe and, therefore, was not likely to take "enough money from us to startle us out of our apathy." She repeated the conclusions of Herbert Spencer and the beliefs of America's upper class that almshouses were filled not with the "unhappy and guiltless poor" but with the vice-ridden and the slothful: "Nine-tenths are in almshouses because they have not wit enough or energy enough to get into prison"; "between half and two-thirds are of foreign birth." Her remedies were equally conventional—better facilities, separation according to sex and age, and vigilance by "good citizens."

Her exaltation of acquisitive virtues seemed clear common sense to the Gilded Age and caused the *Nation* to praise "this brilliant Frenchman" and his contributions to social reform.[3] The popular mood of the nation in the 1880's was increasingly one of humanitarianism and reform. Concern for the impoverished, the sick, and the insane was becoming a social duty for well-placed public-spirited ladies. The governor of New York had appointed the first woman to the New York State Board of Charities in 1876, and the governor of Iowa, taking to heart Alice's call for public vigilance, offered to appoint her to the State Visiting Committee—the kind of central inspecting authority she had advocated in her essay, with powers to correct abuses and make improvements in insane asylums and poorhouses.

[3] Quoted in Clio Harper, *Library of Southern Literature*, ed. Edwin A. Alderman (New Orleans, 1909), p. 1714.

Alice refused. It was too difficult, too unpleasant. The day after Christmas, 1881, she wrote to her school friend, Anna Dawes:

> [The duties, which would pay] $4 or $5 a day, and 5¢ a mile when actually employed, have no charms for me. There would be sure to be some awful abscess which would stare me in the face, so that I should have to get into a row with some superintendent; or else I should be utterly swindled by some cunning maniac and have her let out on the community to kill her relatives, whose ghosts would haunt my pillow. You make my blood run cold when you call me a "philanthropist." I am only a student of economical subjects, and I am just as interested in banking as I am in paupers and lunatics. I am rather more interested in the labor question than either, and my interest in them is all purely an intellectual feeling. Why, then, do I go into that unpleasant line of business? Two reasons: one, an unaccountable liking for the subject; the other because that line isn't over-run.[4]

Public interest was also focused on another social question, the "bachelor women" who had risen in number and in public esteem after the Civil War. By the end of the century, fewer ladies in "blessed singleness" were becoming family dependents, frail vessels of Christ assigned to third-floor bedrooms and the care of their nieces and nephews. Early in 1882, Alice sent a manuscript on spinsterhood to *Harper's Bazar*, which published it as an unsigned editorial, "A Neglected Career for Unmarried Women," and sent her ten dollars for it. She used the money to buy copies of the magazine for her friends.

Alice was thirty-two, and she had made up her mind not to marry. She saw no reason, and no real opportunity, to change her comfortable situation for one that might diminish the pleasures of her private life and career. It was a decision she had reached slowly out of inclinations that she shared with many other nineteenth-century women writers, who seemed to marry not at all, like Sarah Jewett and Mary Noailles Murfree, or badly, like Mary Wilkins Freeman.

Later in 1882, Alice submitted another brief essay to the *Nation's* editor, Wendell P. Garrison:

DEAR SIR:

> If the enclosed Mss is suited to your paper will you let me know. If not I enclose stamps for its return. Address, Miss French, 217 11th Street, Davenport, Iowa.

---

[4] Quoted in Tucker, "'Octave Thanet,'" p. 50.

I may perhaps be pardoned for saying that I write from experience as well as observation.

Very truly yours,

ALICE FRENCH

(Octave Thanet)[5]

The *Nation* accepted the essay and printed it unsigned as "The Decline in Hospitality." The last paragraph of the letter, Alice's announcement that she wrote from observation and experience, was a statement customarily repeated by those submitting manuscripts to editors caught up in the vogue of the new realism. Editors were besieged by hopeful contributors who testified to the authenticity of their material, as Alice had or as Constance Fenimore Woolson had when she wrote: "All I write is founded, and intended to be founded, upon actual realities. I have no interest in anything else."

In the summer following her trip to Europe, Alice reworked the material in her tour journal and sent it off to *Lippincott's*, which quickly published it in September, 1882, as "Through Great Britain in a Drag." More than a dozen of her essays had now been published, almost all of them in respectable, even formidable, journals. But she had not managed to sell a short story since "The First Xerxes Loan Collection" had appeared in the *Californian* two years before. One short story, "Sister Dora," had unsuccessfully made the rounds of the editors until, remembering the request of Ella Pratt, Alice had finally submitted it to *Wide Awake*, but even there "Sister Dora" had no more success than the earlier "A Friend of a Dog." The manuscript had now gone out to so many editors that it was dog-eared when it finally returned from *Wide Awake*, and Alice wrote in her diary, "I don't know where to send 'Sister Dora' now."

Rejections of her stories shattered some of the aggressive self-assurance with which Alice had armored herself, but when they came, she tried to work her way through them, perfecting her style with constant practice and intense effort, sitting in her room on the second floor of the house in Davenport, writing and rewriting, editing and correcting; and when she failed to stick to her work schedule, she would note it in her diary: "Mrs. Wilson, the dressmaker is here, and I did nothing all day. That is the worst of me. I can't put in odd moments."

[5] Alice French to Wendell P. Garrison, November 2, 1882, Newberry Library.

She was not a magazinist grinding out material, but she had a magazinist's sense of the issues that were insistent in the life she knew; and now, following her earlier success with laborers and poorhouse inmates, she turned to prohibition. Agitation for temperance had been going on for years—since her grandfather had been president of the National Temperance Union before the Civil War, and even before that. By the 1880's temperance movements were flourishing: the Prohibition Party was only a decade away from its greatest strength at the polls, and teetotalism was discussed in vestibules and saloons by children and grownups who sang popular songs like "I Never Drank Behind the Bar" and "Boys, Take Mother's Advice." But prohibition laws were more often ignored than observed in Davenport; and to Alice, temperance legislation was impractical and unenforceable, a restriction of individual liberty advocated by muddled utopianists, Christian Scientists, and radicals in the woman suffrage and the labor movements. As a result, she wrote an article attacking the prohibition movement and sent it to *Lippincott's*, which had published her earlier essays on labor. The manuscript came back. She then submitted it to the *Atlantic*, which had accepted her two-part "The Indoor Pauper" the previous year. But if tramps, workingmen, and paupers were not subscribers to the *Atlantic*, prohibitionists were, and Thomas Bailey Aldrich, the editor, returned the essay. When the manuscript arrived again in Davenport, Alice recopied the first six pages and erased the editorial marks from the others. Then she sent it off to the newly formed *Century Magazine*, which had aroused the wrath of righteous literates by publishing Washington Gladden's controversial discussion of divorce. The *Century's* editor, Richard Watson Gilder, also returned the essay, but he sent a letter of rejection that was more palatable than the others had been. Gilder was renowned for the gentle way he rejected manuscripts, a gentleness so sublime that "disappointed scribblers came to him from hundreds of miles away to thank him for his kindness and stay to dinner."[6]

Gilder had read Alice's work in *Lippincott's* well before she had submitted her essay on prohibition; and in his letter accompanying the return of her manuscript, he advised her to develop her obvious talents for fiction—to write stories in the simplest possible way, to let the story be told by the characters, and to stop wasting her talents on nonfiction.

[6] Mott, *History of American Magazines*, III, 473.

It was good advice. Short fiction was coming into great demand, for after the Civil War technical improvements in presses, engraving, and stereotyping and a rapid growth in national advertising had started a boom in magazines. In twenty years, from 1865 to 1885, the number of periodicals published in the nation rose from 700 to more than 3,300. As the number of magazines increased, their proportion of short stories rose to replace traditional and leisurely travel articles and long serials. The *Atlantic* customarily ran three short stories in each number; magazines such as *Sunday Afternoon* carried even more, and all created a vast new market that stimulated native writers, for while novels could be pirated from British publishers (the international copyright did not come until 1891), short stories were homemade. Furthermore, belles-lettres in America had ceased to be the creation of New Englanders; and as readers and authors increased and diversified, the topics and locales they read and wrote about diversified with them until the writing of fiction that was regional, distant (yet American), and picturesque became an industry.

Literature had become inductive; readers were now more interested in external phenomena, more interested in "real" details of the life of western miners or southern freedmen than in examples of universality found in Concord, Massachusetts. Gilder and other successful editors of the eighties and nineties were more interested in what was "good" and "true" than in actual realism or the emerging naturalism, and they were exquisitely sensitive to the public taste they served. The new species of fiction such men helped call forth was named local color. Its first appearance in America has sometimes been identified as Bret Harte's *The Luck of Roaring Camp and Other Sketches* (1870). That colossal success outsold any collection of stories ever before published in America, surpassing even the sales of Horatio Alger's *Luck and Pluck* to become, along with Fitzgerald's *Rubaiyat*, the best seller of the year. Harte's sketches, which he had originally published in San Francisco's *Overland Monthly*, while not the origin of local color in America, were the first popular examples of that particular amalgam of realism and romance which eventually became one notable literary expression of late nineteenth-century America. Romantic plots studded with realistic details, regional settings, dialect, and rustic hearts of gold had all appeared before, in Washington Irving and Cooper, in Longstreet's *Georgia Scenes*, in the New England characters of the *Biglow Papers* and Harriet Stowe's *The Minister's Wooing*. But local color combined all these with elements of the frontier tall tale, Scott's border romances, and other European literary conventions and examined not fundamental similarities in men, but surface differences, cataloging things open to immediate observation—speech, customs, sights, smells, and sounds. It was novel, regional, hopeful (or complacent), romantically picturesque, and populated with exemplary blacks or odd whites. At its best it was skillful and perceptive, and in the case of such an expert as Mary Wilkins Freeman or Sarah Orne Jewett or Alice French it was sometimes even moving; but it was never profound.

Local color existed as an appendage to the realistic movement of the last of the century, but local colorists, while numerous and diverse, were seldom realists. They lacked the assumptions which realists made about the world. They tried to describe what was real, what seemed to be actual southern Negroes, New England virgins, or western roughs, and like Alice French they could claim that what they wrote had really happened, or was possible, or even likely, but while they were armed with the critical terminology of Frenchmen like Zola and had a spokesman in Howells, their writing derived more from Dickens and Scott than from Zola or Flaubert.

Nor were they rudimentary naturalists. The verisimilitude of local colorists had the appearance of truth, but the events of their narratives lacked the arithmetic probability of events described by naturalists. Local colorists lacked the ability to perceive and sustain a novel, and their use of short fiction precluded the piling up of details required in literary naturalism to suggest irreversible natural forces inexorably proceeding. Furthermore, they were not determinists—even for a literary pose. They found the world moral and therefore rational if not always attractive. Their responses were partly shaped by magazine editors, always victims of received opinion and in the 1880's and 90's men who demanded a moral lesson in literature. That in turn required a moral world which, fortunately, could exist in the distant places described by local color. Heroes might no longer be knights and nobles, but they were congealed in the same morality.

Much local color was written for women, by women—who had become the dominant cultural force in the nation in the last decades of the century. Ladies' journalism was beginning to flourish and by the eighties both the *Ladies' Home Journal* and *Good Housekeeping* were large and prosperous magazines.[7] To supply them and their competitors,

[7] The *Ladies' Home Journal* was the first magazine in the United States to have a circulation exceeding 500,000. In 1891 its circulation reached 600,000.

a host of literary ladies followed in the wake of Harte, preempting one region after another, attending to accurate detail, and usually avoiding subsurface complications. The majority were literary map makers who might have written short romantic verse in previous decades—now they sketched out plots set in quaint locales. The best of them were well established when Alice began to follow Gilder's advice and concentrate on fiction. Charles Egbert Craddock (Mary Noailles Murfree) was writing of the Tennessee mountains; Sarah Orne Jewett and Mary E. Wilkins were writing of New England and New Englanders, while Constance Fenimore Woolson wrote of the Great Lakes regions, Kate Chopin of the Creoles, and Mary Catherwood of middle westerners and French Canadians.

Marketable as such regional fiction was in the eighties, it was two years before Alice produced a short story with the salable characteristics of local color. Life's duties intruded repeatedly on her writing, and she lacked the poverty that traditionally drove nineteenth-century women either to scribbling or to moral ruin. Her family's money meant she could indulge herself with travel and elaborate socializing with her friends in the East or with Jane Crawford in Davenport and Nora Scott in Chicago. The Frenches had known Nora and her sister, Nannie Field, and Nora's brother-in-law, Marshall Field, for years; and Alice had visited Nora and Nannie at the Field mansion on Prairie Avenue in Chicago, stopping there on her trips through town or during shopping visits from Davenport.

The winter after Gilder advised Alice to write fiction, her girlhood friend Jane Allen Crawford left Davenport to tour Europe, and her leaving so distressed Alice that when Nora Scott suggested a winter trip to Aiken, South Carolina, Alice quickly agreed.[8] Aiken, then a resort and spa in the tradition of Saratoga and Newport, was a refuge from the rigors of the northern winter for those who could afford

[8] In her old age Alice recounted for an interviewer who was compiling biographical material the matter of Jane Crawford's departure: "When . . . Jennie went to Europe, Alice wept bitter tears over her going and wrote voluminous and daily letters. . . . Jennie wrote calmly in reply, while Alice wept, this time with delight, over each precious missive from her 'Dear.'"

The exaggeration implicit in the account may merely have been due to Alice's faulty recollection at long distance of her feelings for a friend with whom she subsequently shared the major portion of her life. Such companionable arrangements were common enough for nineteenth-century ladies of means and place and notably so for women writers; Sarah Jewett had Mrs. Fields, and Constance Fenimore Woolson had hoped to have Henry James.

relief. The trip from Chicago to Atlanta and Aiken was Alice's first visit to the South, and she took with her an idealized image gathered from romantic ante-bellum novels. Reality was a disappointment—but not wasted, for she used her own reactions as those of her next heroine:

> I have lost faith in Southern manorhouses. Ever since I came South I have sought them vainly. All the way from Atlanta I risked my life, putting my head out of the car windows, to see the plantations. At every scrubby-looking little station we passed, the conductor would say, "mighty nice people live heah; great deal of wealth heah before the wah!" Then I would recklessly put my head out. I expected to see the real southern mansion of the novelists, with enormous piazzas and Corinthian pillars and beautiful avenues; and the white-washed cabins of negroes in the middle distance.... All I saw was a moderate-sized square house, with piazzas and a flat roof, all sadly in need of paint.[9]

Aiken shared the characteristics of other elegant nineteenth-century American resorts, and Alice and Nora moved into one of the hotels to join in the round of prescribed socializing and outings. Alice's disappointment over the absence of southern splendor was soon forgotten in her interest in the "crackers" of South Carolina and Georgia, and their dialects. With Nora she toured the countryside, listening to their talk, jotting down interesting sayings, noting their attitudes toward the winter visitors. She also observed her fellow northerners parading in lobbies, sitting on piazzas, showing off in carriages and on horseback and holding arch conversations at sedate teas and parties where mothers chaperoned their eligible daughters but not too strictly. Alice and Nora stayed through the worst of the winter, and when they returned early in the spring, Alice had a notebook filled with scraps of information—dialogue in dialect, character sketches, descriptions of scenes and events. She had collected plenty of material for such a short story as Mr. Gilder had suggested, but there was no hurry.

Alice passed the summer of 1883 in Davenport and wrote nothing. That fall she decided to take another trip, a longer one this time, all the way to California. But preparations were altered when Jane Allen Crawford, whose husband had died and who had returned from Europe, invited Alice to accompany her on a trip to Arkansas. Jane, her mother, and her brother had inherited from Jane's father a share of a five-thousand-acre plantation in northeastern Arkansas at Clover Bend

[9] "The Bishop's Vagabond," *Atlantic Monthly*, LIII (January 1884), 26.

on the Black River. The Allens were going to inspect their property, and Alice agreed to begin her trip to the West by joining them on the journey to Clover Bend.

In the autumn of 1883, when Jane, her mother, her brother Ernest, and Alice, arrived at Minturn, Arkansas, on the Missouri Pacific line, six miles from Clover Bend, they were met at the railroad station by the other shareholder, the plantation manager, Colonel F. W. Tucker. The party and their luggage were loaded onto a buckboard drawn by a team of mules, and they set out on their journey through the cypress swamps to the plantation, over a floating corduroy road of logs laid side by side through the swamp mud. It was a vast change from the coach-and-four that had swept Alice through the well-cultivated English countryside two years before. Here there was nothing as civilized as an English lane, and the first real sign of civilization along the road was the plantation windmill, with its blades rising above the line of cypress and walnut trees that obscured the horizon. But when the wagon rolled into the settlement area, Alice could see that Clover Bend was only a slightly more rustic version of the elegant plantations she had hoped to find on her trip to Aiken the year before. There were no "Corinthian pillars and beautiful avenues," but set back from the willow-shaded river was a large planter's house with piazzas enclosed by lattices covered with honeysuckle. And there were tenant cabins scattered in the middle distance, some white-washed, others painted variously blue, pink, or yellow—a variety that was the result, Alice later discovered, not of artistry but the fluctuating paint supply at the plantation store. Near the river stood the mill where the cotton was ginned and the corn ground, the plantation store, a smokehouse, barns, and an icehouse. Half a mile away was a schoolhouse, periodically empty when all the children were sent to the fields to "make a crop."

The plantation and its history soon absorbed the northern visitors. French pioneers had settled the land when it was part of the Louisiana Territory. Spaniards had come later, and part of the plantation was adjacent to what was still known as the "Spanish Grant"; years afterward Alice described the "original grant kept in our safe for a long time; a queer old yellow parchment sealed with the arms of Spain." [10] The first planter in the area had brought slaves and built a mill and the

[10] "Plantation Life in Arkansas," *Atlantic Monthly*, LXVIII (July 1891), 32–33.

store, and Clover Bend had remained one of a dwindling number of feudal empires in the postwar South, with five thousand acres undivided since Reconstruction. The plantation was almost self-sufficient. It was eleven miles from the county seat and six miles from the nearest railroad, through the "worst swamp in Arkansas." The settlement was directly accessible only by steamboats coming up the Black River from its junction with the Mississippi. Other than the river, the only regular communication with the outside was either by the wagon drawn by six oxen which carried supplies, including ice and fresh beef, from the railroad station at Minturn, or the rider who brought the mail to the desk that served as the post office in the plantation store.

Clover Bend was managed by Colonel Tucker, a lawyer, marriage counselor, judge, doctor, policeman, and expert in all things except two—he declined to write love letters for plantation illiterates and he refused to pull teeth. Most of his duties were performed at the plantation store, the social center of the community, where plantation loungers gathered each day under the wide gambrel roof to discuss crops and beasts. The store was grocery, millinery, pharmacy, hardware and farm implement store, gunsmith's, meat market, and jeweler's. And it was also the courthouse where the plantation manager, as the justice, held court in an office separated from the rest of the store by a glass partition. When the court was in session, loungers gathered in the middle of the main room to watch law dispensed on the other side of the glass partition and to listen to the proceedings through the iron grill set in the wall. Trials were short and unhampered by judicial formality, but punishment was mild and patterned on local customs.

The sharecroppers, black and white, operated under a system of economic bondage wherein plantation land was rented on shares returned to the owners by the tenants—one-fourth of a cotton crop, one-third of a corn crop. An additional one-sixth was charged for grinding corn in the mill. For such payments the sharecroppers received use of the land, a cabin, and credit at the store for the potential value of the crop. It was a system full of abuses, but it had one overriding virtue: even the penniless could begin farming without money, equipment, or land, and they could make enough to survive, if eternally in debt.

Alice's visit, originally planned to last a few days, stretched into six weeks and the trip to California was abandoned. Alice and Jane and her family were entranced by the primitive southern atmosphere that seemed a compound of warm moonlit nights, homemade whiskey, swamps, and the rural pomp of Clover Bend, surrounded by villages with names like Bug Tussle, Hog Scald, Yellville, and Jenny Lind. Alice and Jane decided to make one of the larger plantation cottages into a permanent home where they could return each winter to enjoy the mild weather that remained cool enough during the late spring so that, as Alice later described it in the *Atlantic*, "We sleep under two blankets, like the dwellers in St. Augustine, Nice, Algiers, and I dare say all the citizens of the equator that respect themselves." [11]

When Alice returned to Davenport from Clover Bend, she began to write, now with a seriousness not apparent before. She worked in her room through the morning, sometimes straight through the day, as much as ten or twelve hours at a stretch, using the material she had collected and listed in her ledgers and notebooks—the interesting words, phrases, characters, and plots—and she returned to reading Samuel Johnson and gave some of her days and nights to Addison and Steele in hope that she might be able to absorb and reproduce the quality of their prose. The first result was "The Bishop's Vagabond," which was published in January, 1884, her first short story to appear in the *Atlantic*.

The story was set in Aiken, South Carolina, in the spring. The title character, modeled after Alice's uncle, was an Episcopal bishop from the West, and "so English" that he was admired by all female guests at the hotel. The Bishop's daughter, Louise, was courted by the immensely wealthy Mr. Tallboys—he was short. The story's conflict rose out of Mr. Tallboy's pursuit of Louise and the attempts of a southern poor white named Demming—the Bishop's vagabond—to swindle the Bishop. Following the conventions of other local-color fiction filled with romance and strange people in a unique setting, it was burdened with dialect that often required explanatory footnotes to lead readers through jungles of apostrophes and phonetic approximations. It was Alice's first use of extensive dialect transcriptions,[12]

[11] *Ibid.*, p. 47.

[12] As with other local colorists, her dialect was sometimes inaccurate and often superfluous. She frequently used "frum" (as in the quotation below) and "wuz" and "sez," which sound identical to "from," "was," and "says." Such conventions suggest that local colorists copied each other as well as the rustics they described. Yet true phonetic reproduction was less important than suggesting realism to readers, for all of which "frum," "wuz," and "sez" at least served better than the apostrophes.

and it revealed not only her attempts at realism but also the perseverance and tolerance that magazine writers and editors could expect from their readers, as when the Bishop is asked to conduct the funeral for Demming's wife:

> If you all 'd kin' o' gin me a small sum, and ef you'd jes start a paper as 't were, and al-so ef you'-self 'ud hev the gret kin'ness ter come out and conduc' the fun'al obskesies, it 'ud gratify the corpse powerful. Mistress Demming'll be entered * then like a bawn lady. Yes, sir, thet thar, an' no mo', 's w'at I'm emboldened ter ax frum you.

For which Alice added the footnote: "*It is supposed that Mr. Demming intended to say 'interred'."

Demming was a cracker with the same virtues the author saw in the poor whites of Arkansas: "Ah! The Cracker has his virtues . . . not the cardinal New England virtues of thrift and cleanliness and energy; but he has his own. He is as hospitable as an Arab, brave, faithful, and honest, and full of generosity and kindness."

The story had some of the strengths of her later local-color stories. She had the evocative power to recreate a scene and characters as a traveler might have seen them. But the story also had the weaknesses of the feminine tradition of the eighties, with a dramatic rescue, reconciliation of lovers, and a moment of sudden and revealing insight. Once again, young lovers explored an interesting locale, and the beautiful heroine, who knew more than all the men around her, moved confidently amid the aura of opulence that arose partially from descriptions of delightful picnics, like those Alice had read of in Jane Austen, abounding in hampers full of delicacies. Carnegie had been right to appoint Alice stewardess of the coaching party; she liked to eat and to write about it.

The story revealed how Alice looked at the world in which she traveled and lived. Beyond suggesting that she believed the New England virtues of "thrift and cleanliness and energy" were the cardinal ones, the story made slight attempt to appraise American resort manners before lapsing into conventional romantic adventures. But the formula was successful, and Alice had a chance to use it again. In the summer of 1884, following her first visit to Clover Bend, Alice, her brother Nathaniel, Nora Scott from Chicago, and Nathaniel's wife, Marian, set out on a long trip through Canada. Their first stop was at St. Alphonse in Quebec, just north of Lake Champlain. From there, they went to Montreal and boarded a river steamer for a three-hundred-mile trip down the St. Lawrence to the mouth of the Saguenay River and to Ha Ha Bay.

At a resort hotel on Ha Ha Bay, the quartet rode horseback in the woods and went boating on the river, once getting caught out in the bay during a frightening storm—Alice was not at all distressed. The women amazed the other tourists by rowing and hiking, and bowling on the lawn, and by playing billiards in the hotel, a game that Alice had learned in childhood. Alice and Nora Scott went among the French Canadians searching for interesting types, Nora speaking to them in French having only English inflections and Alice speaking poor French rapidly by saying everything in the present tense and the masculine gender.

The natives, with their European customs and language, provided Alice with more details for her notebooks; and when the party returned at the end of summer, she began to work on a short story incorporating the sounds and sights of French Canada, exposing to view the customs, dialects, and quirks of the inhabitants. The plot was familiar: honeymooning newlyweds, the wife lovely and remarkably perceptive, came to Ha Ha Bay, where they reunited quarreling lovers, saw the sights and picnicked among craggy scenes and rustic folk, calmed a runaway horse, and charmed another recluse. The story carefully explained customs and language and introduced characters to match the wilderness. That fall Alice submitted the story to Thomas Bailey Aldrich of the *Atlantic*, who bought it and published it the next year under the title "The Ogre of Ha Ha Bay."

In the winter following the trip to Canada, Alice and Jane Crawford returned to Clover Bend to set up their winter home. They were met at the railroad station in Minturn and rode the same mule-drawn buckboard along the corduroy road through the swamp to the plantation. During their absence, their cottage had been painted red and had been moved back from the river bank and the danger of spring floods.

In the red cottage Alice installed equipment for a carpentry shop, where she made shelves, picture frames, chairs, a chicken house, and even fence gates—ten of them eventually placed around the area to direct the flow of animals and humans in an orderly New England fashion. Carpentry was the first of several hobbies Alice pursued with characteristic vigor, for it provided an outlet for the energy and emotions not consumed by her writing. She saw something symbolic in working with tools, a significance that had come to her while she was depressed over the rejections of her manuscripts. She named the period her "bad time" and thirty-five years later, in a speech she made on her development as a writer, she described it:

> We who write are punished with knotted cords for all our sins. I knew, as I began to write that to understand writing I must understand life; and life loomed big and dark, no more within reach of my inexperienced girlish hands than my own shadow. The more I lived the more I studied and observed, the worse it grew until I felt like a lost soul. That bad time lasted two or three years and it was BAD. I never spoke of it to anyone. There was no reason for speaking. Yet what, in the end, comforted me, was simple enough. It happened one day as I wrote on the plantation, I heard the drone of a saw and the hiss of a plane. A right good carpenter was at his work in the sunshine and whistling as he worked. He wasn't wretched because he was not an architect. He was happy, because he was the best carpenter he knew how to be. He put as loving care into his perfect joints and mortices as an architect could into his plans. And while I watched him, it came to me that our great mistress, ART, needs us all, carpenters as well as architects. The best artisan is always a bit of an artist, and the "backbone of the army is the non-commissioned man."
>
> The substance of this parable so heartened me that I began to write again with fresh courage, resolved to see as clearly as it was given me to see, nor to speak until I did see; also to do the best work in me, not lashing my soul whether someone else were doing better. . . . I have had nasty returns of that night that covered me . . . particularly over proofs, but they are . . . pacified by the consolation of the great "hanging judge":
>
>> "I do my best,
>> God take the rest!" [13]

One virtue of plantation life was that servants were plentiful, if not very reliable. First the two women hired a Negro cook named Jinny, and a "gnome-like darky" named Steve, who tended the fires in the house. Eventually dependable servants were imported from the North but the two women often had to fend for themselves, repairing their primitive drainage system, painting, hanging paper, once even building a chimney out of old bricks and a mortar of sand and whitewash.

[13] The quotation "backbone of the army . . ." is from Kipling's "The 'Eathen," which she often used. She liked Henley's "Invictus" even more, and for the same reasons. Alice gave this address on several occasions after the turn of the century, most notably in Indianapolis. The manuscript, in several forms, is in the Newberry Library.

In that second winter at Clover Bend, Alice got a closer view of the plantation's inhabitants. Half of the tenants and servants were black. They were convivial, slow, and warmly erotic compared to the New Englanders from whom Alice French took her morality. The Negroes were the first completely submerged group Alice had confronted, and they mystified her as they did most of her contemporaries. They lacked cardinal New England virtues, ran away from store debts and oppressive wives (a divorce cost twenty-five dollars). They were immoral; the Northern ladies were shocked by young girls who repeatedly had "misfortunes" while unmarried. All the tenants, black and white, disturbed Alice's sense of Yankee thrift and neatness by burning fences for stove wood, letting cows and pigs wander in their yards, and spitting on the floors of their cabins. And they seemed lazy, working only long enough to get money for immediate needs. She was observing actions common to many nonindustrialized people unused to wagework; and in spite of all her historical reading, she seemed unaware that the need to store up wealth, the Protestant work ethic of Massachusetts and Iowa, was a dubious principle to much of mankind.

Equally distressing to her was their brutality.

The most repulsive trait in the negro's character is his atrocious relish of cruelty. It exceeds apathy over the other creatures' pain; it is veritable enjoyment. Look at the flashing of teeth at the struggles of a broken-backed cat or a half decapitated chicken. . . . Yet in these brutal torturers of animals you may find not only ardent affections and a pathetic loyalty, but generosity, cheerfulness, sunny good humor, the social instincts, and an amazing meekness under provocation.

. . . My own notion of the explanation is that the cruelty of the negroes, like the cruelty of children, comes from a torpid imagination. They have not sense enough to realize the misery they inflict. It is the grotesque antics, not the suffering, of the cat or chicken that delight them.

The plantation's poor whites, on the other hand, had their virtues:

To one element in the Arkansas rustic's composition I give a hearty respect, namely his robust independence. He is no man's inferior, and every black man's superior. For this very reason, because he is so secure in his self-respect, he has not an atom of the naturalized American's surly assertion; he does not "mutter in corners and grudge against the rich" any more than he truckles to them; and he never presumes a hair's breadth.[14]

[14] "Plantation Life in Arkansas," *Atlantic Monthly*, LXVIII (July 1891), 37, 42–43.

Alice had heard some of the plantation's legends on her first visit. Now she collected them for her notebooks. The plantation had its own conjurer—a regular tenant who sold potions and charms (the skin of a rabbit's stomach relieved a teething baby when tied around the infant's neck). He claimed the power, when suitably irked or rewarded, to spread sickness and "blast crops," and Clover Bend Negroes who suffered from his spells could either pay him to pacify the spirits or take the strong remedy—Epsom salts—offered free as a psychic nostrum by the plantation manager.

There were stories of ghosts and "ha'nts" enough to satisfy any Northern visitor. One ghost inhabited the loft of the plantation store. Another gibbered and shrieked and rolled in the mud before a cabin in which a tenant had died from the bite of a rabid dog. Another ghost, a murder victim, had haunted its murderer for years and repeatedly brushed a cold dead hand against his cheek until he killed himself. Colonel Tucker told Alice a story of a fanatic who had lived at Clover Bend and had appointed himself "regulator" of the people's morals, threatening some backsliders into righteousness, beating those who ignored the threats. One night when the "regulator" was walking through the garden of the house Alice and Jane shared, he was shot from ambush, and his body was carried into the dining room. In 1891, in writing on plantation life for the *Atlantic*, Alice reported that on the rising of the night wind, ghosts bearing the "regulator's" body would come to the house, "their invisible fingers lift the latch; we see it rise; the door swings open; it swings back; they are in the room."

The most renowned ghost of all was the specter of the original owner of the plantation. During the Civil War a cavalry force had been stationed in Arkansas, from which raiding parties were sent into Missouri. In 1864, with the end of the war less than a year away, the troops were withdrawn south, destroying everything left behind. The original planter, a "secessionist" but with "no mind to waste his cotton on a funeral pyre," had buried his silver, meat, salt, and even his cotton to hide them from the retreating Confederates and the approaching Union troops. Tradition held that his sudden death had prevented him from removing his hoard, and in spite of the belief that the planter's ghost guarded the treasure, the land around the house was pitted with holes dug by treasure seekers. Shortly after Alice first came to Clover Bend, treasure digging (done mostly by moonlight) began again when one of the renters reported seeing a figure standing at the edge of a field, dressed like the old planter, with an immaculate white suit, a broad-brimmed white hat, and carrying a riding whip in his hand.

Other stories were more factual but no less frightening. During the Civil War marauding groups of guerrillas, "graybacks," belonging to neither side, had pillaged the countryside. From every window of the red cottage Jane and Alice occupied, they could see places where men had been killed. Across the river, in a small cypress brake, the ruins of a cottage indicated where the guerrillas had murdered a family and burned the house over the bodies. Colonel Tucker told Alice all the tales of guerrilla tortures with hot coals on the victim's back, fingernails ripped out, and men and women flogged to death. Early one afternoon while driving Alice and some visitors to Portia, Arkansas, nine miles away, he stopped the wagon so often to point out scenes of local murders that his exasperated sister finally exclaimed, "If you're going to stop at the scene of every killing, we won't get to Portia before night."

Such scenes and events were exactly what regionalists were using elsewhere so successfully, but the legends and the characters of Clover Bend did not yet appear in Alice's fiction. Early in 1886, after "The Ogre of Ha Ha Bay" had been published in the *Atlantic*, she left Clover Bend for another trip to Aiken and from there to St. Augustine. When she arrived in St. Augustine, she visited the fortress and the ancient houses, some of them still showing signs of destruction from the Union occupation during the Civil War. But America's oldest town was a disappointment. The flowers were not as lovely as she had expected, the weather was wet and cold, and even the orange trees were drab. And her hotel, like all the others in St. Augustine, was full of tourists complaining to each other of the weather and the townspeople and the fact that the cobblestoned streets made strolling unpleasant.

Nevertheless, she prowled the town and its landmarks, jotting down her impressions of the scenery and the natives. Working up such details had become her custom; and by the time she returned to Davenport in the spring, she had accumulated material for two short stories set in St. Augustine. The first, "Six Visions of St. Augustine," appeared the following August in the *Atlantic* and described the locale and the complaints of disappointed visitors, in a story of lovers united. Once she had completed the story and sent it off to the *Atlantic*, she began working on her first sketch of the people of the cypress swamps at Clover Bend. For more than two weeks she sat at her desk in her second-floor room, writing and rewriting laboriously in precise long-hand, trying to recreate her impressions of the Arkansas tenant farmers.

Southern poor whites, like Bret Harte's western miners and noble gamblers, had by then emerged as respectable fictional characters, for the South, far more so than even the West, had developed into a land of profitable literary exploitation. In the five years from 1882 to 1887 more than half as many magazine articles about the South appeared as had been published in the preceding eighty years, and to feed the new interest came the local colorists George W. Cable, Joel Chandler Harris, Thomas Nelson Page, Kate Chopin, Charles Egbert Craddock, and essayists like Edward King, whose series of articles on "The Great South" had appeared in *Scribner's* in 1874.

Accompanying the rise of interest in the South and its people came an emphasis on the dialect story, an interest which continued well beyond the 1880's, when Page's "Marse Chan" and Charles Egbert Craddock's *In the Tennessee Mountains* were published and set extremes in the literary uses of dialect. All local colorists seemed to have discovered an esthetic power in the contracting apostrophe and phonetic approximations of the colloquialisms of outlanders. Their counterparts in the North, in murky, sodden mill towns, had yet to become literary subjects—what was picturesque or colorful about a twelve-hour shift in a cotton mill?

Alice had attempted to catch the Georgia and South Carolina poor-white dialect in "The Bishop's Vagabond," and on her previous visit to Clover Bend she had recorded some unusual qualities in the Arkansawyers' speech, the talk of her household help and of the renters in their cabins and in the fields. She wanted to study people as Balzac had, so she spent afternoons sitting in the office of the plantation store, listening unnoticed through the iron grill, jotting down in her fine hand the unvarnished talk (but not the swear words) of black and white shoppers and loafers inside the store. It helped her to achieve a command of the plain style and to escape the tradition of ornate rhetoric evident in American fiction of the early half of the nineteenth century. The Arkansas dialect, which like others seemed to spring only from an earthy and ignorant rusticity, was actually a preserve of French and archaic English. The Clover Benders said "boy dark" (bois d'arc) for "hedge," and "bateau," "pirogue," and "levee." They said "you was" as eighteenth-century English gentlemen did,

Scene on the Arkansas plantation where Alice spent much of her time

From Alice's book Adventure in Photography

and "holp" for "help," "ax" for "ask," and "a power" and "a heap," "triflin'" instead of the New England "shiftless," and "fitified" for "having a fit." Many terms Alice recognized as those she had read in the reprints of writings by Latimer, Ridley, and Cranmer owned by her uncle, the Bishop. And all of the speech was mingled with colorful local metaphors like "mud shoe-mouth deep."

Combining the local dialect with the Clover Bend locale and portraits of poor-white sharecroppers, Alice wrote her first Arkansas story, "Ma' Bowlin'," and submitted it to *Harper's Weekly* early in 1886. When the story appeared (January 15, 1887), it presented two departures from conventional American fiction: it was set in the Arkansas back country and its heroine was a feeble-minded child, Ma' Bowlin'.

Ma' lived in a rural settlement beset by feuds and located on the edge of a vast cypress swamp. Early in the story she wandered into the swamp, got lost, and thus made necessary a full-scale search of the swamp and elaborate descriptions of its character. Then, when all seemed hopeless, the child floated out of the dangerous wilderness in a boat poled by a stranger who, it then turned out, was none other than a man her father was supposed to have murdered long before. With the "victim" thus in full sight, all was forgiven, and incredibly, "Ma'," who had by then managed to reconcile man and wife, reunite old friends, halt a feud, and stop the persecution of an innocent man, topped it all in the midst of the general felicity by miraculously regaining her wits.

The story was noteworthy in its description of the customs, speech, and emotions of the tenant farmers, of their attitudes toward vengeance, death, God's punishment and His benevolence, and in its intense descriptions of the swamp. Southern swamps had already provided Sidney Lanier, Constance Fenimore Woolson, and George Washington Cable with the opportunity to indulge in florid descriptions of nature, a convention that the local colorists used to direct the responses of their readers and that eventually became a routinized technique for describing characters by reciting the details of their environment.

In 1886, Edward Burlingame, the editor of the reorganized *Scribner's Magazine*,[15] wrote Alice to ask for just such a story as "Ma' Bowlin'"

[15] In 1881, Scribner and Company sold *Scribner's Monthly* to the Century Company, which changed the name of the magazine to the *Century Illustrated Monthly*. In the sale agreement, Scribner and Company agreed to keep the

for the new magazine's first issue. Burlingame had read Alice's work in the *Atlantic* and the *Century*, and he had plans to publish such regionalism as a means of making the new *Scribner's* the fourth quality magazine (along with *Harper's*, the *Atlantic*, and the *Century*) in America. Burlingame's letter was a milestone for Alice. No such eminent editor had ever before sought her out for a story, and she set out to write the kind of regional tale Burlingame had wanted by working up the material she had gathered on her trip to St. Augustine. The first issue of the new *Scribner's* contained the beginning of Harold Frederic's novel of upstate New York, *Seth's Brother's Wife*. The second issue (February, 1887) carried Alice's "Half a Curse."

The story was set in St. Augustine and began in 1862, while the city was occupied by Union troops. The characters included the conventional beautiful heroine, an army captain, a Negro servant, and a carpetbagger from Tennessee. Through a ruse the carpetbagger had succeeded in buying the heroine's ancestral home; but as soon as the war ended, the captain returned to St. Augustine to help restore the home to its rightful and beautiful owner. He was successful only with the aid of a voodoo curse conjured up by the ex-slave, who then died as a result of her spiritual exertions—as she knew she must. The two lovers were then united over the coffin of the loyal Negro.

The story followed the romanticized tradition of post-bellum southern fiction with its mansion, its southern belle, and its Negro mammy, a loyal and noble illiterate providing wisdom and salvation for her betters. The resolution brought by the union of the Yankee officer and the southern maiden, reuniting the North and South, was an equally overworked convention that had appeared as early as 1867 in John De Forest's *Miss Ravenel's Conversion* and that Alice had read in Albion Tourgee's two best sellers, *A Fool's Errand* (1879) and *Bricks Without Straw* (1880).

The story lacked the local-color realism of those descriptions of poor people caught in ignorance and cupidity that later characterized her work. The heroine and hero of "Half a Curse" followed patterns that had appeared before in her stories of intelligent women worshiped by devoted gentlemen. Alice's fiction suggests that she never

Scribner name out of the magazine market for five years. At the end of the five-year period, Charles Scribner's Sons began *Scribner's Magazine* as competition for the *Century*, with Edward Burlingame as editor. See Mott, *History of American Magazines*, IV, 717–732.

discovered passion; love was simply social parley, humanitarianism, and a fond heart. No impassioned men brought such women to wedlock or a detailed ruin; heroines were always in command of their honor, permitting themselves to be adored only within the bounds of modesty.

In April, 1886, Alice completed her second local-color story of Arkansas and sent it to the assistant editor of the *Century*, William Carey:

> It is in two (short) parts. Clover Bend, the scene is a real plantation where I go autumns. The legends alluded to are equally real and so in the main is the story of Whitsun and Boas, while the characters are sketched from life. I am prepared to wade through any amount of—ink, in defense of my dialect. The most interesting feature of the Arkansas dialect is its composite character. It has borrowed from Tennessee a great deal but it has some queer little Yankee terms (picked up during the War I fancy) and some odd survivals from the French and Spanish of the early setlers. All over the South now we hear "I guess" and particularly the Southern "I don't *guess*." They never say, as Yankee's do (myself, I am a Yankee by the way) "I guess so"; they say simply "I guess," in response. I don't know but I should have put a footnote to some expressions like "much" for to pet or caress, "can't make a riffle," "can't make a wiggle," "lit a shuck" ect. [*sic*]: but I am not fond of footnotes for stories. We spend our autumns as I have said in, Clover Bend, and live among the people, so that you may depend on the realistic treatment—the artistic is another thing a *painfully* other thing I often find it. . . .
>
> Very gratefully yours,
ALICE FRENCH [16]

She added a postscript—"Perhaps it would be better to call the tale, 'In the Cypress Brake'"; but Carey, who had changed the title of one of Frank Stockton's short stories from "The King's Arena" to "The Lady or the Tiger," left it as it was—"Whitsun Harp, Regulator."

Alice had made the legends of Clover Bend into one of her best stories. Whitsun was drawn from the self-appointed regulator of morals who had been ambushed in the plantation garden. Driven by a call from the Lord, Whitsun had set out to beat virtue into the sharecroppers, "ye cayn't talk folks decent, but ye kin lick 'em decent." Boas, another character taken from Colonel Tucker's tales, was

---

[16] Alice French to William Carey, April 19, 1886, *Century* Collection, New York Public Library.

haunted by a ghost as punishment for having committed a murder. By the end of the story, lovers were united, and as the Clover Bend legend had it, Whitsun was murdered and Boas died, finally released from the touch of the ghostly hand.

Even with true love finding a way at the end, the story was a realistic and often harsh appraisal of the life of the people in the Arkansas back country, and Carey was interested enough to pass the story on to Richard Watson Gilder, editor of the *Century*. Gilder wanted some changes. He thought it stylistically ornate, burdened by too much Arkansas dialect and weakened by inadequate motivation— he called it "subtley remote"—but he offered to accept it for the *Century* if Alice would revise it. Gilder was wary of dialect, even as early as the eighties. He had accepted "Marse Chan" from Thomas Nelson Page in 1881, but held off publishing it until 1884 because of excesses his refined sensitivity detected in the story's Negro dialect. Gilder agreed with Howells that an editor should "print nothing which a father may not read to his daughter, or safely leave her to read herself," and he thought dialect tended to corrode principles and rhetoric. Gilder had been educated as the only male student in his father's Flushing Female Academy in New York, and his critics said he, like Howells, was a "male bluestocking"; William Randolph Hearst called him a "tender apple-blossom" and a "quivering mouse." He was, as Dr. Arnold had been, "alarmed by the want of Christian principle in the literature of the day," and his self-confident and lofty prudery often led him to repair that want by editorial interference: He bowdlerized the portions of *Huckleberry Finn* that appeared in the *Century* in 1884 and 1885, cutting out such things as the Duke's famous comment on the play bill: "Ladies and Children not Admitted. 'There . . . if that line don't fetch them, I don't know Arkansaw,'" and omitting such vernacular phrases as "in a sweat," "dern your skin," and "hogwash."

But in the eighties and nineties all popular magazines were a force for literary conservatism and propriety; Crane and Dreiser had to be published elsewhere, for magazine literature took its directions from its genteel mass audience, and editors had learned never to offend their readers. The *Atlantic* had lost fifteen thousand subscriptions following the shocking revelations of Harriet Stowe's "True Story of Lady Byron." Gilder, who was afraid to endanger the *Century* by any similar error, declined Cable's "Posson Jone'" because of its picture of a drunken minister, and rejected Crane's *Maggie* because it was "too cruel"; but in 1887 he could announce that the *Century* had the largest circulation of any quality magazine in America. By the end of the decade the *Century* was receiving more than four thousand manuscripts a year and had become so prosperous that it could pay more to serialize a novel than most writers got for the subsequent book.

Such economics made magazine editors imperious and writers compliant. When Alice received Gilder's complaints, she rewrote the story and sent it back:

> I don't wish to be "literary" at all, in any style, so I have carefully gone over Whitsun and tried as hard as a Russian nihilist to simplify myself.
>
> "Subtle remoteness" is pretty bad, anyhow, and it certainly is a fault in art to fly over the heads of one's characters.
>
> I tried other places to put the Arkansas thought into English. The difficulty is that their vocabulary of sentiment is so amazingly limited. Fancy describing the emotions of people who never use the word "love," or even say they are "fond" of each other.
>
> But I think the story is the better for the overhauling, and I am glad you gave me the chance.[17]

When the story appeared in the May, 1887, *Century*, it impressed the editors of Houghton Mifflin and Company, who asked Alice to collect a number of her short stories to be published in one volume. She began assembling stories in the spring, at the same time that Mary Wilkins was preparing *A Humble Romance and Other Stories* for August publication by Harper's and the same month Scribner's brought out Thomas Nelson Page's *In Old Virginia*. Alice collected nine stories that had been published in the *Century*, *Harper's*, the *Atlantic*, and *Scribner's Magazine* and sent them in a paper-wrapped bundle to Houghton Mifflin in Boston. She had made few alterations, the major one being a different title for "Communists and Capitalists." In an attempt to avoid the suggestion that it was another of her essays in economic history, she had changed the title to "A Communist's Wife."

The book appeared in the fall of 1887. Small, with a green binding, it sold for $1.25 and had the baffling title *Knitters in the Sun*, taken from *Twelfth Night*, Act II, Scene IV, and the Duke's reference to

> The spinsters and the knitters in the sun,
> and the free maids that weave their thread with bones.

[17] Alice French to Richard Watson Gilder [May 1886], *Century* Collection, New York Public Library.

Alice had wanted to add a preface, explaining that the title referred to the optimism of her characters, saying, "Americans are all knitters in the sun, working out their dreams in the sunlight happily," but the editors of Houghton Mifflin convinced her that it wasn't needed, and the unfortunate title remained unexplained.

The book was not a best seller, but for that matter, neither was *A Humble Romance* nor *In Old Virginia*, nor were they expected to be. The last years of the eighties and the decade of the 1890's saw the appearance of an enormous number of short-story collections—nearly two hundred in the 1890's alone—but none of them ever duplicated the success of Bret Harte's *The Luck of Roaring Camp*. Local-color short stories were now proving to be too rich an offering when collected in one volume; and the local colorists, whose work no longer seemed so central to the day's issues, received scant attention from the book-buying public in 1887, a year whose best sellers were H. Rider Haggard's *She*, Frances Burnett's *Little Lord Fauntleroy*, and Palmer Cox's *The Brownies, Their Book*.

VIII. Everything Ending Happily

The New York *Tribune* reviewer called *Knitters in the Sun* "one of the best collections of short stories the reader can find anywhere. . . . As a story teller, Octave Thanet has no superior and very few peers." Alice clipped out the review as a memento and wrote on the margin, "Christian at work." Other critics rated the collection equal to Cable's *Old Creole Days* and Thomas Nelson Page's *In Old Virginia*, but William Dean Howells, house critic for *Harper's Magazine* and the decade's literary assessor, dissented when he reviewed *Knitters in the Sun* in his "Editor's Study." Howells had a simple definition for realism: "the truthful treatment of material"; and while he granted that Alice French had "greater power" in some respects than even Mary E. Wilkins, he objected to the "'goddess type' of dimly accounted for countess" who was the heroine of "A Communist's Wife." [1] And in "Whitsun Harp, Regulator," the best story in the collection, he judged the author had resorted to an unrealistic ending to save the hero from sin. Howells liked to see wickedness punished, but in a manner consistent with Matthew Arnold's definition of God, and not in a way that would weaken "moral fibre" or "clog the soul with unwholesome vapors."

> When men are bent on sin, not so does "the power not ourselves, that works for righteousness" save them by melodramatic accident. It saves them in their own free wills, or, if they resist, it saves them not at all; it is bad art and mistaken morality that teaches them otherwise. The Good Fairy conception of the Divine government of the world should be left to the cruder theologies: it is wholly unworthy of fiction. [2]

[1] Alice used three "dimly accounted for" countesses in her first two years of short-story writing. Each such aristocrat was an ark of social wisdom and provided the ethical machinery with which Alice could fulfill a moral purpose in fiction without directly intruding in the narrative.

[2] "Editor's Study," *Harper's Magazine*, LXXVI (January 1888), 321–322.

The January issue of the magazine, with Howells' criticisms, arrived in Davenport two days after Christmas, 1887. That same day, Alice mailed her reply:

My Dear Mr. Howells;

Will you pardon a few words (to yourself alone) from a writer whom you have accused of the one particular sin which she has most scrupulously tried to avoid.

In your kind review of Knitters in the Sun, you mention Whitsun Harp and say that Lum Shinault went out to kill him but was saved from murder by finding Harp killed already.

Then you most justly remark that a fairy providence is unworthy of fiction and find the whole proceeding wrong and unnatural.

I quite agree with you. Only, dear Mr. Howells, *I didn't do it.*

Lum was not turned from his purpose by any such artistic trash. As the author of his being I should be ashamed of him if he had been. Lum went to kill Whitsun Harp but (this page you must have skipped somehow) Whitsun met him at the store and publicly apologized before "the store" (which is the Arkansas public). . . . *Therefore*, Lum was reconciled to him; and . . . having been reconciled to him, he went shooting (for squirrels *not* for Whitsun) and found the body. . . .

To my mind Lum *couldn't* have been saved from killing Harp by any direct appeal on the sin of murder. I know those people (I have often dined with Whitsun's real murderer—for all the characters in the story had a real existence) and they do not yet, and certainly did not, then, think that murder is a sin. But all the same, Lum was saved by the good in him, by his unselfish pity.

The power that makes for righteousness does not always work on a straight line. But the work is none the less effectual, and though you have always been my literary master, I still believe that it was a truer art (because more natural) to save Lum in the only way in which I knew of a man of his kind and his locality being saved.

I am rather glad that you said this (in Harper's) since it has given me an opportunity to thus confess my artistic faith in you, namely that an artist's business is simply to tell the truth. I have *no* moral purpose in anything that I ever wrote; but if study and patience, observation and hard work and the constant effort to be fair can make a person tell the unvarnished truth; then I have told it.

There is only one exception. The Communist's Wife was the first thing that I ever wrote and I was rather frightened when I found it had slipped into the bundle which I sent to Houghton, Mifflin and Co.[3]

[3] In spite of her disclaimer, moral purpose was evident in most of her work and would surely have been apparent but not necessarily repugnant to Howells, who

Forgive so long a letter, intended for you only and believe me

Very Truly Yours

ALICE FRENCH

(*Octave Thanet*)

Perhaps you will excuse my mentioning that Whitsun Harp is almost entirely a true story. Harp lived and died as I have tried to picture and Boas was haunted as I have described and (though not in Clover Bend) I know of a Lum saved as Shinault was. This is no excuse for me if I haven't made the story real: I only mention it to show that I have no such notions as you impute to me: but am as uncompromising a realist as lives. I have tried not to idealize my friends of the Cypress Swamp, one atom. . . .

The stolid way in which they bear things is a part of these people's nature.

A. F.[4]

Howells' reply was apologetic. He had indeed misread the story and promised to retract his comments. And he asked permission to quote from her letter in his "Editor's Study." All that was more than she had hoped for, and she quickly wrote again:

I think that I am fortunate in having you do me a slight injustice since you make such large amends.

It is to *you*, to whom I wished to justify myself, rather than the public: still, I am not of the Vanderbilt opinion and the letter is at your disposal; only should you use any of my words I hope you will include some of those which avow my faith creed. It is only a question of fact on which I should venture to appeal, not of law. I do not wonder at your skipping a short paragraph in dialect and you might very properly give me a little "whack" for entrusting so vital a part of the plot to the dialect. . . .

I am inclined to think that it does take some courage to be a realist and believe with Plato that The Beautiful is the glory of the True though why is it right to lie in fiction [more] than in life? We all do more or less of it, there,—to keep the peace; and it appears that we [are] expected to do it in art, also, for the same reason.

I am grateful to our "late little misunderstanding" for one thing; it gives me a chance to tell you that I am most grateful to you for the article which you have written in the Editor's Study. I have a right to say that;

---

had moral purposes of his own. Furthermore, Alice's implication that "A Communist's Wife" was included in *Knitters in the Sun* by mistake was particularly unlikely in view of the fact that she had changed the story's title for its appearance in the collection and had corrected proofs before the book was published.

[4] Alice French to William Dean Howells, December 27, 1887, Harvard College Library.

because I discarded a most promising effective incident in a story, believing that while it was possible it wasn't probable and trusting my *denouement* to the simplest means I could find. You may be sure that you have done me service to the public and I am sure that you have helped other artisans who want to be artists just as you have helped me. Thank you.

Very Truly Yours,
ALICE FRENCH [5]

Howells' recantation appeared in the March, 1887, issue of *Harper's*:

How very fallible criticism is at the best and under the most favorable conditions, may be conceived from the cruel error into which the Study itself—mirror of impartiality and balance of justice as it is—fell into lately concerning Octave Thanet's admirable group of sketches, *Knitters in the Sun.* . . . we were able to convict that clever writer of lese reality in an important point and to deliver a very pretty lecture on the "ways of God to man," in censuring her for romantically misrepresenting them. We were as usual, perfectly right in our opinions, but we were wrong in our facts; we had overlooked a passage in the story reprehended which gave it a wholly different complexion, and confirmed it to our own ideal. . . . we wish we could truthfully say that it gives us pleasure to make this correction. It does nothing of the kind; it is extremely distasteful, and nothing could oblige us to do it but the love of justice, and the hope of breaking down any small remnant of respect for criticism generally which might be left in the mind of our readers of the Study's past attacks on it.[6]

Much of the pride in being a realist that Alice displayed in her letters to Howells was justified. In the pursuit of local-color exactitude, she scrupulously sought out obscure facts to lend realism to her stories. Once work on proofs for *Knitters in the Sun* had been completed and returned to Houghton Mifflin, she had taken only enough time to make a hurried trip to Chicago to attend a charity fete sponsored by Marshall Field's wife, Nanny, and then to travel to Cincinnati for a music festival, before she was back, gathering details for her next short story. Her zeal for authenticity was revealed in a letter she wrote to William Carey, assistant editor of the *Century Magazine*, explaining the pains she had taken in preparing a story based on a cyclone in central Iowa in 1882, five years before:

[5] Alice French to William Dean Howells, January 4, 1888, Harvard College Library.

[6] "Editor's Study," *Harper's Magazine*, LXXVI (March 1888), 643–644.

DEAR SIR:

I send you here the Cyclone Story which I spoke of a long time since, but have been too busy to write. I went to Grinnell, went over the track of the Cyclone interviewed eye witnesses and got the Grinnell papers of the time. . . .

I enclose directed envelope and if the story is not "available," I will send stamps for its return.[7]

May I trouble you, should Mr. Kuble come in the office of the Century, to thank him for me for his capital illustrations of Whitsun Harp. . . .

Very Sincerely Yrs.

ALICE FRENCH

P.S. As I shall be in N. Y. sometime this summer or autumn, I shall call at the Century building; not because I have any manuscripts to sell or a serial story to propose or some poetry "which my friends" ect ect; but simply from curiosity (natural to the provinces, you know) to see a great magazine and "you all."

A. F.[8]

Five months later, in October, 1887, she wrote to Carey again, this time offering to write an article, "An Irish Gentlewoman in the Famine Time":

It describes the literal experiences of an Irish lady who had an estate in County Cork. The lady in question is still living, nearly ninety. . . . her letters, diary ect are most thrilling. I happen to know her and this, because my brother [Nathaniel] married her grandniece. At Dunmanway they used to have to draw the dining room curtains to keep out the sight of the starving faces pressed against the glass.

I should not mention her name . . . but I should give the facts literally. . . . My position would be neutral but certainly the impression that the landlords are all grasping absentees is not true in some cases. I have twice before been to Ireland.

If the idea doesn't strike you favorably it may Mr. Alden or Mr. Burlingame or Mr. Aldrich.[9] And (business being business) if such an article were to your mind . . . how much would you pay for it?[10]

[7] The *Century* rejected it and it appeared in *Scribner's* in March, 1888, ten months later.

[8] Alice French to William Carey, May 18, 1887, *Century* Collection, New York Public Library.

[9] Henry Mills Alden, editor of *Harper's Monthly*; Edward L. Burlingame, editor of *Scribner's*; and Thomas Bailey Aldrich, editor of the *Atlantic*.

[10] Alice French to William Carey, October 22, 1887, *Century* Collection, New York Public Library.

Since she had begun to follow Gilder's advice on writing a little more than three years before, such editors as those whose names she invoked had come to welcome her work. Her stories of Arkansas were among the most memorable of those created by the nineteenth century's local colorists, and they came at a time when short stories were ceasing to be a literary trifle. Authors less often called them "sketches," a term Alice had used as Twain had before her.

During the next decade Alice would write seventy short stories, a total of ten volumes of letters, essays, and fiction. And as she wrote, her work became more complex, less repetitious. Her writing changed from the romanticism of "Hugo's Waiting" to didactic stories of labor and capital and to Arkansas and Iowa local color. She reduced the dialect that choked her earlier work and cut down the number of repeated stock figures that were imbedded in her early stories, although she continued throughout her life to use upper-class men and women as reservoirs of knowledge and goodness. Such devices kept her readers attentive, and editors like Gilder knew she was successful. One week after receiving her offer of the Irish famine essay, Gilder replied, urging her to submit the essay to the *Century* and also to send more fiction. She answered quickly:

DEAR MR. GILDER:

I shall like to do the article. I can do it either "with or without," (as they say in Skat) I mean going to Ireland. . . .

As to fiction I can send you an Arkansas tale sooner than anything else. I have had some amusing experience apropos of my Arkansas stories. A young lawyer in the vicinity was supposed to be an author of them and received some very interesting letters. I have had some funny letters myself. The writers are, generally, very cordial and pay me the compliment of supposing me to be a native—and a man.

If you have had too much Arkansas already, I can give you a Western sketch. You know you have one of mine on hand, "The Governor's Prerogative."[11]

Her stories grew from material such as she had collected on the Irish famine, much of her fiction having its genesis in anecdotes and newspaper stories. In October, 1887, *Scribner's* published a story inspired by a newspaper account Alice had read of a woman who

[11] Alice French to Richard Watson Gilder, November 3, 1887, *Century* Collection, New York Public Library. "The Governor's Prerogative" was published in the *Century* in February, 1888.

had mortgaged her child. Alice considered the mother, with her indifference to responsibilities, to be an Arkansas type,[12] and the story that Alice eventually wrote was a blend of the news story and the memory of a woman Alice had seen near Clover Bend tramping through the swamp at twilight, following a gypsy wagon. Alice named her character "Headlights" because of her fiery eyes, and because Headlights abandoned her son Jeffy and ran off with her lover, she was eventually distinguished as one of the most immoral women in all of local color.[13] But she was witless rather than evil. A roving cotton picker who merely displayed the mores of her group, she eventually repented only to die while struggling back through the swamp to the plantation carrying money she had saved to redeem her pawned child.

"The Mortgage on Jeffy" was full of swampland scenery and perceptive descriptions of what the poor did and believed and how they were alien to the respectable society, whose standards intruded in their lives. Yet Headlights was still a local-color figure with much of the sentimental limitation that the term implies, and her death paid the debt to society she had clearly incurred through her shameful behavior. Her author was seldom able to overcome a belief that decency, or reason, or esthetics, or the rules of the magazine trade required a demonstration of the necessity for redemption and the prevalence of moral retribution in the world. Such displays of authorial faith partly distinguished local color from the kinds of naturalism and regionalism that superseded it. In the world of most local colorists, moral law had been pretty largely revealed in the principles of white protestant Anglo-Saxon capitalism and in the rules of a society whose chief virtue was its solidity.

Yet it is a mistake to think that local color was a point on a continuum of morality that began in romanticism and led to naturalism. Some of Alice's characters were as immoral (but not as amoral) as Dreiser's Sister Carrie or Stephen Crane's Maggie. Alice pictured ignorance, brutality, hunger, greed, and cruelty, but these were all difficulties which might be conquered. She never fixed upon the hereditary

[12] Years later Alice said, "I have tried to draw types rather than individuals and at least I can put my hand on my heart and say that I never knowingly have described any living person to his hurt."

[13] Shields McIlwaine, *The Southern Poor-White from Lubberland to Tobacco Road* (Norman, 1939), p. 158.

weakness of a character to explain his woes as an unavoidable taint or as the working of a predetermined fate, devices which literary naturalists used with brutal irony to shock a comfortable society by suggesting that good men did not thereby triumph or the wicked suffer.

Most local color used the details of naturalism while retaining the moral vision of popular romantic fiction, a mixture evident in an essay, "The Short Story," which Alice wrote for the June, 1888, issue of *Literature: A Weekly Magazine*. She announced that the old method of describing characters as gentle or endowed with a "noble brow" was no longer adequate. Authors must give clear and lengthy detail: "A modern writer must picture [a character] in his habit as he lived, with detail enough to satisfy the police." On the other hand,

> There is a spurious sort of realism in vogue, a superstition of the commonplace, one might call it, which would eliminate the thrilling. Art, say these prophets, should act like an insurance company and concern itself only with averages. . . . They tell us, truly, that dull lives are worth description; but it is a *non sequitur* that therefore only dull lives should be described. By all means let Miss Wilkins and Mrs. Wyman show what beauty and grace animate the gray days of plain people. . . . Art only soils her white feet when she prys into the vile by-ways of the human heart; and the dissecting room belongs to the doctor.

At Clover Bend during the winter of 1887–88, she wrote a short story dealing with the brutalities of the prison system in Arkansas that exhibited just the blend of naturalistic detail and the romantic triumph of received morality her essay advocated. She named the story "Trusty, No. 49" and sent it off in the spring of 1888 to Gilder at the *Century*.

> I send . . . the Arkansas story. . . . It deals with the Arkansas convict camps. I have not ventured to relate anything that has not happened and I have softened the picture a good deal. Some things are too ugly for art.
>
> I'll send Irish Gentlewoman soon. Let me know if you want Trusty No. 49 before 5 August because I go to Canada then and I have so many orders I want to know whether it's yours—or another's.[14]

Gilder accepted the story (if she would make revisions) and asked once again for the article on Ireland she had failed to send. Her excuse was lack of suitable details on the famine, but in the middle of August, only a few days before leaving for Canada, Alice wrote again:

> I am greatly obliged to you for your promptness in Trusty No. 39's [*sic*] case. I have tried to show my gratitude by being prompt in return;

[14] Alice French to Richard Watson Gilder, July 15, 1888, *Century* Collection, New York Public Library.

my Irish papers ect came and I put off my departure for Canada for a week to complete and send the article to you. The MS isn't as neat as I like to have it; but I hope you will pardon the chisel marks. The price we agreed on was $250.00 [15]

Alice's price, about two and one-fourth cents a word, twenty dollars a printed page, was high payment in the 1880's, when only quality magazines offered over one cent a word and standard payment was usually three-fourths of a cent a word. Magazines had yet to enjoy the high profits that came with the rise in sales and the increased advertising profits of the nineties.

In August, Alice left for her Canadian vacation and took the convict story with her. Gilder wanted less detailed descriptions of the beating suffered by convict laborers. On August 23, she wrote from Ha Ha Bay about the manuscript:

> Have made the changes you urged in Trusty . . . I'll return it by next boat—no R R's here.
>
> I hope it gives the reader the impression of a sleepy out at elbows Southern town, just beginning to stir; and the story, you know, hangs on the nature of the people being just what it is.
>
> I *knew* you would object to the blood, but I put it in after a good deal of consideration because that ghastly little touch gives just the horror and squalor and *brutality* of the scene. . . . However, I am not 'biggity'. . . . Perhaps poor Stowbay's back will give enough brutality to the scene.[16]

Alice originally had planned to return to Davenport by sailing up the St. Lawrence from Ha Ha Bay, but shortly before she was to leave, news came that her father was ill, and she went instead to Pocasset, on the Massachusetts coast, where her parents were spending the summer of 1888. George French had hoped that a summer vacation on the Atlantic shore would help restore his failing health, but by late summer he had grown so ill with abdominal pains that he was taken back to Davenport, where he was forced to remain at home virtually an invalid, leaving his son George with the management of the plow factory. Morton had left for New Mexico to be a mining engineer; but Fanny and Alice were at home, and so was Robert—though shortly he would be in Andover, at the academy.

[15] Alice French to Richard Watson Gilder, August 13, 1888, *Century* Collection, New York Public Library.

[16] Alice French to Richard Watson Gilder, August 23, 1888, *Century* Collection, New York Public Library.

On the morning of October 13, 1888, a little more than a month after his return from Massachusetts, George French died.[17] He was sixty-three years old, and the autopsy disclosed what had been feared all along—cancer of the stomach and liver.

The city newspapers carried lengthy articles describing his achievements and his service to Davenport and Iowa. At his funeral, his friends eulogized him, and the Unitarian preacher reminded mourners that such a man's death was a loss not only to his family but to all who stood "in the midst of unsolved questions in regard to higher welfare of the workingman." George French's life seemed to have embodied all the canons of expectant capitalism. In place of the jealous New England God whom his ancestors had lost, he had substituted another image that was no less exacting and no less ambivalent. Unlike most of the westward-moving emigrants of the nineteenth century, he had not fled to escape a society whose economic system had oppressed him. He had gone West to labor after respectability and success only in terms of that society he had left behind.

To Alice, her father had been an ideal of goodness and wisdom who possessed those "cardinal New England virtues" that she cherished. George French's beliefs, as well as his character, had been the large part of his daughter's education, and for that reason she had grown devoted to the ideals he personified. She had the rhetorical skill and the perceptive eye for detail that were often missing in contemporary writers whose realism and naturalism now seem to speak more profoundly for their age; it is tempting to contemplate what she would have written had she not been dominated by the social morality she had received through her father and by the requirements of the timid editors she wished to please.

Shortly before her thirty-ninth birthday, Alice received a letter from the editors of the *Book Buyer*, a New York monthly and the house organ of Charles Scribner's Sons. The magazine, which devoted itself to literary news and reviews and capsule biographies of authors, asked Alice to send a photograph to be used with a biographical sketch scheduled for spring publication. She submitted the photograph, and when the April, 1889, issue appeared, it carried a full-page picture

[17] With their father's death, Alice's brother George became president of the Eagle Manufacturing Company, and Nat, who had been practicing law in Davenport, retired from his law partnership and joined his brother in operating the company.

of her handsome face with the large eyes, strong mouth, and full, plump jowls that made her look younger than her thirty-nine years.

The magazine's laudatory article announced that her stories were "conspicuous for their dramatic power, truth to human nature, simplicity, pathos and quiet humor." Such judgments were customary to the age, especially for such reviews as the *Book Buyer*, which had practical reasons for its attention.

Alice was writing a full-length novel based on Clover Bend legends and set in the Arkansas swampland. After five winters on the plantation, she had built up a store of usable details and impressions of the region's history of backwoods feuds, skillful and unpunished murders, and the colorful rustic existence of a rural people suffering from ignorance and fear and even malaria picturesque enough to draw her misgivings for the future, when "the country will be so well drained that it cannot even summon an old time chill."

Alice filled her novel with blood and turbulence, using the stories she had heard of raids by marauding "graybacks" on civilians during the Civil War. In mid-February, 1889, she had written to E. L. Burlingame at *Scribner's*.

MY DEAR MR. BURLINGAME:
Should you care to "examine" a story in three parts of Arkansas life during the last part of the war—an epic of the guerrillas? The hero would be a young Arkansan educated in England by his uncle who comes back to Arkansas to his broken old father when both his brothers are killed. . . .

The family has dignity, the father was a sort of slipshod hidalgo, you understand. . . .

The son is a handsome, sweet tempered fine fellow, but unhappily a constitutional coward. The plot turns on the attempts of the guerrillas to secure 2000 dollars cotton money sent to this Colonel Rutherford. The first messenger is killed, but has so artfully secured the money (real life again) that it is saved.

Then the son takes it, is captured and tortured and his courage gives way enough to confess that he has given it to a certain Presbyterian Minister, a character in the region, the best of men, but a keen horse trader. . . .

You can see the rest of the story—Rutherford's remorse "the only Rutherford ever was a coward"; his attempts to right himself by bravery afterward. Attack on the plantation by the guerrillas. . . . ect-ect- everything ending happily.

You may think it too sensational. It isn't quite so bad as it sounds and the Expiation idea (Expiation is the name of the story) is that no matter how a man has sinned, remorse does no good except so far as it leads to active restitution. . . .

I don't know whether you will like the story but if poor I know it is honest and drawn from life. I have spared the reader the dialect as much as possible.[18]

Burlingame liked her outline and suggested that the novel be published both by Scribner's Sons and serialized in *Scribner's Magazine* —a common enough practice and profitable for both the publishing house and its magazine, as well as for the author. Alice completed the novel in less than three months and wrote Burlingame on May 27, 1889, to announce that she had sent her "epic" on by express. Burlingame replied on June 9, accepting it for publication and announcing that the famous A. B. Frost would illustrate it.

The completed novel had thirteen chapters (about forty thousand words), and ran in *Scribner's Magazine* for four months (from January, 1890, to April, 1890). In May, 1890, shortly after Alice's fortieth birthday, it was published in book form.

Expiation followed the outline Alice had sent Burlingame. The novel began in 1864 with a description of its hero, Fairfax Rutherford, traveling along a corduroy road through an Arkansas swamp and dressed in a "bush" outfit he had purchased in London for his return to his family's plantation on the Black River. Suddenly a horse came charging down the road, with a corpse lashed to its back. On the corpse was a note directing Fairfax to go to a cabin in the swamp, where he learned that hidden in the rags around the corpse's feet was twenty-five thousand dollars (Alice had increased the amount from the two thousand dollars she had originally suggested), which the dead man was delivering to Fairfax's father at Montaigne, the family plantation. Fairfax then mounted the dead man's horse and rode through the swamp to hide the money at Parson Collins'. From there, he set out once again to make his way to Montaigne, but was shot and captured by the graybacks, and under torture revealed where he had hidden the money. Then the graybacks descended on Parson Collins, only to learn that the Parson had given the money to "Slick Mose," a simple-minded inhabitant of the swamp who talked to animals and lived with snakes. Enraged at the loss of the money (they knew they would never

18 Alice French to E. L. Burlingame, February 1889, Newberry Library.

catch Slick Mose), the guerrillas tied up the Parson, pinned a target to his breast, and forced Fairfax (by pouring hot coals down his back) to shoot him—or so Fairfax and the assembled rascals believed.

Fairfax was then abandoned by the graybacks, who left him to die of his own wounds; but he nonetheless made his way to Montaigne, where he collapsed and during a delirium confessed his crime against the Parson, thus revealing himself to be the first Rutherford coward. But only briefly, for once recovered, Fairfax set out to expiate his sins by eradicating the graybacks and bringing peace back to Lawrence County, Arkansas, all of which "Fair" Rutherford did. He then returned to Montaigne, where he learned that the Parson still lived; he had not been shot by Fairfax after all. Thus the plantation was saved, the Rutherford name was rescued from ignominy both by good works and a turn of fate, and all neighborhood rascals were put to rout.

The story was romantic, dashing, and melodramatic. And it clanked with such Victorian machinery as torch-light processions, solemn vows, wondrous coincidences, secret parleys in the swamp, horses galloping in all directions, and a villain so mean and low he was called "Jew-Indian" by the poor whites to indicate his worthlessness.

The novel's weaknesses, which force summary into travesty, exist because the edifice of incidents and noble gestures have no actual foundation. And while *Expiation* generates real excitement in its semblance of drama, it fails even as simple entertainment because of its disconnected structure, a weakness caused by Alice's inability to rise above the limits of her talent for short fiction. The novel is only a sequence of energetic scenes: Fairfax galloping along the corduroy road, the graybacks torturing their victims, and, what struck readers in the 1890's as especially vivid, the death of the chief villain in the swamp. The novel was incompletely plotted—unanswered questions intrude and puzzling events lack explanation or motive. Alice shared another failing with her betters: although she labored hard not to make them so, her villains were more interesting than her hero.

She did avoid the rotund prose and rhetoric of the historical romances that were popular at the end of the century. She had finally achieved a colloquial style touched with provincialisms and more like Hugh Latimer than Addison and Steele; but while avoiding fine and noble writing, she employed the fine and noble sentiments of historical romance, showing that even among the wicked and the rustic, simple virtues were imperishable and decency immutable. Alice wrote of middle western laborers and bumpkins and of southern hillbillies and crackers who displayed rough-neck qualities traditional in regionalism, but in *Expiation*, as in most of her short stories, she expressed a romantic faith by thrusting characters into worlds based on the chivalric myths of the southern plantation or the variants that Horatio Alger created for the northern entrepreneur.

The reviews of *Expiation* were generous. The Boston *Beacon* announced that the author had "taken her place among the very foremost of American writers of fiction." [19] The *Dial*, while complaining "there is a little more of the element of dialect than we can accept with unalloyed pleasure" (four explanatory footnotes appeared in the novel's first seven pages), still praised her and added that while Octave Thanet was really a woman, Alice French of Iowa, she nevertheless wrote like a man. [20]

The *Nation* said of Octave Thanet that "his" novel was "vigorous" and "straightaway" and praised "him" for abandoning the romantic villain and substituting one of plain evil. [21] Not surprisingly, Scribner's own *Book Buyer* called *Expiation* one of the most noteworthy pieces of fiction to appear in years. [22] Yet Scribner's gave the novel little publicity other than its review and brief public and trade announcements of its availability at fifty cents in a paper cover, one dollar clothbound.

Shortly after the novel started to run in *Scribner's Magazine*, the publishers began negotiations with the English firm of Frederick Warne and Company, which wished to publish the novel in the United Kingdom. Contracts were signed late in the spring of 1890. On April 22, 1890, Alice wrote Scribner's about the first royalty payment she had received:

DEAR SIRS

Your favor, enclosing check for ninety-seven dollars and sixty cents from Frederic Warne and Co. has just reached me. Please accept my thanks for the excellent bargain which you made for me. Indeed, I do not see how even the most irritable and suspicious of the *irritable genus* could find any

---

[19] Quoted in *A Book of Iowa Authors by Iowa Authors*, ed. Johnson Brigham (Des Moines, 1930), p. 87.

[20] *Dial*, XI (May 1890), 13.

[21] *Nation*, LI, No. 1311 (August 14, 1890), 136.

[22] *Book Buyer*, VII (April 1890), 113.

chance for fault finding with such uniformly considerate and generous publishers as I have always found "you all".

(And, I am not irritable, I am very good tempered.)*

I do hope that you won't find me a bad investment. Please thank Messrs. Warne and Co. for me.

Very truly yours
ALICE FRENCH

* Excuse frankness.[23]

The English edition was published in July, 1890. The following month, London's *Athenaeum* carried a review that caused a minor literary skirmish. The reviewer recommended *Expiation* to "those who think that blood shed keeps fiction pure," adding:

> The volume is unpleasant to read. The paper is exceedingly stiff, like that used too commonly for novels in America. The spelling is American. It would have been more convenient if the publishers had stated whether the book was published with the author's permission, and whether it has already appeared in America.[24]

Aroused by the peevish criticism and hints of piracy, Alice's English publishers replied to the *Athenaeum*, which then printed their statement:

> The novel has been running in the numbers of *Scribner's Magazine* which have been sent to you monthly for review, and . . . our firm are the sole agents for that magazine in England. . . . The volume, on the back of the title page, contained the very information your reviewer has quibbled for.[25]

To which the magazine responded by asking how it was supposed to know that

> "Copyright. Entered at Stationer's Hall (All rights reserved)." means this is an American novel, originally issued in *Scribner's Magazine* and now reprinted by arrangement with the author.[26]

The argument sputtered on until the *Athenaeum*, made ingratiating by talk of legal action, apologized and announced that it had no intent to suggest that the publishers were not men of respectability and good faith.

[23] Alice French to Charles Scribner's Sons, April 22, 1890, Newberry Library.
[24] *Athenaeum*, No. 3276 (August 9, 1890), p. 189.
[25] *Athenaeum*, No. 3277 (August 16, 1890), p. 228.
[26] *Athenaeum*, No. 3278 (August 23, 1890), p. 259.

To Alice, the brief argument on the other side of the Atlantic was far less interesting than the fact that *Expiation* aroused critical attention at home, even bringing acclaim from Dr. Barrett Wendell, the Harvard literary scholar and friend of Horace Scudder of the *Atlantic*. Wendell, Scudder, and other pillars of taste and gentility responded to the novel's exciting picture of the Arkansas back country as much as to the romanticism of its happy ending and its antiseptic love affairs, two elements that reduced the realistic grimness of some of the novel's details and demonstrated how distant Alice's work was from American literary naturalism.

Alice continued to write Arkansas stories. Most of her work was now done at Clover Bend, in her study in the cottage or in the attic above her bedroom when noisy house guests were present. Her system was businesslike. She had bought a typewriter and was learning to use it for writing first drafts. With a plot taken from the local legends and traditions, or from her reading, she collected all her notes, assembled her ideas, and began her story, fitting in the varieties of interesting words and phrases she had collected. From a history of nineteenth-century France she drew up "A list of potentially useful words and phrases":

> A factory like an obelisque
> perspicacity
> azure slated
> Café de la Paix
> Marching down the Rue Montmarte
> In the cemetery of Père La Chaise the communists made their last stand
> Vigier Baths
> Mérgon etching
> Cicatrix
> The dome of the Invalides "damascened with gold"
> interpenetrated with ruddy light
> The tragic prolegomena to
> Cross gulls [*sic*] on a field argent
> penumbra
> Seven Against Thebes
> Matrix

Other details came from the life that surrounded her, and she sought them out as she had the dialect of the poor-white renters. In the 1890's, writers were increasingly drawn to slums or villages to see how the other half lived. Stephen Crane went to the Bowery to sit with the tramps and listen to their talk. Alice would have reported the same facts, but she was constitutionally unable to express in her fiction the same bleak and bitter view of life.

She subscribed to a weekly Arkansas newspaper to read the details of local crimes, and like the natives, she went to nearby Walnut Ridge when the court calendar seemed interesting. There the judge and jury were no less notable than the murderers and burglars they tried, and it was from such observations that Alice had written "Trusty, No. 49," which, with much of the blood and beatings intact, Gilder had eventually accepted for the *Century*. The story appeared in June, 1890, and even the expurgated version condemned convict-leasing in Arkansas with pungent details rare in local-color writing.

The story described the trial of a poor-white sharecropper who had killed a gambler. Near the end of the trial—which was presided over by a judge who carried a rose in his teeth—the jury withdrew to reach its decision. Thereupon one juror suggested that the guilty man either be executed or set free, for no human being deserved to be sentenced to the horror of a leased-convict camp in Arkansas. Then followed a description of life in one Arkansas prison camp where convicts suffered from malaria, dysentery, and brutal floggings by the penal camp boss. Then when the juror had completed his tale of brutality, he revealed that he himself had served time in the prison camp he had described and that the murdered gambler was none other than the notorious prison camp boss who had brought suffering and death to so many men. Whereupon the jury set his murderer free.

Grim as the story's naturalistic details were to readers living in the genteel tradition of the early 1890's, "Trusty, No. 49" demonstrated clearly how Alice was enveloped in the traditions of sentiment and romance and dependent on the kind of fairy providence Howells had thought he had seen three years before. But her yoking of a social tract with the blessings of romantic fiction was still polished enough to bring her increased popularity in the 1890's. Realism had arrived and naturalism was on its way, but the English-reading world preferred Stevenson, A. Conan Doyle, Anthony Hope, F. Marion Crawford, Kipling, and Richard Harding Davis. In America it was an age of Thomas Bailey Aldrich and James Whitcomb Riley rather than Henry James.

When "Trusty, No. 49" finally appeared in the *Century*, Alice was visiting in Boston, where she paid a call on the Horace Scudders. Scudder, had become editor of the *Atlantic Monthly* the preceding April, 1890, and was thus a member of that Brahminical community which one of the members described as an "Apostolic Succession" of distinguished men. Scudder thought of editors as "acolytes serving the altars of literature,"[27] and he read Greek and Latin authors for a half-hour each morning just so he could "keep his ear attuned to style." Houghton Mifflin had published *Knitters in the Sun* three years before; and when Scudder met Alice, he suggested that Houghton Mifflin might be interested in publishing another collection of her short stories. When she returned to Davenport, Alice wrote him about the suggestion:

> I enclose a list of the stories that occurred to me for the book. By the way, I will tell you in a deep confidence (you and Mr. Houghton) that I had a letter from the Scribners, wanting to publish my short stories. I was glad that their fate was settled.
>
> You are so generous at 4 Park Street that I know you will be glad that *Expiation* is "going off capitally." [28]

During the following winter Alice worked intermittently at selecting and revising suitable short stories. She had saved the issues of the *Century*, and *Scribner's*, and *Harper's Bazar* that carried her work; and now she revised her stories by cutting out magazine pages, pasting them onto larger sheets, and altering the order and form of sentences and paragraphs with scissors and glue. Awkward as it was, it was better than retyping them on her cumbersome typewriter.

While she worked on the stories for Houghton Mifflin, she began a book of a different sort. A. C. McClurg, the Chicago publishers, had asked her to edit the letters of Lady Mary Wortley Montagu (1689–1762) for McClurg's series entitled "Laurel Crowned Letters." Alice's edition appeared in December, 1890. She had based her selection on Lord Wharncliffe's 1837 edition, her principal contribution being a dedicatory letter commending the literary ability of Lady Mary,[29] if not her personality or her appetite for gossip about polite English society. The publication of the letters created little response except from Scudder, who wrote to Alice pointedly asking about progress on the work she had undertaken for Houghton Mifflin and raising questions

[27] Ellery Sedgwick, *The Happy Profession* (Boston, 1946), pp. 154, 156.
[28] Alice French to Horace Scudder, July 31, 1890, Harvard College Library.
[29] Alice addressed her as "Lady Montagu."

about the prevalence of dialect in the stories she was including. In her reply Alice agreed:

> I'm afraid there is a load of dialect in the stories written before I tried to reduce my dialect to the smallest proportions. As I do now. . . .
>
> Should we include other stories, there are two courses open. We might call the book "Old and New Poor Folks," and add two stories of the time of Edward VI . . . or we might add, instead, (a more feasible scheme, I fancy) three Western Stories, The Governor's Prerogative, The Day of the Cyclone and The First Mayor. I will send you the stories tomorrow and you can judge for yourself about their value.
>
> Were the book only about Arkansas, I should call it By the Cypress Swamp; but if we mix it up with the West, that won't do.
>
> I will try to evolve a title.
>
> As to the contract, the book is an indulgence of my own; and I am not trying to make money by it. I told Mr. Houghton I would like to have the same terms as for Knitters In The Sun.[30]

The book appeared in June, 1891, and contained ten stories, all of which had originally appeared in popular magazines. Six were stories of Arkansas, four were set in a western village—Davenport in disguise. Both "Old and New Poor Folks" and "By the Cypress Swamp" had been ruled out as titles, and Alice and Scudder had agreed that the volume be named for the first story in the collection, "Otto the Knight."

The book aroused more critical response than *Knitters in the Sun* had. The *Nation* rose to oriental eloquence with "there is but one Arkansas, and Octave Thanet is its prophet."[31] Scribner's *Book Buyer* was only slightly less generous when reviewing a book published by Houghton Mifflin and announced that all were good stories except the title story, which dealt with the conversion of Otto Knipple from trade unionism to Americanism, all of which the *Book Buyer* found "shadowy and ill-defined."[32] The reviewer in the *Dial* commended Alice's picture of benevolent capitalism, observing that many of the stories "touch upon what are known . . . as questions of the day. . . . The admirable work of this writer is distinguished by its undercurrent of earnest thought."[33]

[30] Alice French to Horace Scudder, December 31, 1890, Harvard College Library.

[31] *Nation*, LIII (October 1, 1891), 264.

[32] *Book Buyer*, VIII (July 1891), 261.

[33] *Dial*, XII (June 1891), 51.

The *Atlantic Monthly* originally praised the stories for their "pene-tration," "sympathy," "power," and "pervasive humor,"[34] but the following year, the magazine carried a critical article on the short story by C. T. Copeland, who cited them as poor examples of the short story form:

> Whatever time of day it is with Octave Thanet, and whether she says the sun is shining or the moon, the light is too often supplied by the footlights. In "The Day of the Cyclone" ... the thunder sounds tinny, and the elements themselves are enlisted as *dramatis personae*. A soberer method, less of an effort after brilliancy in dialogue at the expense of nature, and a lighter touch where pathos is the thing touched would commend her undoubted gifts more highly to the judicious.[35]

But the light touch would have ill suited the didactic motives Alice exhibited in *Otto the Knight*, especially in her stories of union members. She had made her position clear four months earlier to Richard Watson Gilder of the *Century*:

> It is a misfortune (the gravest kind of misfortune) that gradually, all the sentiment, all the feeling of duty to his fellow citizens (the patriot's instinct, in short) in the case of the workingman is being diverted to the one perilous channel of *class feeling*! He is a workingman before he is an American—or a man!
>
> The secret societies of labor appeal to the best and the worst in their members. ...
>
> I have tried to show ... what seems to me the most terrible most hopeful secret of moral law. I mean that even as the best in us may drag us to the pit, so sin itself can purify. The evil that we do out of an un-selfish heart is not hindered in its outward destruction, but it may actually elevate instead of degrade the evil doer.[36]

It was befuddled ethics, clearly not realism, but it helped make her short stories popular enough among readers and editors. *Expiation* had not been a popular success—early in 1891 she received only $219 from Scribner's on royalties for four thousand copies sold for fifty cents each—but in her letter to Gilder she announced that her price was "$200 or $200 and something dollars" for another story for the *Century*; and not long afterward, Hamlin Garland reported, she was

[34] *Atlantic Monthly*, LXVIII (November 1891), 70.

[35] "The Short Story," *Atlantic Monthly*, LXIX (February 1892), 265.

[36] Alice French to Richard Watson Gilder, February 13, 1891, *Century* Collection, New York Public Library.

getting an astounding "300 dollars for a story of 6,000 words—fabulous!" [37] Her price per word had risen to five cents at a time when Garland was lucky to be paid half a cent.

In 1891, following publication of *Otto the Knight*, a new edition of *Knitters in the Sun* was issued by Houghton Mifflin, and that fall D. Appleton's published *We All*, a juvenile novel set in Arkansas. The story used characters patterned after Alice's nieces and nephews and told of a Chicago boy, the son of a railroad magnate, who visited an Arkansas plantation where life was filled with midnight galloping through the swamp, Negro haunts, and boys with real pistols. Such exertions only briefly obscured the presence of a "silver lining" in every cloud. The *Book Buyer* said the writing was "wonderfully fine." [38]

In the last years of the eighties, Alice had managed to write five or six stories each year. By the nineties she was writing eight or ten a year, most of them stories set in Arkansas or in middle western variants of Davenport. In 1892, she wrote eight short stories, an article on Arkansas folklore for the *Journal of American Folklore*, and a poem, "United States to Russia," published in the Abbot Academy *Courant*.

Most of the stories had been written at the request of magazine editors. The poem came in response to the famine following the Russian crop failure of 1891 and the organization of Russian famine relief commissions in America. The relief movement began on November 13, 1891, when the Red Cross met in Boston and Clara Barton made a Thanksgiving appeal for funds. The Russian crop failures threatened almost fourteen million persons with starvation, and at the Boston meeting two hundred dollars was collected to be sent to Countess Tolstoy to be spent on food for the hungry.

The movement spread to the Middle West when William C. Edgar, the editor of Minneapolis' flour trade journal, the *Northwestern Miller*, set out to collect "six million pounds of cargo" for the starving Russians, motivated partly by the knowledge that the United States had a surplus of flour and that giving away one free shipload would "call world-wide attention to America's plenteous store." In Iowa, the editor of the Davenport *Democrat* joined with Alice and her brother George and the Davenport Unitarian minister to form the Iowa Russian Famine Relief Commission, with a prominent person in each

[37] Hamlin Garland, *Companions on the Trail* (New York, 1931), pp. 460–461.
[38] *Book Buyer*, VIII (December 1891), 536.

congressional district appointed by the governor to serve on the Commission.

Russian relief became an Iowa crusade to collect corn as Minnesota had collected flour. The members of the Iowa Commission stumped the state, making speeches in lecture halls and private homes throughout Iowa. Alice and her fellow members drove through the countryside asking individual farmers for a share of each corn crop and conducting campaigns among townspeople to get money to buy corn and ship it. By such methods and by organizing operettas, concerts, and even a mock political convention at the state university in Iowa City, the Commission raised forty thousand dollars in money and corn.

Plans for the transportation of the relief supplies to Russia met with difficulties at first. Assistance from the federal government was opposed by politicians who held that the Russian government could care for its own if it would. Furthermore, it became apparent that much of the Russian food shortage had been caused by grain hoarding by speculators, who objected when the American aid threatened to depress their grain markets.

It was then suggested that relief supplies be sailed across the ocean in the *Constellation*, but the U.S. Navy, which used the vessel for training midshipmen at Annapolis, refused to release it, pointing out that its capacity was much too small and many of its timbers were rotten. Eventually, Alice obtained free transportation from the railroads and succeeded in getting reduced freight rates on cargo vessels.

As a result of the Iowa campaign for Russian relief, 225 railroad carloads of Iowa corn went to Russia in five ships in 1892, accompanied by an expert to set up kitchens and teach Russian peasants how to cook corn dishes. And as a result of Alice's work on the campaign, the governor of Iowa appointed her secretary of the Iowa women's auxiliary to the Red Cross. She also received a letter of thanks from the pastor of the Anglo-American Church in St. Petersburg, but her most cherished return was a leather portfolio sent by the grateful peasants of Kazan.

Russian relief was the kind of nineteenth-century philanthropic adventure that lifted the hearts of the donors and set no precedents for future obligations (the famine worsened in subsequent years, but a second call for funds met with little response). The famine itself served as an inspiration for those who speculated that starvation was the result of communal land ownership systems or the work of

"Narodniks," Russian Populists bent on embarrassing their government.

In January, 1892, Alice had written to Richard Watson Gilder asking him to urge George Kennan of the Red Cross to speak for Russian relief when he came to Iowa on a lecture tour. Kennan had written his famous series of articles, "Russia and the Exile System," published in the *Century*, in 1888; and Alice thought he would help the cause, in spite of the fact that he had left people with the impression, which she conveyed to Gilder, that he was "a nihilist, an anarchist and does not really care whether the peasants starve or not, if their starving will only injure the existing government." [39]

The poem Alice wrote for the Abbot *Courant*, appeared in June, 1892:

UNITED STATES TO RUSSIA

O sorely smitten brother, O ancient friend of ours,
Above your vast dominions the hunger spectre towers;

We clasp our children closer, while Russian mothers weep,
And welcome in their anguish the merciful last sleep

That stills the moan of famine and cures their
            children's pain.
Yet in *our* mortal peril, with every nerve a-strain,

When brothers were our foemen, and friendship stood aside,
The flag with the Russian eagles, the ships of the
            white czar's pride

Came swiftly to our harbors, to help us in our need,
A menace to the sullen powers they could not choose
            but heed! [40]

O sorely smitten brother, O ancient friend of ours,
Above your vast dominions the hunger spectre towers,

[39] Alice French to Richard Watson Gilder, January 24, 1892, *Century* Collection, New York Public Library.

[40] The "sullen powers" were England and France. In 1863 the government of Alexander II had sent naval fleets to New York and San Francisco, a move northerners interpreted as a gesture in support of the Union in the Civil War and a threat against British interference in favor of the Confederacy. Actually, the fleet movements had been preparation for a privateering campaign against British shipping in the event Britain and France interfered with Russian suppression of the Polish revolution.

Our turn, O friend and brother, to send a fleet to you,
With every masthead flying the red, the white, the blue!
But no guns scowl through the portholes, and 'neath
          our ensign fair,
Flutters the flag of mercy that the world knows
          everywhere.
And the cargo that we carry is hope for starving men—
Lo! for the lives you saved us, render we lives again.

While working on Russian relief, Alice fell behind in her writing, and at one time seven editors were waiting for her work, among them Edward Livermore Burlingame of *Scribner's Magazine,* who had contracted some time before for a series of six stories. Alice had sent the first of them to him in March, 1892. They finally appeared as "Stories of a Western Town," beginning in the August, 1892, issue of *Scribner's* and continuing intermittently until February, 1893. The stories were set in Davenport, and several characters were modeled after members of Alice's family. Another source was less direct. In February, 1893, she wrote to Robert Bridges, book critic and columnist for the old *Life:*

M. "Drooch":[41]
During the progress of Stories of a Western Town which have been appearing in *Scribner's Magazine* for some months, the author has been desirous of acknowledging a little fact about them that may have an interest to you. It is simply that an article written by you in "Life," last year or earlier, was their inspiration. This article mentioned how rare it was that any novelist took for a hero "a *good* citizen," a man who simply without any noise and quite as a matter of course, is doing his best for his community and his country. And yet as you most truly say, there are thousands of such men in every state; they it is who make Democracy possible. I was impressed by your words. I thought of them, often. In the end, the character of such a man occurred to me—as well as many real men whom I know; and I have in Harry Lossing tried to draw just such a good citizen.

In the last story of the series ["Harry Lossing"] I have contrasted him with a man who is *not* a good citizen. He is given the alternative of losing his sweetheart or doing something what he believes injurious to the town of which he is mayor. He takes the Western way out of the dilemma—he declines both alternatives. He will neither give up his conscience nor his sweetheart; and he proceeds to have both.

[41] A misspelling. Bridges signed his column "Droch."

Excuse so much about stories that you may not have seen at all. I have been grateful so long, however, that I could not resist the temptation to express the feeling. May I add that I always go first to your comments and criticisms in "Life," and enjoy them just as much when they do not express my sentiments as when they do. But, most times, they have the peculiar attraction of saying what I think better than I could say it, myself. And, you know that is always an oblique compliment to one's sagacity.

For all of which reasons I am,

Your obliged and grateful reader,

OCTAVE THANET.[42]

In April, 1893, *Stories of a Western Town* was published in a single volume, and that month Alice wrote to Scribner's, "I trust [the book] will sell. I have had plenty of successes 'd'esteme.' I should like now a success de pocketbook." It was her first short-story collection published by a company other than Houghton Mifflin; and Horace Scudder, who had edited *Otto the Knight* and *Knitters in the Sun* for Houghton Mifflin, reviewed *Stories of a Western Town* in the November *Atlantic*:

"She is content with obvious construction for her stories. . . . She is a reporter of life, it is true, rather than an artist. . . . If she poured the best contents of two or three stories into one, and refined that by repeated processes of writing, she might produce work which would not only reflect the life in which she is so much interested, but have a lasting life of its own."[43]

It was the first time she had not been treated charitably by the *Atlantic*'s reviewers, and at the end of the year, when she drew up a list of her literary friends, Scudder's name was omitted.[44] But other critics were more complimentary. One of them, Marie Therese Blanc, a French critic for the Parisian *Revue des Deux Mondes*, even compared Alice's storytelling ability to that of De Maupassant.[45]

Another project for Scribner's was under way as soon as Alice had

[42] Alice French to Robert Bridges, February 6, 1893, Robert Bridges Collection, Dickinson College Library.

[43] "A Few Story Tellers, Old and New," *Atlantic Monthly*, LXXII (November 1893), 698.

[44] The list included Edward Burlingame of *Scribner's*, Henry Mills Alden of *Harper's*, Richard Watson Gilder of the *Century*, and J. S. Phillips of *McClure's*.

[45] Th. Bentzon [Marie Therese Blanc], "Dans l'Arkansas: A Propos des Romans d'Octave Thanet," *Revue des Deux Mondes*, CXXXIII (February 1, 1896), 542–572; tr. Evelyn Schaeffer, "In Arkansas Apropos of Octave Thanet's Romances," *Midland Monthly*, VI (July 1896), 43.

completed work on the proofs of *Stories of a Western Town*. At Christmas, 1889, Alice had given Jane Crawford a camera as a present. Soon the two women had a darkroom at Clover Bend and were making and printing their own photographs, even making sensitized plates for the camera. One of the hazards was unique at the plantation: because of the primitive drainage system and the high water table, developing chemicals that were poured down the drain often seeped back to the surface of the ground and poisoned Alice's chickens. But the two women had the drain tiled and deepened and continued making pictures until they became experts. In March, 1890, Alice wrote Burlingame to suggest a series of articles on photography for *Scribner's*. Burlingame countered with the suggestion that instead of articles, Alice write a book on her photographic experiences and illustrate it with her own pictures. She began work later that year and continued fitfully through 1891, finally completing it in 1892. Much of the book was filled with photographs, but it took a month, from mid-February to March, 1893, for her to complete work on the proofs of the text. On March 14 she sent the manuscript to Scribner's, which published it three months later as *An Adventure in Photography* and bought all rights for five hundred dollars.

Now a fixture in *Scribner's Magazine*, Alice was turning out material with regularity. Each story took about three weeks to complete, though when she was behind schedule, she could work on two at once, writing as long as twelve hours a day. In the spring of 1893, she wrote "The Proud Pynsents," working from May 1 to May 23; while at the same time, starting May 4 and finishing May 24, she wrote "The Labor Question at Glasscock's."

In Davenport she now worked on the second floor of the house in a room formerly occupied by her father, which she described for the readers of the *Book Buyer*:

> [The room] is hung in olive green paper of a small conventional design, and the woodwork is in light shades of olive. There is matting on the floor and some Indian rugs. On the walls are some etchings and water-colors, and a couple of bas-reliefs. . . . The leather covered arm chair before the table is more than a hundred years old, and once was a legislator's chair in the Pennsylvania Senate.[46]

Literary journals of the 1880's and 90's reported on writers' homes and carefully documented their likes and dislikes, seeking out their

[46] Mary Jane Reid, "Octave Thanet in Her Davenport Home," *Book Buyer*, XII (February 1895), 24–25.

opinions in surveys and questionnaires with an interrogatory high purpose duplicated in the twentieth century only by pedagogues and social scientists. In the 1890's, the *Book Buyer* sent a questionnaire to Alice asking about her favorite authors, books, and mottoes and printed her replies along with those of Eugene Field, Robert Grant, and Richard Harding Davis. Alice listed her favorite authors as Montaigne, Scott, Lamb, and Thackeray for prose, Browning and Lowell for poetry. She had no favorite composers: "I don't know enough about music to venture to have a favorite." She reported that *Henry Esmond* was her favorite book and *Much Ado about Nothing* her favorite play. Her favorite fictional characters were Rebecca of *Ivanhoe* and Thackeray's Colonel Newcome, and as her favorite heroes in real life, she listed magazine editors and good cooks. She most enjoyed, or so she said, playing with children; she most detested getting the bottom of her gown muddy; and for her motto she offered, "Neither forget yesterday nor tomorrow." It was the kind of promotional game that magazines in later ages played with movie stars, but Alice took it seriously, more so at least than either Richard Harding Davis, who listed himself as his own favorite author, or Robert Grant, who reported his motto for life was "Use Pear's Soap."[47]

Literary journals like the *Book Buyer* seemed to reflect a world that was comfortable enough in its solidity to be frivolous. Critical magazines were not the reservoirs of discontent with America that they became in the next century. They often existed above the distractions of the nineties, an age that was sometimes gay but was more often gaudy, spendthrift, wasteful, and greedy, yet still a time of great national achievement. In 1892 the New York *Tribune* and the New York *World* surveyed America's rich and discovered that enormous private fortunes had been accumulated: the *World* found 3,045 millionaires in America, the *Tribune* found 4,047. The nation's wilderness had been conquered: the 1890 census reported that for the first time a continuous line no longer marked a frontier of settlement. But the nation that was now both rich and civilized was moving toward one of the worst depressions in its history; and by 1892 rising unemployment, strikes, tight money, and increasing poverty seemed to imply that something was wrong with American democracy.

As if to commemorate its excesses and in spite of gloomy forecasts of impending depression, the United States prepared to celebrate itself in 1892 with the World's Columbian Exposition in Chicago.

[47] *Book Buyer*, X (February 1893), 11.

Plans for the fair had begun in 1890, when President Harrison approved an Act of Congress providing for an "international exhibition of arts, industries, manufacturers, and the products of the soil, mind and sea." Its avowed purpose was to celebrate the 400th anniversary of the discovery of America, but plans for the exposition became so grandiose and the complexities so massive that the fair's opening had to be delayed until 1893 and the 401st anniversary. But the year's delay only aroused greater interest, for the whole nation seemed to be prepared to flock to Chicago and the enormous exposition buildings laid out on bog land at the shore of Lake Michigan.

Shortly after the fair opened, Alice wrote again to Burlingame at *Scribner's* to propose a series of articles on the fair, not its buildings or its displays, but on its visitors. They were coming by the millions and ranged from the Infanta Eulalia of Spain and Archduke Ferdinand of Austro-Hungary to laborers, businessmen, country bumpkins, and armies of professional thieves. When Burlingame accepted her proposal, Alice went to Chicago to watch the crowds laboring solemnly through the great buildings as Henry Adams had, "looking like an owl" at the dynamos and the steam engines. She watched them gawking at white palaces built of iron and stucco that gleamed from the sun in the day and glistened from Edison's light bulbs at night. And she watched them being entertained: Lillian Russell's voice rose shrilly over the heads of her audiences, and on the Midway Plaisance sightseers could ascend 600 feet in the air in a captive balloon or ride 250 feet above the ground on George Washington Ferris' marvelous wheel. More famous still was a performer named Fahreda Mahzar, who was billed as Little Egypt and danced so that spectators could see the diamonds on her garters and "every muscle on her body at the same time."[48] With elephants to ride and Indians and pygmies to watch, crowds flocked to the Midway; it was more fun than the dynamo and more respectable than Chicago's elegant bagnios, and certainly cheaper—during the fair, brothel rates in Chicago tripled.

Before leaving Davenport for Chicago to collect material for the *Scribner's* series, Alice had received a letter from Marshall Field inviting her to stay in the Field home during her visit to the fair; and when she arrived in July, she went to the three-story red brick palace on Prairie Avenue with its ivory and gold drawing room and clock that was wound only once a year. From the Field mansion she commuted to the exposition grounds each day, returning early in the evening

[48] Emmett Deadmon, *Fabulous Chicago* (New York, 1953), p. 107.

when she didn't stay late to see the fireworks displays or to watch the anonymous throngs that wandered at night among the brilliantly lighted buildings.

Some in those crowds had not long to wait for fame: Casey Jones was driving an Illinois Central shuttle train between the fairgrounds and the Van Buren Street station, and an obscure poet named Edwin Markham saw an inspiring reproduction of Jean François Millet's "The Man with the Hoe" in the Fine Arts Palace. Alice saw the same picture, and to her it seemed to reflect the heavy but noble burden of honest toil that good men should accept. She liked Hovenden's "Breaking Home Ties" even more, and in that she was not alone; it was the most popular picture at the exposition.

"Art" and "Culture" dominated the fair with statuary, architecture, and designs that strained at beauty but succeeded in being only large and numerous. Whole civilizations of classical art seemed to have been gathered in single groups set on stuccoed barges in the lagoon or mounted on ornate pedestals. With few exceptions, the fair's retrograde architecture set American design back into a wilderness of flossy classicism, but the buildings were nonetheless awesome. The Manufacturers Building was the largest in the world; its proud builders announced that seven million feet of lumber had gone into the floor and five carloads of nails held it down. On her first day at the fair, Alice walked through it to see the book publishers' exhibits; Harper and Brothers had on view the first book they had published, a translation of Seneca's "Morals." The Century Company displayed the first draft of Thomas Nelson Page's "Marse Chan" and the original manuscript sheet on which was written the last sentence of Frank Stockton's "The Lady or the Tiger."

The Women's Building was an Ionic pile designed to demonstrate woman's noble role in the world. On its paneled walls were portraits of representative women of the world, among them Howells' daughter Mildred. The building held everything from a Japanese boudoir to a collection of four million abstinence pledges, all signed by children, and had been dedicated by the regal Mrs. Potter Palmer, who did so while draped with a dog collar of 2,268 pearls and a tiara of diamonds as large as lima beans. Queen of Chicago society, the nearest thing the Middle West had to an indigenous royalty, she joyfully symbolized the sumptuous materialism of her world when she consecrated the building by driving a gold nail into the wall—for the "golden touch."[49]

[49] Attendants pulled it out as soon as the ceremonies ended.

For the Middle West, the exposition meant that art had come to what had recently been (and some said still was) a cultural wasteland. Yet Chicago in the nineties was growing self-consciously literary and was beginning to celebrate the presence of midlanders such as George Ade, Robert Herrick, and Harriet Monroe. Hamlin Garland was attempting to establish Chicago as a literary center, although America's favorite literature was seldom what was written by Herrick, or Moody, or those like Dreiser, Sandburg, and Anderson, who followed. When the president of the Massachusetts Free Public Library Commission addressed the congress of librarians gathered at the fair, he announced that "Scott is attracting more readers than formerly, and Dickens fewer," adding that the most popular book in the libraries of America was *Uncle Tom's Cabin* with *Ben-Hur*, *Lorna Doone*, and *The Scarlet Letter* close behind.

The fair was like a crystal ball or a catastrophe of nature—those who witnessed it found in it confirmation of their predispositions: Henry Adams came twice and despaired because the fair revealed that Americans had no direction in their lives. The *Critic* conducted another survey; Alice's response was carried in the November 25, 1893 issue: "More and more I found the architecture significant as well as harmonious. And more and more its wonderful and pathetic beauty grew upon me. Next to the architecture and the landscape I was impressed by the crowd." Mary Hartwell Catherwood, a devotee of historical romance, not surprisingly liked best the picturesque architecture of the Spanish buildings and the primitive natives displayed on the Midway. Joseph Kirkland, consistent with the grim realism of his fiction, announced to the *Critic* that he was most impressed by the presence of so many deformed and crippled spectators. He "met at every turn, some form of bodily disability or deformity. Men and women tottering with age, babies encumbering poor parents, invalids sustained by patient friends. . . . and the pat—pat—pat of the cripple's cane broke the soft rustle of the Art gallery. . . ."

Writers and scholars convened a series of congresses during the summer, and at the congress of historians, Frederick Jackson Turner read his paper, "The Significance of the Frontier in American History," which became one of the most influential statements about America produced in the nineteenth century and created as many historical truths as it reported; but the champion of the frontier in literature, Hamlin Garland, was unaware of Turner's pronouncements, and in the

Critic Lucy Monroe's report of the meeting of historians failed to mention either the frontier hypothesis or its creator.

In July a congress of authors gathered in the old Art Institute, a castellated stone mass on Michigan Avenue, and Alice read a paper on the short story before an audience that included Charles Dudley Warner, Hamilton Wright Mabie, George Washington Cable, Hamlin Garland, Joseph Kirkland, and Walter Besant, a delegate to the fair from the English Society of Authors.

Alice explained the theories she had made apparent in her fiction: the short story must be true to life, must be honest, but ought not wallow in filth and despair. It was a repetition of her statement in *Literature*, five years before, that "Art only soils her white feet when she prys into the vile by-ways of the human heart." Reporters found her remarks "clever and well-constructed," but it was a morning session, and the audience was small compared to the crowds that came to the afternoon meeting that had advertised poetry readings by Eugene Field and Hezekiah Butterworth.

George Washington Cable presided on the final day of the congress. Richard Watson Gilder spoke briefly, and then Cable read a paper, "The Uses and Methods of Fiction," saying that the novel "elevates our conceptions of the heroic and opens our eyes to the presence, actuality, and value of a world of romance." Mary Hartwell Catherwood spoke on "Form and Condensation in the Novel," and was then followed by Garland.

Garland had been omitted from the original program of speakers, but when Thomas Nelson Page and Moses Coit Tyler, who had been scheduled to speak, failed to appear, he substituted at the last minute with a paper entitled "Local Color in Fiction." He announced that "every novelist should draw his inspiration from the soil, should write of nothing but the country he was bred in and the people most familiar to him." Joseph Kirkland was scheduled to speak next, but before he properly began, Mary Catherwood stood up in the audience and began to speak in defense of the romantic heroes who had not received "due reverence" from Garland. Then she turned to the spectators seated around her, "Think of the work that Frenchmen did on this continent two centuries ago! Why should these men be forgotten merely because they are dead? Why should we consider time in the kingdom of art, where there is no past, no present, no future, where it is all one eternal now?"

It was a hot day and the audience was sleepy, but when Mary Catherwood finished, they gave her an excited burst of applause. Cable then reintroduced "what is left of Mr. Hamlin Garland," who rose and began to assail the belief that American literature could "be built up out of romantic tales of medieval France . . . stories of country life will be false if they deal only with June, sunshine, roses and strawberries. . . . We must base our fiction on reality." And he added that he saw something comic in the fact that "the Lords and Ladies of romance appeared to be making a last desperate stand in the home of Milwaukee beer and Chicago port." Alice then stood and announced that she agreed with both Garland and Charles Dudley Warner that art must be realistic, but that art also demanded the idealization of nature.[50] Forty years later, in *Roadside Meetings*, Garland recalled speaking in opposition to " Alice French, whose work I admire. She was essentially on my side, but like many other prosperous town dwellers, was of the opinion that I had over-emphasized the dirt and toil and loneliness of the farmer's life."[51]

Garland had said, "What do you know of the farm realities I describe? You are the daughter of a banker in the country town riding up our lane in a covered buggy. Yet you look across the barbed-wire fence and you see two young men binding grain on a Marsh harvester. 'How picturesque,' you say. 'How poetic!' But I happen to be one of those binding the grain. I have been at it for ten hours. . . . I know western farm life. No one can tell me anything about it. . . . You city folk can't criticize my stories of farm life—I've lived them."

Eugene Field entered the controversy through his newspaper column, "Sharps and Flats," in the Chicago *Record*. He announced that "Mr. Garland's heroes sweat and do not wear socks"; he also called Howells "the Mohammed of the realistic religion," and Mrs. Catherwood, "the queen of Western romanticism." When the controversy faded, he announced that Alice and Garland were reconciled and speculated that they were preparing an Arkansas expedition to hunt down rare local-color material that had never yet been "treated by the pen of novelists."[52]

By then Alice had returned to Davenport to write her series of articles on the fair for *Scribner's*. She completed them in December, 1893, and

[50] *Critic*, XXII (July 22, 1893), 60. See also Donald Pizer, *Hamlin Garland's Early Work and Career* (Berkeley, 1960), pp. 115, 116, 118.

[51] Hamlin Garland, *Roadside Meetings.* (New York, 1930), pp. 252–255.

[52] Pizer, *Hamlin Garland's Early Work and Career*, p. 118.

they appeared as "Sketches of American Types" in 1894. In spite of the optimistic spirit the fair had generated, she found as many reasons to complain of the greed and loutishness of her fellow Americans as she found to congratulate them for their sturdy virtues and their opulently staged accomplishments. She found the number of Americans who were crude, boorish, and unawed by what was elevating a poor omen for America's future.

In July, before she had left Davenport for Chicago, a letter had come from Andrew Carnegie. Upset over labor trouble, he confided paradoxically that while he didn't believe in fighting labor, he would "*shut down* when things become intolerable." [53] Carnegie's distress had started when the Homestead strike had begun at the Carnegie mill the year before and his man Frick had set the hated Pinkertons on the strikers. Peace came only when public opinion shifted to the side of management after Frick was stabbed and shot twice in the neck by a Russian anarchist.

Out of such strife in the early nineties came privation to much of the middle and lower classes and a depression that exceeded even the hard times of 1873. The federal Treasury eventually was unable to meet its outstanding drafts; the Santa Fe, the Union Pacific, the Erie, and the Baltimore and Ohio railroads went bankrupt, and the stuccoed remnants of the buildings of the fair housed only Chicago's derelicts and unemployed. Tramp armies reappeared; one host of vagabonds, led by Jacob Coxey, who rode behind a span of horses valued at forty thousand dollars, marched on Washington to demand relief, a move that was likened to the march of the mob from Paris to Versailles. Editorial writers in English newspapers seriously forecast a revolution in the United States; but fewer than a thousand Coxeyites gathered in the capital at any one time, and Congress paid no attention to them.

For Alice, 1893 was a good year. Two of her books were published, her short stories and essays appeared in half a dozen different magazines, and she reviewed thirty-six books, although she received only $1.50 a book and did it merely as a service to publishers and her fellow authors. According to her accounts in her notebooks, her writing earned $2,210 in 1893, but that sum hardly matched the income she received from investments in her brothers' manufacturing companies plus the usual returns on her savings bank stock—at 12 per cent.

[53] Andrew Carnegie to Alice French, July 9, 1893, Newberry Library.

IX. Loitering in Comfort

By the end of 1893, the depression had closed five hundred banks; almost one-fifth of the nation's labor force was unemployed, and the Pullman strike had begun.

George Mortimer Pullman, when faced with decreasing orders for his railroad cars, had first cut his labor force and then reduced wages—about one-fourth—although, as economists pointed out, he could have maintained both and still have earned a profit. On May 11, after Pullman fired members of the workers' grievance committee who had sought an audience with him, three thousand employees went out on strike. Mark Hanna called him a "damned idiot" for not being willing to "arbitrate, arbitrate, and arbitrate," but Pullman announced, "workers have nothing to do with the amount of wages they shall receive; that is solely the business of the company." [1]

In 1894 the strike reached Davenport, and the Frenches' manufacturing works were closed. When that happened, Alice decided to go to Chicago with her youngest brother to study the strike at close range. Robert French, just out of Harvard, was working as a laborer on a twelve-hour shift in the Bettendorf Steel Mills near Davenport. Alice rose before dawn each morning to have breakfast with him and discuss labor problems before he left for work. She wanted to see him well trained for his future role in life; and she believed their breakfast discussions would become more meaningful if both went to Pullman, the workers' village just south of Chicago, where they could see clearly the effect of large-scale labor agitation. At the end of July they arrived in Pullman at the Florence Hotel, which George Pullman had named for his daughter, and which, through his dispensation, was the only place in the village where liquor was sold. From the hotel Alice and Robert went out daily, walking the streets, talking to strikers, and attending rallies, parades, and union meetings, Alice trying to

[1] Ida Tarbell, *The Nationalizing of Business 1878–1898* (New York, 1944), 235.

give what she called "hypodermics of common sense" to the strikers. She once angered a crowd by asking unsympathetic questions, whereupon "a rabble of sullen men" made a "moblike atmosphere for a few minutes," but she was undismayed: "I know the poor things well enough not to mind, and it ended by the boys running off with some candy and one of the men asking me into his house—an honest good fellow." [2]

She also talked with officers of the Pullman Company and assembled a file of newspaper articles on the strike. On July 7, 1894, the Washington *Post* pictured Chicago as the scene of wild lawlessness where anarchists and socialists were preparing to blow up the Federal Building to get at the money in the Treasury vaults, but three days later the New York *World* reported, "Of mob rule and riot . . . there has been none." Mob rule or not, Alice wrote Horace Scudder (who had returned to her list of friends), no strike in history was ever more devoid of "real moral bottom." [3] She felt the commonality had managed to disgrace itself once again: "The unions are steadily degrading labor, not capital. . . . This socialist business is like a beautiful fruit, rotten at the core." [4]

Alice returned from Pullman still unable or unwilling to distinguish between the labor movement and social revolution. Her opinions appeared in the *Forum* two months later in an essay, "The Contented Masses," which announced that in spite of all signs to the contrary, a general uprising by the "canaille" was impossible; the people outside the large cities, the "contented masses" would not revolt. She cited Iowa as a center of contentment since its total population of two million contained only four hundred thousand persons who were born out of the country. Furthermore, Iowa's foreign-born were from "Germany, Sweden and Great Britain rather than the mongrel races of Southern Europe." Her conclusions were common in the nineties, and her faith in the virtues of native-born Americans was shared by good and gentle people everywhere, among them the Brahminical Thomas Bailey Aldrich, who had been troubled enough to compose a rhymed warning about "unguarded gates" and the foul immigrants who were coming through them.

[2] Rebecca Sewell, "Alice French: The Octave Thanet of Literature" (Master's thesis, Southern Methodist University, 1934), p. 55.

[3] Alice French to Horace Scudder, July 18, 1894, Newberry Library.

[4] Mary J. Reid, "Octave Thanet at Home," *Midland Monthly*, III (January 1895), 36.

The problems brought by mass immigration were compounded by technical progress, continuing political corruption, and wild financial expansion. In the first half of the 1890's, the number of millionaires in the United States rose above four thousand, even while the value of the dollar steadily appreciated, having risen 300 per cent from 1865 to 1895. Such events affected literature. In the 1890's, more novels were published that dealt with economic issues than had appeared in any preceding decade in history.[5] Realism was flourishing and naturalism was clearly on its way, in spite of the fact that the world that received *Maggie: A Girl of the Streets* and was preparing for *McTeague* and *Sister Carrie* was simultaneously enjoying an upsurge in genteel novels and the melodramatic romanticism of Graustarkian tales.

The popular interest in economic novels and Alice's experiences at Pullman gave her the idea for a novel in which she could trace the economic education of a young man like her brother, a novel in which she could weave her interests in sociology and labor and her solutions for America's dilemmas. But while she didn't know it then, the novel was ten years away. Other things transpired in the summer of 1894. Her essays on "American Types" at the Columbian Exposition were appearing in *Scribner's* and were so successful that Edward Burlingame, the editor, sent her a special letter of congratulation.[6] Shortly afterward Margaret E. Sangster, editor of *Harper's Bazar*, requested a short story of four thousand words but offered only $150 for it, far less than Alice was accustomed to receiving.[7] Henry Mills Alden, editor of *Harper's Magazine*, had written her in January, 1893, offering six cents a word for stories under seven thousand words—almost double the *Bazar's* offer. For stories of more than seven thousand words, Alden would pay only five cents a word—the shorter the story the better, to allow more space for illustrations.[8]

McClure's was another matter. Founded only a year before with less than eight thousand dollars in capital, the magazine was losing money, surviving only with loans from A. Conan Doyle and A. A. Pope, the bicycle maker. The magazine had published three of Alice's short stories, and by November, 1894, its circulation was up to sixty-five thousand; yet the same month, S. S. McClure's partner, John Sanborn

[5] More than 170 between 1890 and 1899. (Walter Fuller Taylor, *The Economic Novel in America* [Chapel Hill, 1942], p. 58.)

[6] Edward Burlingame to Alice French, April 11, 1894, Newberry Library.

[7] Margaret Sangster to Alice French, July 20, 1894, Newberry Library.

[8] Henry Mills Alden to Alice French, January 31, 1893, Newberry Library.

Phillips, wrote Alice asking if future story payments could be made by installments until the magazine became more profitable.[9] McClure had the habit of paying writers ten or twenty dollars down and using the remainder of what he owed them as working capital. Sarah Orne Jewett insisted on her regular price and immediate payment, but most writers were willing to wait; Alice was. In 1894, *We All*, the novelette, had sold only 2,250 copies, but D. Appleton and Company bought the copyright for three hundred dollars,[10] raising her income from writing in 1894 to three thousand dollars—seven hundred dollars more than the year before.

Alice spent much of her money on Clover Bend. Shortly after she listed her 1894 income in her ledger, she and Jane Crawford made their annual trip to Arkansas. As usual, the women had to hire plantation hands to polish the furniture, wash the linen, and drive the pigs from the yard. Alice began to lay in supplies of food—mushrooms, rabbits, wide-mouthed bass, and the home-grown vegetables of Clover Bend. Stores of candy were brought in from St. Louis, and even greater delicacies were ordered from S. S. Pierce's in Boston—caviar, special tea, preserves, boned chicken, and canned squab. To insure proper treatment of such elegant eatables, Alice brought her personal maid, Johanna, and as many of the other servants from Davenport as would come for three or four months in the swampland of Arkansas.

A large staff was needed to care for guests, for the two women were prodigal with invitations to their families and friends and to Alice's literary acquaintances. In 1894, Marie Therese Blanc, the French literary critic who had translated *The Hoosier Schoolmaster*, was touring the United States collecting material for a series of articles on American writers for the *Revue des Deux Mondes* of Paris. Her tour had taken her to New Orleans to visit another Abbot Academy girl, Kate Douglas Wiggin, the author of *Rebecca of Sunnybrook Farm*; and there Alice had written to Mme Blanc, inviting her to visit Clover Bend on her way north from New Orleans. Alice offered to meet her on the steamboat landing at Memphis: "You will recognize me. I shall wear a green cloth gown and shall hold a rose in my hand."[11]

[9] John Sanborn Phillips to Alice French, November 16, 1894, Newberry Library.

[10] Ripley Hitchcock to Alice French, November 7, 1894, Newberry Library.

[11] Kate Douglas Wiggin, *Memories of a Southern Woman* (New York, 1932) pp. 199–201, gives the date of Mme Blanc's visit to Clover Bend as 1896. Tucker, in "'Octave Thanet,'" gives it as 1894; and in "Miss French of Clover Bend,"

In mid-February, when the riverboat carrying Mme Blanc arrived in Memphis, Alice was standing on the levee wearing her green dress and holding a rose, yellow for contrast, in her hand. As soon as their greetings were over, Alice oversaw the collection of the Frenchwoman's luggage and completed arrangements for the trip the next day from Memphis to Portia, Arkansas, by train and from there to Clover Bend by hack. Later, in the *Revue des Deux Mondes*, Alice's guest described the house at Clover Bend as properly rustic from the outside, "as befits the environment, but scarcely is the threshold passed before one finds one's self in the midst of all the refinements of comfort and all the aesthetic pursuits which can be found in an English country home." During her visit Mme Blanc met Uncle Nels, the last of the ex-slaves, and visited the school, where she distributed dolls that Alice had made for the occasion and spoke some French to the students. She was fascinated by the plantation children, who worked in the fields when they weren't in school, either studying or stretched out on the benches, "jes' chillin' with malaria." Their mothers, she observed, were "very fat and stood in great need of corsets." [12]

Mme Blanc stayed for two weeks, touring the plantation and discussing writing with Alice, talking of the Empress Eugenie, Daudet, Bourget, Zola, Victor Hugo, Browning, Tennyson, and even Henry James. The Frenchwoman congratulated Alice for her regionalism; and shortly after her guest departed, Alice wrote to Scribner's asking that two copies of *Expiation* be sent to Mme Blanc, for "she is going to introduce me to the French public."

Soon after Mme Blanc left for New England to visit Sarah Orne Jewett, Alice and Jenny returned to Davenport. Three days later the house at Clover Bend burned to the ground. Everything was gone but the silverware. The library corner with its bookcase and picture of the Grand Canal in Venice, the photographic laboratory, Alice's study, all disappeared in flames. Even the household ghosts were destroyed, along with more important spirits—a collection of wines and liquors its owners thought the best between St. Louis and New Orleans and that had taken ten years to collect. Alice lamented that some of it could never be replaced:

Publications of the Arkansas Historical Association, II (1906), 344–351, the date is 1895.
[12] "Dans l'Arkansas," pp. 542–572.

Alice, left, with Mme Blanc, in the carriage

The '49 Port or the '69 Chateau Yquem, or some Steinberger Cabinet I was hoarding (The Johanisberger was not so fine, but it was good enough for most topers), or the 1802 Brandy or some of the Tokay. I had ... some Imperial and some of Ignatz Flandorff's and some of Androssy's.— Well, peace to their gases. I fear they have not left so much as an ash.[13]

But the house could be rebuilt on an even more lavish scale. In 1895, Alice's investments paid high dividends and her writing earned her more than $3,600. Henry Mills Alden had bought a short story, "The Missionary Sheriff," for $620, the most she had ever received for a story, and it was her first to be published in *Harper's Magazine*. Shortly after it was accepted, Harper and Brothers sent a letter asking that she write a series of short stories to be published first in *Harper's Magazine* and then to be issued by the publishing house in a single volume in 1897. Alice agreed and confidently set to work, writing eight stories that appeared in *Harper's* in 1896 and 1897, six of them in the last nine issues of 1896. In April, 1896, when *Harper's* carried "The Missionary Sheriff," another of her stories, "The Son of the Revolution," was published in the same month's issue of the *Atlantic*. If ever before one author had appeared in two such august journals in the same month, it would surely never happen again, at least, Alice thought, not to any teller of tales from the Midlands.

The event marked the decade that saw her rise to the peak of her popularity. From 1896 to 1900, fifty of her short stories appeared in magazines, and five single volumes of her stories were published by Harper and Brothers, Scribner's, Herbert S. Stone, and Way and Williams. Her early work had often been, like the rest of local color, literary expeditions to obscure corners of the country by an observant visitor intent on documenting nature's caprices and mankind's eccentricities. She had never been a master of plot and situation, although she could sometimes create intense melodramatic moments; no local colorist ever managed to create memorable characters like Huckleberry Finn or Captain Ahab. But her greatest failing had been her inability to rise above the lure of American success and to establish a firm and independent vision of her own. There was rebellion apparent in the best literature of the age, rebellion against conformity, or property, or received morality, or against insensitivity. James, Howells, and Cable all made departures from their backgrounds or from the standards of

[13] Tucker, "'Octave Thanet,'" p. 102.

the world that honored them. Alice French did not. Instead, she sought an identity with the age by accepting the commercial principles of decency and justice prevailing in the New England and the Middle West she understood. When the ideas of the world changed, the pleasures that her work could grant diminished. But in the 1890's, Alice's writing brought her fame and money, even the attention of such literary historians as Barrett Wendell and Henry Pancoast, whose *Introduction to American Literature* (1897) ranked her with Eggleston, Kirkland, and Garland as a chronicler of the West.[14]

During the period of her greatest literary success, Alice continued her civic duties and club work. The years following the Civil War had seen the rise of religious and social clubs and fraternal bands that satisfied all needs, from pomp and panoply to self-improvement. Clubs and lodges developed secret rites and ladies' drill teams, bringing ritual and plumage into barren middle western lives in the form of Knights of Pythias, Owls (the Concatenated Order of Hoo-Hoo), Eagles, even American Druids. Others made a collective assault on culture. Alice joined Davenport's literary Tuesday Club, and she and her friends formed the Bric-a-Brac Club. In the midst of a changing social order, it was comforting to turn to commemoration of patriotism and filial piety, all of which renewed interest in family genealogies and the tombstones of New England. Alice joined the Iowa Society of Colonial Dames [15]—it was more exclusive than the DAR, restricting its membership to descendants of those who lived in or served the colonies before 1750.

On May 20, 1896, Andover, celebrated its 250 years of incorporation and invited Alice, as one of its famous daughters, to attend. She was not expected to perform, although she had begun to give dramatic readings of her stories, using them when requests came for her to speak. She gave so many that it was sometimes difficult for her to keep from repeating herself before an audience. Her most splendid success was "The Golden Story Book," in 1896, "A Collection of Tales with Illustrations Told by Octave Thanet," which she gave at the state

[14] But Pancoast's literary history made no mention of Herman Melville or *Moby Dick*.

[15] She also belonged to the Society of Mayflower Descendants, Descendants of Colonial Governors, Sentinels of the Republic, American Red Cross, Society of Midland Authors, the Illinois, Iowa, and Arkansas Press Associations, the Woman's Council for Defense for Iowa, and the Chilton and Mayflower Clubs, as well as other organizations.

university in Iowa City in a ceremony in which she joined with the university band to raise money for the athletic association.

Such demands upon her time meant that most of her writing had to be done at Clover Bend, where she was free of interruptions. By the summer of 1896 the new house at Clover Bend had almost been completed. From there she wrote her girlhood friend Celestine Fejervary, who had returned to live in Hungary, following her father's death. The letter told of Alice's success with the short story "The Missionary Sheriff" ("you will like to know that I made quite a hit in the April Harper's"), and she described life at Clover Bend—her chicken raising: "We have at present 180 to 190 young lives (half of whom will never know a mother's care) in the shell. I presumed our incubator was naturally of a good ... disposition but ... it is about as much care as a teething baby at night." [16] Unfortunately, all but forty-six died in the incubator, and most of the remainder burned when the brooder, which Alice herself had built around an electric light bulb, exploded into flames.

In the nineties, the bicycle became a national rage, especially after low wheels and soft tires appeared. A special drop frame could be provided for ladies who wanted to ride in skirts; and for the most modest gentlewomen, detachable screens for the front of the machine protected ankles from prying eyes. At first, moralists announced that unrestrained bicycle riding by women created such anatomical damage that it threatened to extinguish the race.[17] But by 1897 more than fourteen hundred Iowans had joined the National League of American Wheelmen, and eventually even Frances Willard turned author with *A Wheel Within a Wheel: How I Learned To Ride the Bicycle.* In "Authors on the Wheel," another survey of literary notables, the *Critic* reported the bicycling habits of American writers: George W. Cable, Theodore Roosevelt, and Julian Hawthorne wrote that they used "the wheel." Edward Eggleston, T. B. Aldrich, and Eugene Field did not. Alice answered the questionnaire with simply, "I do not ride a wheel." [18] But the next Easter, 1896, Nathaniel bought his sister a bicycle, and Alice learned to ride, wisely confining her efforts to

[16] Alice French to Celestine Fejervary, March 21, 1896, quoted in Tucker, "'Octave Thanet,'" p. 98.

[17] Nor were fears allayed by a survey of "fallen women" in Boston that reported that "30% had been bicycle riders at one time." (Mott, *History of American Magazines,* IV, 378.)

[18] "Authors on the Wheel," *Critic,* XXVII (O.S.) (October 12, 1895), 228.

Clover Bend. Shortly after beginning, she wrote to Celestine Fejervary in Hungary:

> Strange to say they tell me that I look well on the wheel. Perhaps it is because of the swell bicycle suit. I am black and blue from my ankles to my waist and feel like the naughty boy who had received the reward of naughtiness, for,
>
> > "If I stand or rise or sit,
> > I cannot smile one little bit."
>
> But lame as I am I can do five miles without wincing. We have a track laid out in the pasture, which has almost the advantages of city life since we meet the three horses and the three cows and any number of pigs, at short intervals and can do steering. I still look as sad as a gold-delegate in a Western Democratic convention, but I am in hopes this "bicycle face" will pass.[19]

The allusion to politics was timely. By 1895 it was increasingly apparent that Cleveland could not win nomination for a third term as President. The nation's economy had collapsed, and in the face of demands for social and economic reform, Cleveland had firmly aligned himself with conservative eastern capital. With farmers in the West and South suffering from low prices and crushing debts, he had opposed increased currency circulation; and over the objections of the Governor of Illinois, he had sent federal troops to Chicago to put down the Pullman strike.

Industrial unrest was widespread, but dissatisfaction was most acute among the farmers in the West, where expansion of farmlands and a drought that had begun in the last years of the eighties brought poverty and foreclosures and resulted in the formation of the People's party. Populism attracted farm groups, labor unions, utopianists following Edward Bellamy's philosophy, and tax-reform followers of Henry George. It advocated a graduated income tax, the direct election of senators, initiative and referendum, and the free and unlimited coinage of silver; thus "free silver" became the catchwords of the impoverished, who saw their relief in the coinage of silver dollars and an increased currency supply.

In June, 1896, the Republican Convention met in Chicago, where Mark Hanna directed the nomination of Governor McKinley and the convention voted in a platform opposing the expansion of currency, in effect supporting the gold standard. The July Democratic Convention

[19] Quoted in Tucker, "'Octave Thanet,'" p. 99.

in Chicago then became a refuge for pro-silver Republicans, Populists, and farmers from the West and South united by their debts and their opposition to the gold standard.

The profits of the Frenches' farm machinery plant had fallen sharply when farm prosperity collapsed as corn fell to fifteen cents a bushel and cotton to five cents a pound. Nevertheless, Alice's brother George went to the Democratic Convention to seek out delegates and urge support for the gold standard, for the nation's businessmen saw the doctrine of "free silver" as a greater economic threat than the depression, which was, after all, "only a temporary condition." But conservatives had lost control of their party to Populism and silver Democrats, and the convention adopted "free silver" for its platform and chose for its candidate the

> Prairie avenger, mountain lion,
> Bryan, Bryan, Bryan, Bryan....

With the nomination of Bryan, conservative gold Democrats split away to form the National Democratic party and summoned a convention at Indianapolis on September 2. Alice went to the Indianapolis convention with her brother. She and Bryan had the same birthday but shared little else; and when the gold Democrats' convention had ended, she wrote to Celestine:

> McKinley's dignified and sensible course during the campaign has reconciled a vast multitude of Democrats to his coming on the stage. Meanwhile, we had an almost ideal convention at Indianapolis. The delegates were eminently respectable; North and South fraternized and there was a platform of principles; not a trap for votes. Probably the most patriotic, the most unselfish convention that has ever met in any political party. They were there simply to save their country first; and their party, second. And their ticket will insure the defeat of Bryan.[20]

The convention was united because the delegates had a common purpose in opposing Bryan and Populism. Few gold Democrats had illusions about winning the election on their own, although the new party shrewdly courted votes with its choice of candidates—Generals Palmer from the North and Buckner (for Vice-President) from the South.

The election of 1896 was one of the most bitter in American history. Bryan's campaign was weakened by the splinter Democratic party and

[20] *Ibid.*, p. 101.

by an inadequate campaign fund, reportedly less than a tenth of that collected by the Republicans. And Bryan suffered mightily from attacks by opponents like Theodore Roosevelt, who compared him to Altgeld, Debs, and Robespierre. Bryan's defeat stemmed from eastern fears of anarchy and from his own inadequacies. With the Republican victory, western radicalism, Populism, farmer protest movements were all put down. The country had voted for big business, the gold standard, high protection, prosperity, and equilibrium. And the upper classes once more could reassure themselves that the inscrutable yet sanctified machinery of capitalism had triumphed, that for the second time in only thirty years a great nation had been led out of a wilderness of anarchy and sectionalism; Republicanism had saved the country from disunion again.

During the campaign Alice prepared *The Missionary Sheriff* for publication in 1897. Her seventh book, it contained the six stories that had appeared in *Harper's* the preceding year. Alice had tried to show a western character's life and attitudes, and into her hero, Sheriff Amos Wickliff, she put all the masculine virtues she could muster for a rough man. It was an age when eloquent and ardent lovers were either foreigners or untrustworthy, a stereotype that has lingered in western adventure stories. Alice gave her hero a homely and manly inability to convey his emotions; he longed only to kiss the hem of his true love's skirt.

The stories mixed blunt realism with snug romanticism in displays of asexual love and details that were meant to be pleasing and to convey the gentle goodness of Sheriff Wickliff: his jail had chintz on the prison cots and bowls of nosegays on the cell tables. But the stories were well received and their incongruous and unlikely details were ignored by the reviews, among them the *Nation's*, which praised *The Missionary Sheriff* in the same issue that expressed complaints about the quality of Henry James's *The Spoils of Poynton.*[21]

After *The Missionary Sheriff* appeared, the Chicago publishers Way and Williams asked to publish a collection of Alice's stories, and she began work on her eighth book—her fifth volume of short stories. But in October, 1897, before the job was completed, news came that her youngest brother, Robert, was ill.

To learn more of the steel business, Robert had gone to the Carnegie mill at Homestead and from there to Sharon, Pennsylvania. In the fall

[21] *Nation*, LXV, No. 1670 (July 1, 1897), 17–18.

of 1897, with his training completed, he was returning home through
Canada when he came down with typhoid. When Alice heard of his
illness, she put aside her writing and left for Toronto immediately.
When she arrived, Robert had improved, and on November 2, 1897,
she wrote to the poet Julia Caroline Ripley Dorr: "I am here with my
brother who is dangerously ill with typhoid fever, and I am hardly an
hour away from him. We think he has turned the corner, however." [22]
But she was wrong, and Robert died four days later. The loss was even
more painful to Alice than the death of her father had been, and she
tried to convey her despair to her diary:

> The hardest thing to understand is why our purest, most true, deepest and
> longest love is punished, in the desolation of loss of the loved one, most
> cruelly. . . . A real love of the soul is never consoled when thus wounded.
> Such wounds are not only wounds; they are mutilations.

On the black-bordered stationery that she now began to use she wrote
to Celestine Fejervary in Hungary:

> Sunshine is not sunshine since he died. Perhaps I know, better than anyone
> else, what everyone has lost. George and Nat had discovered his extra-
> ordinary business insight; the men who worked with him [had] an un-
> bounded admiration for him as well as love; and we, his own people,
> knew his lovely nature; but he let me see his whole heart, and perhaps even
> better than his mother, I saw all sides of him—and I know that next to
> her, he loved me the best. Never anywhere did I know a man with a more
> sensitive nature or stainless honor. He never told a lie or broke a promise in
> his life. [23]

Colonel Robert Ingersoll, her father's old friend, wrote to his former
law clerk, Alice's brother Nathaniel:

> To die when you are old and gray and decrepit, when the day of usefulness
> is gone, when the eyes are dim and the senses dull and the heart slow, is
> bad enough. But to die in life's morning, when you are young, full of hope
> and joy, surrounded by the ones you love, is tragical beyond words. [24]

Alice found some solace in reading William Ernest Henley's "Invictus."
Later, she copied the poem in one of her notebooks, adding the

[22] Alice French to Julia Ripley Dorr, November 2, 1897, Julia Caroline
Ripley Dorr Collection, Abernethy Library of American Literature, Middlebury
College.

[23] Quoted in Tucker, "'Octave Thanet,'" p. 103.

[24] Colonel Robert Ingersoll to Alice French, quoted in Tucker, "'Octave
Thanet,'" p. 105.

comment, "I read this first in a Toronto Hospital." After returning to Clover Bend, she wrote to Henley in England, thanking him for his poem:

> DEAR MR. HENLEY:–
>
> I have always felt the power and the charm of your poetry, but your lines
>
> > Out of the night that covers me.
>
> had the fortune to be my greatest help in a cruel sorrow.
>
> On my unconscious way to it I read them in the November McClure's; and (little dreaming of their office) I learned them by heart. They came to me and steadied me through all the hideous days and weeks that have followed. I clung to them as a drowning man to a raft. Thanks to them more than any outside help I was able to be calm so long as my composure was needed.
>
> I thought you might like to know what you had done for one human soul.
>
> At first I did not intend to sign my name; but I never have written an anonymous letter and it is too late to begin; besides I hope if you ever are lured to America to be able to tempt you to see a Western town or an Arkansas plantation.
>
> > > Very sincerely and
> > > gratefully yours,
> > > > ALICE FRENCH
> > > > (*Octave Thanet*)
>
> CLOVER BEND, ARKANSAS
> February the twentieth, 1898 [25]

Henley replied, thanking Alice for her letter and complimenting her *Otto the Knight*.[26]

Shortly after Robert's death, the short stories Alice had been assembling for Way and Williams appeared as *A Book of True Lovers*. The stories were meant to show that "nothing is sweeter than love," and a preface, in counterfeit seventeenth-century English, announced that her subject was love, love proven in the "ireful acid" of marriage. The first of the stories, "The Strike at Glasscock's," was based on an incident described by Colonel Tucker of Clover Bend and was a parable for labor, showing the plight of a rural Arkansas mill owner

[25] Alice French to William Ernest Henley, February 20, 1898, Pierpont Morgan Library.

[26] William Ernest Henley to Alice French, quoted in Tucker, "'Octave Thanet,'" p. 104.

whose wife had gone on strike "just like the people in the city."
Another story, "Sir Guy the Neuter," set in Queen Mary's England,
drew a letter from Andrew Lang correcting Alice for her use of the
eighteenth-century word "buccaneer" in a story of the sixteenth
century. Lang also thanked Alice because she had quoted some of his
poetry in "The Captured Dream" and had thus "immortalized" his
"superannuated verses." [27]

A Book of True Lovers came out at a time when editors were pleased
to take anything she wrote. Her income from writing had increased
almost $2,000 over two years before. The sales she listed in her
ledger at the end of 1897 totaled $5,390 for the year. Much of the
money went toward the restoration of the house in Arkansas, which was
finally being completed during the summer of 1897. Alice and Jenny
named their new home "Thanford" for Thanet and Crawford.
Running water was piped to both floors, a washing machine was
installed in the laundry room, and an upper gallery around the house
was completely screened against the mosquitoes. Adjacent to Thanford,
an icehouse and shops for carpentry and plumbing were built—"everything needed on a plantation where labor unions cease from traveling"
—there was even a stable with quarters for a coachman. A kitchen
garden was planted behind the house, while the front and side yards
were covered with flower gardens and lawn, and all was surrounded by
a dense privet hedge. Inside the house Alice had her own study
furnished with a roll-top desk and a typewriter on a stand. The room
had a brick fireplace and a bookcase that Alice filled with autographed
gift books. Across the hall from the study was the living room, its
walls covered with brown Chinese grass paper. There the two women
and their guests assembled each day for muffins and special Russian
tea and sat in furniture, much of which was like Alice's short stories,
good respectable stuff fashioned out of the local materials. Alice had
made some of it, for when she wasn't writing or visiting around the
plantation, she was carpentering in the shop, making bookends and
towel racks, even tables and chairs.

Alice oversaw construction of the drainage system, while Jane
Crawford laid out a formal garden with beds of tulips, roses, and white
lilacs that brought bees and humming birds and large colorful butter-
flies swarming around the house. And the two women continued to

[27] Andrew Lang to Alice French, May 17, 1897, quoted in Tucker, "'Octave
Thanet,'" p. 88.

raise chickens for their own table and to grow strawberries, dewberries, and raspberries for the elegant meals they served their guests.

Caring for it all were eight, sometimes as many as ten, black or white servants, including a coachman, gardeners, a groom, and even a butler. One visitor reported that petals from the roses covering the house sometimes blew onto the floor of the porch, and after each "zephyr showered the floor," Alice, who was termed "New England tidy," [28] would instantly call the maid to sweep up.

In February, 1898, William Allen White and his new bride, Sally, came from Emporia to visit Clover Bend. He later described Alice and the splendor of the plantation in his autobiography:

> [She] was one of the best short story writers of the nineties [and] lived in the winter on this Southern plantation. There survived the civilization of the old South. The freed men were only nominally free. They lived with the land and on it, virtually serfs, and because she was passing rich, Octave Thanet lived in feudal splendor. There, for the first time, we had high class Southern cooking—turkeys stuffed with chestnuts, and roast pig stuffed with apricots and almonds, quail fried exquisitely, and all manner of gorgeous pastry. Chauncey Williams, who was about to publish one of Octave Thanet's books, also was her guest, and for four days she put on a real gastronomic parade. Miss French, who weighed something over two hundred forty pounds in her six-foot stature, enjoyed stuffing us as much as a taxidermist loves his art.[29]

Sally White concluded that nowhere in America or in Europe had she eaten as she had at Thanford. As a new bride, she was most interested in the planning of meals, noting that each morning, as the first duty of her day, Alice spent one full hour consulting with the cook. Special meats were shipped from St. Louis once a week. Ice came from Poplar Bluff by train. There was grandeur even in the waste: imported delicacies spoiled, and the ice always lost half its weight on the way to the plantation—yet ice was necessary at any cost for making ice cream. Sweet butter was another perishable, but Alice held salted butter was fit only for the uncouth and uncivilized.

She designed special dishes in honor of famous people and noteworthy friends—"Tomatoes Marion Harland," "Czarina Soup," and

[28] Margaret Minor to Rebecca Sewell, March 22, 1933, quoted in Sewell, "Alice French," p. 94.

[29] William Allen White, *The Autobiography of William Allen White* (New York, 1946), pp. 311–312.

later "Venison Haunch Roast, Coolidge." For Teddy Roosevelt she devised a "White House Stew" of mushrooms and glazed sweetbreads. One menu listed:

Mock-Terrapin Soup
Roast Young Duckling with Raisin Stuffing
Glazed Onions   Spaghetti au Gratin
Pickles   Guava Jelly   Chutney
Hearts of Lettuce Salad   Cheese Straws
Strawberries with Clotted Cream   Lady Fingers and Macaroons
Coffee   Rhine Wine

But that was only for a conventional luncheon. She created far more elegant meals in the evenings, when all dressed formally and hovering servants attended the guests, offering them silver engraved with the name "Thanford" and linen with "Thanford" woven in it. After dinner the company was always led into the living room, where a log fire was built to keep out the chill of an Arkansas winter night, and conversation was dominated by the hostess.

While Chauncey Williams and the William Allen Whites were at Clover Bend, news came that the *Maine* had exploded in Havana Harbor. White knew the incident would jar something loose in America. "Manifest destiny" was in the air, fostered by special interests and bellicose patriots like Alice, who was sure the sinking of the *Maine* meant war: "With the Maine blown up, there'll be no stopping us. . . . We have a fine navy and a bang-up army. But I hate to be fighting an undersized nation like Spain. . . . The nation all America is ready and eager to grapple with is Germany, and if we do fight Germany, we will lick her well." [30] White disagreed with most of Alice's political pronouncements, but when he and Sally left Thanford, he wrote in the guest book:

THOUGHTS

(Written while contemplating the unpleasant
prospect of leaving Clover Bend.)

Down at modest Clover Bend
Loitering with comfort here,
Gentle hearts and honest cheer,
Lofty thoughts and soothing beer
meet and greet the stranger—friend,

[30] Tucker, "'Octave Thanet,'" p. 112.

Down at Thanford, Clover Bend,
Kind hearts, Kind thoughts and good wines blend,
And wisdom flirts with comfort here.[31]

With her guests gone, Alice turned to writing once again. In the late nineties, most of her work appeared in *Scribner's*, *McClure's*, and the *National Magazine*, though in January, 1898, *Harper's* published "The Blazing Hen-Coop," recounting the disaster of the burning of the hen house Alice had built. While Clover Bend was the place of her writing, it was now less often the subject and setting. Local-color regionalism was dying out with the change in popular taste away from sentiment and dialect and with the passing of the nation's buoyant sectionalism that had fostered literary descriptions of regional peculiarities.

The rage for dialect had come with America's interest in itself, and writers had flocked to present the speech of Negroes, the Irish, southerners, Yankees, and French Canadians—all better heard than reproduced in stunted words and at confusing length. Objections to dialect had begun to appear in the seventies; the *Atlantic* denounced the corruption of the language by fiction's disobedience to grammar, and by the 1880's, the *Nation* had begun complaining of the "corrupt English" of contemporary fiction. In 1898 even Joel Chandler Harris was apologizing to *Scribner's Magazine* for submitting dialect stories, "That sort of stuff has seemed to be under the ban."[32]

By the 1890's, more local colorists were turning to writing stories of modern realism or historical romance. Alice was contemplating writing another novel. Scribner's had reprinted *Expiation* in 1896 (it had appeared in French in 1894 with its dialect left untranslated), and she was confident she could do as well again, although this time on a more immediate topic—the workingman. She had been writing short stories of northern laborers for *Scribner's*:

DEAR MR. BURLINGAME:
There! Here you have 5 weeks solid work, a whole library of Socialist literature read—just to give a good swing to my hand . . . then two solid weeks of writing and one of boiling the wretched mass down! Don't ask me to write any more such sketches; I can't afford it!

[31] *Ibid.*, p. 116.
[32] F. L. Pattee, *The Development of the American Short Story* (New York, 1923), p. 286.

Do you think $300 is a nice, modest sum for the job? Because I do. I assure you I am just 'worn to a frazzle' by it as we say in the South.[33]

There had been some discussion of Scribner's publishing the stories as a book, but action on it had been slow. She wrote:

GENTLEMEN:

I don't know whether you are thinking of publishing Stories of Labor in book form; but as I have had three inquires about the right to publish them, I want to be able to speak definitely.

Of course I should prefer to have you publish them; and I should not want to deal with anyone else; but I don't like to say "The Scribners have arranged about that" when perhaps "The Scribners don't want the stories."

I think, however, I should like to sell the thing this time outright; and I would sell it and the other books you have ... for 1500$ English and American rights.

If my last book goes on selling the way it is now and the English interest grows, it will be a bad bargain for me, but I have just finished building a house; and I want to have it furnished and everything paid for; and so I prefer the bird in the hand to 2 in the bush.

You may not care to consider the proposition at all, in which case I shall consider it a sign that I *may* make more money in the end the other way; and no harm done. ... In any event I shall feel that our pleasant relations are not in the least disturbed.

Very sincerely yours
ALICE FRENCH[34]

Scribner's published the stories as *The Heart of Toil* in 1898, in a volume with a buff binding and a design of hammers and tongs on the cover. It contained six tales of labor and management, all previously printed in *Scribner's* in 1897 and 1898.

The *American Monthly Review of Reviews* congratulated Alice. She

made the laboring man, the toiler in the mills, of the Middle West peculiarly her property, and it would be hard to pick out any other writer, man or woman, who writes at once so interestingly and with such entire understanding of both capitalist and laborer.[35]

[33] Alice French to E. L. Burlingame, March 14, 1897, Newberry Library.
[34] Alice French to Charles Scribner's Sons, February 24, 1898, Newberry Library.
[35] *American Monthly Review of Reviews*, XVIII (December 1898), 734.

The stories reflected once again the attitudes of "respectable" America in the 1890's. Strikes were shown to be wasteful, futile, and foolish. As the reviewer in the *Nation* pointed out, the book restated her thesis: "That if the mass of day-laborers in America were all or half of American birth and breeding, strikes would have been abandoned by the strikers as a hopeless method of getting what they want." [36]

Another volume, *A Slave to Duty and Other Women*, her ninth book in eight years, also appeared in 1898, a reprinting of stories gathered from a wide variety of magazines and published by Herbert S. Stone in Chicago. For the first time, critical response to her work was almost wholly uncomplimentary, the reviewers announcing that the stories were trivial and unimportant.

In the summer of 1899, Alice's mother died. Shortly after the funeral Alice left Davenport for an extended trip to New England, where she visited Sarah Jewett and her companion, Annie Fields, whose husband, James T. Fields, had been the second editor of the *Atlantic*. Such maidenly visiting was a custom in New England, particularly among literary ladies; and while she was in New England, Alice also called on Mary Wilkins. Miss Wilkins and Alice had much in common beyond their spinsterhood. Alice received a proposal of marriage by mail from one of her readers, and later, when she had returned to Davenport, Mary Wilkins wrote her to recommend a graphologist in Baltimore who would analyze a sample of hand-writing for a dollar and report on the character and health of anyone, even potential husbands. The letter had some ironic implications for Mary Wilkins' own unhappy marriage in 1902, but she didn't realize it at the time: "When you have another offer from a stranger, just send it to Mr. Keene, and you can find out all about him, even his state of health and whether he would be likely to throw chairs at you. There need be no uncertainty in matrimonial matters with the aid of Mr. Keene." [37]

By the end of the century Alice had achieved distinction, if not marriage. The last decade had been the most productive of her life. Ten of her seventeen volumes had appeared between 1890 and 1899, the tenth published in 1899, when Alice became one of Harper and Brothers' "famous authors," an honor conveyed upon her when three of her short stories were published as one of Harper's "Little Books by Famous Authors." The *Overland Monthly* described her and Charles

[36] *Nation*, LXVII, No. 1745 (December 8, 1898), 432–433.
[37] Mary E. Wilkins to Alice French, Newberry Library.

Egbert Craddock as occupying "the same position in American fiction as did Aeschylus and Sophocles in the Greek Drama." [38] In 1900 she was made the subject of an article in Appleton's *Cyclopaedia of American Biography*. Being cited in a reference work meant that she was now a permanent figure in American literature, even though the entry had a bibliography of her works that began with a misspelling—"*Knittles in the Sun*" and presented incorrect publication dates for three of the eight works cited.

At the university in Iowa City, an Octave Thanet Society was formed in 1899 (it lasted until 1933). The aim of the society was "to uplift its members along all lines, especially those of a literary nature"; and to insure its purpose, fines were levied against inattentive members: charges ranged from one dollar for failure to appear on a weekly program to ten cents for failure to march in a parade. For its motto the society selected "The beautiful is the glory of the true," the Platonic phrase Alice had quoted to Howells twelve years before when complaining of his review of *Knitters in the Sun*. The society's colors were white and pink, and it had a cheer:

> Kinne inne wah, kinne inne wah!
> Whoop-a-la, whoop-a-la, whoop-a-la.
> Good to be, hard to beat, Octave Thanet.

When *Little Pilgrimages Among the Women Who Have Written Famous Books* was published in 1902, its authors announced that the scene in *Expiation* in which the villain was killed in the swamp was "one of the most terribly dramatic in American fiction.... For grimness combined with brevity it is unsurpassably impressive." And they quoted the famous poet and editor Richard Henry Stoddard as saying that Octave Thanet was the best writer of short stories in America.[39]

Alice's fame had meaning for Davenport, too. Andrew Carnegie, thirty-two years after promising himself to cast business aside, the amassing of wealth being "one of the worst species of idolatry," had turned to philanthropy and the building of libraries in profusion— three thousand buildings with three thousand "Carnegies" carved on façades that glorified what Finley Peter Dunne called "archytechoor,

[38] Mary J. Reid, "Four Women Writers of the West," *Overland*, XXIV (August 1894), 138–144.

[39] E. F. Harkins and C. H. L. Johnston, *Little Pilgrimages Among the Women Who Have Written Famous Books* (Boston, 1902), pp. 157, 168.

not lithrachoor." In January, 1900, largely through Alice's efforts, Carnegie offered $50,000 to found a free library in Davenport if the city would furnish the site and provide $4,000 in annual support. When the city agreed, Carnegie raised his donation to $75,000.

In 1900, Alice became historian for the Society of Colonial Dames; she was already state president of the Iowa Society. Now she wrote less and less. From 1902 to 1905 she completed only a dozen pieces for magazines; and the June, 1902, statement from Harper's showed a royalty of only $1.87 for fifteen copies of *The Missionary Sheriff*, plus $2.50 for fifty copies of *The Captured Dream*. For the first six months of 1902 her total royalties from Harper's had amounted to little more than $15.00. But her fame had not diminished, and on February 7, 1903, she received a letter from the new President of the United States:

> MY DEAR MRS. FRENCH:
> I doubt whether I have ever seen a story of yours which I have not picked up and read, always with pleasure, and, especially where you deal with labor problems, real profit. But I think that in your last story . . . you have done better missionary work than in almost any other of your stories that I know, save perchance, one or two on acute phases of the labor problem.
> Do you ever come to Washington? Mrs. Roosevelt and I would like so much to see you and have you break bread with us.[40]

Roosevelt believed that statesmen should read poetry and novels, "including short stories under the head of novels,"[41] and he liked for authors to know when he enjoyed their work. His letter began a friendship that was to last until his death sixteen years later, for while Alice thought Roosevelt had some dangerous notions about capitalism, she shared his ideas about action and duty and his thirst for immediate results and his aversion to mollycoddles.

Now was a good time to speak out for capital, and management, and the old durable virtues, and early in 1904 she began to work on the novel based on the Pullman Strike which she had been considering for ten years.

[40] Theodore Roosevelt to Alice French, February 7, 1903, quoted in *The Letters of Theodore Roosevelt*, ed. E. E. Morison (Cambridge, 1951), III, 421–422.
[41] Theodore Roosevelt, *Autobiography*, ed. Wayne Andrews (New York, 1958), p. 175.

Alice French, at the height of her career

Before the turn of the century, novels of social comment were the work of middle-class writers such as Elizabeth Stuart Phelps, who wrote *The Silent Partner* (1871) about New England mill hands, and John Hay, who attacked unionism in *The Breadwinners* (1884).[42] Mary Hallock Foote's antilabor novels *John Bodewin's Testimony* and *Coeur d'Alene* appeared in 1886 and 1894 and, like their predecessors, expressed the views of a society satisfied with the values of the age and frightened by forces that would change them. True proletarian fiction was yet to be written. Existing novels of social purpose usually glorified the creators of wealth and suggested that the entrepreneur was the New World's Aeneas, an industrial Natty Bumppo whose fearless exploits had moved from the virgin forests to the exciting world of commerce and whose enemies were no longer savages but foreign ideologues and union organizers. Thomas Bailey Aldrich's *The Stillwater Tragedy* (1880) called the union organizer "a ghoul that lives upon subscriptions and sucks the senses out of human beings."

But by the turn of the century, even though the depression had ended and America had become the richest nation on earth, there were increasing suggestions that society was ruthless, disorderly, and unjust. Attacks had come in sociological studies like *Wealth Against Commonwealth* (1894), and later in such novels as Frank Norris' *The Octopus* (1901) and *The Pit* (1903) and in Upton Sinclair's *The Jungle* (1906). Protests appeared even in poetry with Edwin Markham's "The Man with the Hoe." Markham had seen Jean François Millet's famous painting "The Man with the Hoe" in 1886 in *Scribner's Magazine* and later he saw it again, as Alice had, at the Columbian Exposition in Chicago. His poem, which appeared in the San Francisco *Examiner* early in 1899, described the common laborer as oppressed and degraded, "stolid and stunned, a brother to the ox." Markham's poem became a text for preachers and orators. Magazine articles that quoted it and journals that reprinted it implied that men were downtrodden even while rich men congratulated each other that it was a democratic age. Ambrose Bierce said the poem was socialistic, and the railroad millionaire Collis P. Huntington offered a seven-hundred-dollar prize for the finest versified rebuttal; but William James said it was "impressive in the highest degree." Literature seemed to speak out increasingly against the basic proprietary rights of ownership, not merely against the folly

[42] By 1905, Hay's novel was thought to be so pertinent again that the New York *Times* announced it would reprint the work as a serial in its Sunday issues.

of individuals such as railroad president George F. Baer, who made the memorable pronouncement that "the rights and interests of the laboring man will be protected and cared for, not by the labor agitators, but by the Christian men to whom God in His infinite wisdom has given the control of the property interests of the country."

Alice had a practiced eye for what she held to be social humbug; and when she began work on her long-delayed novel of the Pullman strike, she set out to expose the fools and lash the knaves who suggested that the resolution of social problems lay in collective action. If the time was out of joint, she would try to put it right by demonstrating her theories of finance and capital, racism, individual responsibility, and society. Her capitalists would be shrewd, competent, honest, and sternly kind; the villains would be union organizers and immigrants.

In the spring of 1904 she outlined the first chapters in Faribault, Minnesota, where she was visiting her nephew Harry; the novel itself was written at Clover Bend and in Davenport, in the study that she had recently redecorated. She sent a complete outline of the novel to Bobbs-Merrill in Indianapolis, who offered her a contract for a book of 80,000 to 120,000 words, first to appear serially in the Bobbs-Merrill magazine the *Reader*, and then to be published at $1.50 a copy. Payment was to be a royalty of 10 per cent and ten free copies when the book was published.[43]

Alice completed the manuscript late in 1904. As soon as he read it, her editor at Bobbs-Merrill, Hewitt H. Howland, prophesied sales of 38,000 to 40,000 copies in two editions.[44] That was good news, for in January, 1905, eight months before the novel was to be published in book form, Alice's brother Nathaniel reported that signs of a forthcoming business slump meant her Republic Iron and Steel stock would probably pay no dividends until July—if then. Hearing that, she wrote in her diary, "It's me to the typewriter and work *hard* as a Dog for a year, I reckon." Five days later she began a short story, "on Business Secret which shall be called Finding of Nicholas." Ten days later, on January 25, she sent it off, and just in time, for the next day proofs of

[43] The royalty payment was low. She was an established author and had received 15 per cent from Way and Williams, the publishers of *A Book of True Lovers*. In 1900, Hamlin Garland was offered 20 per cent royalties on books to be published by S. S. McClure.

[44] Noted in Alice French's diary, November 19, 1905, Newberry Library. All further references to Alice's diary are to the copy in the Newberry Library.

The Man of the Hour arrived. Finishing them in two weeks, she immediately began another short story, which she completed in ten days. She named it "The Greater Courage" and sent it to the *Cosmopolitan*. It had been a busy month—two short stories, page proofs on a novel, and preparations for the yearly trip to Clover Bend.

In February, Alice and Jenny went to Chicago to see *Ben-Hur*, which Alice judged "really very fine as spectacle." From Chicago they went to Clover Bend, where they found Thanford a mess. The windmill pump had broken; the grounds had been flooded by early spring rains; and mud was everywhere. It took more than a week to get everything back together, two weeks before all was running smoothly. By then it was the middle of March, a glum and rainy time. On March 19, Alice entered in her diary, "My 55th birthday—elderly lady now, drat it!" But she received the good news that her Republic Iron and Steel stock had risen to eighty and one-half; and by April the weather was better, the yard was beginning to bloom, and on April 11 she received a check for two hundred dollars from the *Cosmopolitan* for her short story.

At the end of May, Alice and Jenny returned to Davenport, where they had decided to join their households as they had at Clover Bend. They found a house at 1003 Perry Street and soon began readying it for occupancy. Renting an electric car and a driver, the two women went daily to the new house to supervise a force of seven hired workers to set it in shape. New fence posts were put up and the hitching rail was repaired. A special new bath tub big enough for two ordinary people was installed: the old one was too small for Alice. She made a porch chair and an ironing board for the house, sewed curtains for the conservatory, and built her own typewriter table for the study. At the end of summer all work was done, and the women moved in. By then Alice was suffering from acute indigestion—recurring abdominal pains that she attributed to overwork on the new house, but her symptoms were frighteningly like her father's had been. And she was far overweight. William Allen White had called her a "great marshmallow of a woman";[45] and Hamlin Garland, writing not long after, said, "She is huge of body—huger than ever."[46] She tried diets but failed to keep to them, and her bulk continued to expand. A physical

---

[45] William Allen White, *Autobiography*, p. 289.
[46] Garland, *Companions on the Trail*, p. 460.

examination revealed a hernia. Her blood pressure had always been high; now it was worse, and on August 7 a blood vessel burst in her eye and partially blinded her.

Toward the end of the month she began to feel better and could see well again by September 1, when her novel was published. She sent one of her ten free copies to Theodore Roosevelt with a letter explaining that her hero was her own brother. Eight days later Edith Kermit Roosevelt replied, saying the book showed Alice's brother must have been a good man and once again inviting Alice to call at the White House.[47] The novel had interested the President, who had praised its author, saying she knew as much about factories and the machine business as any man.[48]

Alice had dedicated *The Man of the Hour* to her dead brother, "R. T. F. Workingman and Gentleman," and she had set it in Fairport (Davenport) at the end of the century, "a kindly town, where everyone went to the High School before his lot in life gave him college or work for his daily bread; and old acquaintance was not forgot." Among the most elegant of its houses was the grandiose Georgian mansion of Josiah Winslow, a man who was, like Alice's father, a manufacturer of plows and whose name Alice had taken from Josiah Winslow, fifth governor of the Pilgrim Colony and a "true picture of wisdom, courage and generosity." Josiah's wife, Olga, was a Russian princess. Their son, the novel's hero, was named Johnny-Ivan, a compound resulting from the fact that the servants feared to choose between the father's "John" and the mother's "Ivan." Johnny-Ivan and his mother were sensitive and quick to aid the poor, even the undeserving. The father had sterner qualities, the Puritan virtues, having descended from a long line of Puritans. His great wealth had been acquired like George French's: "In the first part of his life he concerned himself with piling up money. . . . Before the war his success was beginning; even in the sixties he was a rich man; the war made him far richer. His great factories could not turn out plows and sulky-rakes fast enough for the teeming soil's demands."

Josiah's wife, Olga, had more distinguished forebears than her husband, but she was a "member of the new order of thinkers in Russia" and set little value on ancestry or property. On her honeymoon Olga gave away a priceless sable coat to a beggar who was cold.

[47] Edith Kermit Roosevelt to Alice French, October 5, 1905, Newberry Library.
[48] Noted in the Des Moines *Register and Leader*, December 31, 1905.

Winslow, a "practical" man, was shocked, for he knew her generosity would only further corrupt the beggar's self-reliance, his character being attuned to deprivation.

Not long after Josiah Winslow returned to Fairport with his new wife, she gathered around her a group of foreigners and radicals, among them a Russian who lived in the town dump. Soon it was apparent that Olga was a nihilist, something incomprehensible to Josiah: "Your serfs are free, free as our niggers; why do you go plotting and conspiring with disgusting people who don't take baths?" [49]

Josiah went to church; Olga stayed home and smoked cigarettes. Josiah was straightforward and brusk; Olga was baffling, with her oriental mind, her worship of Tolstoy, and her "relentless following of logic to its end, whatever or however terrible such end may be." When it became apparent that Josiah and Olga were completely incompatible, Olga left Fairport for France, abandoning her son to the father. Even so, the mother's influence was strong; and as Johnny-Ivan grew older, he developed a social conscience, turned to radicalism, and worked for the labor movement.

After his father's death, Johnny-Ivan was drawn into the Pullman strike in Chicago, where he changed his name to Ivan to match his foreign ideology and gave his inherited riches to the strikers to support them in their struggles. Eventually the Pullman strike was broken, and only then did Ivan begin to see that his help had done nothing but prolong the suffering of the strikers. Realizing that he had led men to hunger and death, Ivan became morose, but reading Henley's "Invictus" restored his courage and finally he realized that his proper role in life was to rise in the world of commerce and industry, where he could serve as an example of what one individual could achieve. He then went to work in the steel industry and soon became a superintendent in a mill across the river from Fairport. A natural leader of men, he

[49] Alice and her contemporaries favored heroes with fine teeth and washed bodies. Cleanliness—or the lack of it—in popular fiction, like the subsequent white horse for western movie heroes, had become a convention for suggesting character. Genteel reviewers often criticized heroes of realistic novels who did not wash as often as they might; and nineteenth-century political radicals, especially anarchists, were constantly reproached for having bad odors and rumpled clothes, their unwashed state being somehow an argument against their doctrines. Dirty heroes did not become popular until the 1930's, when the validity of literary naturalism had become well established, and being unwashed was a sign of proletarian origin.

was called upon to break a strike developing in what had been his father's plow factory. John (his name had changed with his attitudes) then organized for the battle against the strikers by importing scab labor and housing them in the plant. There all lived together, John arming his men spiritually by reading the Bible and Homer to them and sharing all aspects of their hard life—except for a porcelain bath tub he had installed in his office.

The novel's climax came when an army of strikers marched on the plant. In the battle that followed, just when things looked bad for John and the strike breakers, he rallied them by shouting football cheers for "Har—vard," and the attacking strikers were beaten off with streams of water and gunfire, while a child watching on the sidelines sang:

> Gainst the line of crimson
> They can't prevail!

In the battle John Winslow was wounded, but he had completed the circle from labor leader to rugged capitalist; and when he recovered, he learned not only that he would inherit more of his father's money to replace what he had given away, but that his true love had forgiven his earlier follies and would marry him.

It was the fiscal morality of the *McGuffey Readers*. Wealth followed virtue. Alice's commitment to the defense of property and her predilection for considering organized workingmen a threat to society had led to oversimplified answers and naive conclusions. She reaffirmed her belief that supporting unions was foolish because their purposes could not be accomplished. She implied that while the honesty of most labor leaders was beyond rational belief, the right to contravene ordinary moral rules was one of the perquisites of propertied men.

Sprinkled throughout the novel were provoking aphoristic observations:

> The best government is the one that puts the smart man at the top and makes the fools work their passage.

> I met your social labor leaders and your socialist leaders and every other kind of a leader who scorns a nailbrush. . . . I tell you, you are not going to pull people out of the mire by jumping in and getting mired up beside them; you'd better keep on firm ground and throw them a plank!

> The whole socialistic scheme is abnormal. It would only be possible in the millennium when we are all saints—and then it would be unnecessary.

If you've got a little corn crop, as we had last year, nobody can make it into a big one. All the strongest union could do would be to get a fair share. But the biggest share of a small crop mightn't be as big as a small share of a big crop. So I say this question of bullying folks into giving big wages has got its limits. The size of your share don't cut any figure if you've only got an empty basket to divide! The Unions a good deal like a lawyer. If you've got anything coming to you, he'll see you aint beat out of it. But he didn't make it for you.

Alice had been reared and cultivated in an almost sacerdotal society of the rich and successful, and this was the center of her morality. She saw human freedom and man's temporal salvation as residing in reverent support of industrial enterprise, believing that opposition to the natural order of nineteenth-century capitalism would bring only a hungry old age and an unkempt grave. It was the dominant philosophy of her time. Capitalists and industrialists were thought of as pioneer creators of the nation's achievements and responsible for its expansion.

She had been raised on variations of the "Lowell Myth"—benevolent Massachusetts capital concerned for the welfare of the worker, and she saw the solution to economic problems in terms of her father's experiences and what she had seen in Davenport earlier in the nineteenth century. George French had known his workers by name and had sent each a pair of gloves and a turkey at Christmas, and the men had never struck. Alice did not know that her concept of industrial America had long since ceased to be realistic, that individual entrepreneurs like her father were passing and finance capitalism was bringing amalgamations and cartels, consolidations and mergers that controlled at long distance, great sums and great corporations. The rugged individualist was disappearing in the face of competition from trusts, a competition whose ultimate function was to limit competition. Thus her novel offered problems that no longer existed and solutions that were no longer feasible.

Alice wrote of the rise of unions with the open-mindedness of the lord of the manor reporting a peasant uprising. Her workers were intellectually bamboozled by greedy leaders and spellbinding orators, and the crudest arguments for socialism stunned them into rapturous appreciation of foreign rabble rousers who pronounced v for w and cowered in dark corners. She set up her disputatious workers as caricatures, parts of a controlled laboratory experiment in which variables are suppressed so the lesson will turn out right. She could not see that it was feeble capitalism that would collapse when attacked by the assembly of weak minds and impoverished souls she portrayed as union men.

The incredible spectacle of the strikebreakers rallied by cheers for Harvard was not a complete loss of dramatic sanity as much as it was an indication of what she assumed her readers would appreciate and understand. It was her way of suggesting the alliance between property and the learning which she identified with Andover and "Har—vard," an alliance that defenders of the right assumed to exist. She appealed to her readers' uncritical sentiment in hopes of gratifying their appetite for heroes with intelligence, wit, refinement, and resourcefulness; and in doing so she had written a romantic success story in spite of her intentions.

With all its flaws, the novel was a technical improvement over her earlier attempts at long fiction, and the reviewers gave *The Man of the Hour* far more attention than anything she had previously written. The Boston *Herald* called it "the American novel of the year," and the Washington *Star*, the "book of the year."[50] It was judged superior to Edith Wharton's *House of Mirth*, which was reviewed at the same time and criticized for "revealing the coarse phases of wealth" and "the degeneracy in what is falsely called 'the higher circles.'" Critics who had grown weary of pessimism were heartened by the book's "arrant optimism" and its portrait of the "Anglo-Saxon triumphing over the Slav." Thomas Wentworth Higginson wrote to Alice that the novel was a fine social document that could have been but little stronger:

> Johnny-Ivan is the type which our universities frequently send out and the result of whose actions we see, while our fiction hardly recognizes it. It is, perhaps, for this reason that you gave him a foreign mother. But this seems to me needless for that end, as we can see it quite as often in purely American blood and the mixture rather confuses the earlier part of the book. (Perhaps you had in mind Lowell, as an instance of the result of a mixed parentage, and, if so, not without reason.)[51]

When *The Man of the Hour* was published, Bobbs-Merrill announced that it "more nearly approaches the 'great American novel' than any other book of our day." Their advertisement in *Publisher's Weekly*, September 2, 1905, said:

[50] Boston *Herald* and Washington *Star*, clippings in the Newberry Library.

[51] Thomas Wentworth Higginson to Alice French, November 6, 1905, quoted in Tucker, "'Octave Thanet,'" p. 125.

Foreigners don't realize that there is a class in America with traditions of race, with education and with the inherited power to rule which makes poverty only a temporary eclipse and keeps certain families prominent generation after generation. . . . The author has also pictured a decent labor leader and some of his difficulties.

The novel briefly became a best seller, rising to fourth place nationally in September, just ahead of *The Garden of Allah*. In Birmingham, Alabama, it outsold even Thomas Dixon's *The Clansman*. To celebrate what at last seemed a financial success, Alice decided to take a trip to the East. Republic Iron and Steel stock was still rising, and the family's manufacturing company had grown from the old Eagle Plow Works to become the French and Hecht Manufacturing Company and was paying a 30 per cent dividend for the year.

Before leaving for Massachusetts, Alice went to Chicago for dresses from Marshall Field's and then to Frederick's, the jeweler's, to buy a pearl collar and an opal pin. Then she left to visit her cousins in Andover, where her arrival was usually the occasion for some kind of public demonstration: she commonly was called on to address the student body and faculty at Abbot. Two years before, Miss Means, the principal, had held a reception for Alice at the Academy to which the entire citizenry of Andover was invited.

After a week in Andover, Alice went to Boston, where she met Margaret Deland, who took her driving in a new auto. She briefly visited the Barrett Wendells and Sarah Orne Jewett. Then she went to Cambridge to see her nephew at Harvard, taking him and some of his college friends to dinner and a play. One of the young men was Theodore Roosevelt, Jr., and Alice noted in her diary, "I never saw such a battered boy as young Teddy. But he is a fine manly modest fellow." [52] One of the plays she saw was *You Never Can Tell* which she thought an "amusing but Shawish play. I despise that fellow he is only one huge amalgamated POSE!" The visit to Boston lasted one month; and on December 5 she left for New York, where she saw *The Squaw Man* and visited *Scribner's* and *McClure's* and met Ida Tarbell.

In the middle of December she returned to Davenport and began her Christmas shopping, checking at the bookstores to learn that her novel was selling well. She had injured her foot on the trip from New York,

[52] Teddy Roosevelt, Jr., was playing football for Harvard, for which he suffered at the hands of both newspaper reporters and football opponents.

and it was healing only slowly, making walking difficult. Still, she had some help, either her coachman to take her about, or the hire of a new gasoline automobile and driver. That winter, townspeople reported her scorching about Davenport at ten and twenty miles an hour in a new thirty-horsepower Pope-Toledo.

X. A Trump in Every Way

Marshall Field died in January, 1906. Alice noted this portent in her diary. Time was running fast, and age brought disappointment. Yet, the sales of *The Man of the Hour* had totaled about 37,000 by February, 1906, and that brought her more than $5,000 for the year. From *McClure's* Ida Tarbell sent a request for a short story and proposed that Alice permit her name to be submitted for membership in the National Arts Club. Alice answered: "I shall feel proud to have you propose me. I am thinking up one of your short stories. And I bless heaven I met you!" Alice had previously received a gift copy of Ida Tarbell's first book, a biography of Mme Roland, and she added her thanks and some characteristic observations:

> I should have written before thanking you for the life of Mme. Roland were it not that I have been unable to use my right hand . . . and I didn't want to have my secretary write for me. I now understand what seemed to me the untamed enthusiasm of some of my friends about that Book. It is certainly with out any exception the most illuminating book on the subject I know and I have been an omniverous reader of books about the French revolution ever since I read (with much inward revolt, equally at style and sentiment) Carlyle's French Revolution, twenty years ago. You make plain as no one else I know really does, the *two* revolutions; and the artificial character of the second.
>
> You make equally plain the crime against humanity which was committed, in vanity and noble aspiration, by those amiable and imbecile dreamers, the Girondists. . . . Of course you have noted the dreary resemblance between the French revolution and that bloody and futile drama going on in Russia. Squalid farce and grim tragedy in one, isn't it. And the people between, inert and pussilanimous and bewildered just as they were in France.[1]

[1] Alice French to Ida Tarbell, January 1906, Ida Tarbell Collection, Allegheny College Library, Meadville, Pennsylvania.

The day after the sales report on her novel came from Bobbs-Merrill, Alice left with Jenny for Clover Bend, where the two women spent almost a month getting things operating smoothly. The servants were lazy, the weather was wet and chilly, and the whole place was topsy-turvy. On her fifty-sixth birthday she recorded her dismay in her diary: "Horrid Horrid birthday. ... Consider it on the whole the dreariest birthday in a long and ill spent life!"

In April she left Arkansas to attend the annual convention of Colonial Dames in Washington, D.C., taking with her an invitation to dine with the Roosevelts. On May 4, at eight in the evening, she went to the White House for dinner with President and Mrs. Roosevelt, Senator Lodge, and President Butler of Columbia University. It was a small dinner in a year when Roosevelt, interested in the renowned and the literary, bragged of entertaining Alice, in addition to Jacob Riis, Mark Twain, Henry Adams, Bat Masterson, Saint-Gaudens, Howells, and Buffalo Bill.

Roosevelt's years in the White House were rewarding for well-known authors who wrote wholesomely. The President thought Tolstoy was "filthy and repulsive" because he failed to condemn other human vices as much as he did the wickedness of war, and Roosevelt protested against some of Chaucer's tales "on the score of cleanliness." He thought Henry James "a miserable little snob," [2] but he liked Owen Wister, Kipling, Scott, and Alice French. He wrote to his son Kermit, "There is quite enough sorrow and shame and suffering and baseness in real life, and there is no need for meeting it unnecessarily in fiction." [3]

He liked Alice's work because he felt it gave him an understanding of "how people felt in certain country districts." [4] And he liked her view of the world: in 1906 he wrote to William Allen White of the Emporia *Gazette*:

MY DEAR WHITE:
    You are right about Octave Thanet. To me she has always seemed to preach just the social and economic gospel that we as a people need; and, besides the prime quality of being interesting, her books always seem to me might [*sic*] good tracts for the people. She is a trump in every way.
Always Yours,
THEODORE ROOSEVELT.[5]

[2] Roosevelt, *Autobiography of Theodore Roosevelt*, pp. 84, 98, 99.
[3] *Ibid.*, p. 247.   [4] *Ibid.*, p. 208.
[5] Theodore Roosevelt to William Allen White, July 10, 1906, Davenport Public Museum.

On the evening of the White House dinner, Roosevelt took Alice aside to talk of Arkansas politics and a possible appointment for her friend, Colonel Frank Tucker of Clover Bend, an ardent supporter of the Union and a Republican. Roosevelt yearned to strengthen the Republican party in the South, to make something out of what he saw as a wrangling "set of black and white scalawags"; and to do so he planned to make a series of political appointments based solely on merit, a political illusion that led him to seek Alice's advice.[6]

The day after the White House dinner, Alice left Washington for two weeks of visiting in Boston and Andover before returning to Chicago on the *Twentieth Century*, "drawing room fare, $28." In Davenport once again, she began to play golf, displaying more fervor than skill (136 strokes for nine holes), but she enjoyed the exercise and the socializing; it had become fashionable to spend the afternoon on the new course laid out on Rock Island. There the annual summer golf tournament was held amid an exhibit of middle western pomp:

> The links were full of carriages. We observed the Ransom Cable's magnificent landau motor, the Smith Northern, the Rosenfeld White-Steamer, the Cable brougham, the Nat French's beautiful Victoria, the Lardner T-Cart, one of the smartest traps in the 3 cities, the Skinner golf wagon, the Deere's double phaeton, and George French's and Nutting's park wagons and a multitude of others. In the main, the effect was brilliant, but we were pained to observe a laxity in coachmen's cravats which verges on the barbaric. There is NO option in coachmen's cravats. The man on the box can only wear white pique. And one may mention that legs in plaids and feet in unblacked shoes do not look well with silver buttons and silk hats.[7]

The golfing continued through summer, interspersed with visits and visitors; young Arthur Ficke sometimes called and read his poems,[8]

[6] On November 16, 1908, Roosevelt wrote to Richard Watson Gilder of the *Century*: "I tried to strengthen the organization by appointing the very best Republicans I could find, and also by recognizing certain Gold Democrats like Luke Wright and others. I did the same in Texas and Louisiana, where I found thoroly respectable white Republican parties. I did the same in Arkansas, getting, curiously enough, a recommendation from Octave Thanet (Miss French) as to the Republican leader whom I could thoroly trust." (Roosevelt, *Letters*, VI, 1362.)

[7] "Perry Street Prowler," a family newsletter which Alice distributed to friends and relatives.

[8] Twenty-three-year-old Ficke, who was studying law and teaching English at the university in Iowa City, was preparing his first book of poetry, *From the*

and later in the year Celestine Fejervary returned from Hungary, bringing her niece on a tour of America.

In September, Alice went to Colorado Springs for the Colorado centennial celebration. She was part of a Woman's Day program that included Agnes Repplier, Jane Addams, and the president of the Daughters of the American Revolution. Before an Opera House crowd so large that the city stationed firemen throughout the hall to prevent fire and panic, Alice spoke on "The Wider Life of Women in the Twentieth Century" and boldly attacked the doctrines of the suffragettes.[9]

When the centennial celebration was over, Alice returned to Davenport. The year 1906 was the first since 1883 that her work had failed to appear in print, and she had still not written the short story she had promised to send Ida Tarbell. But by January, 1907, she had begun work on a second novel for Bobbs-Merrill, a mystery story written to capitalize on the vogue of detective fiction that had followed the successes of A. Conan Doyle's Sherlock Holmes stories and Ann Katherine Greene's *The Leavenworth Case.*

Alice named her novel *The Court of Last Resort* and began working on it with characteristic vigor, although she reported in her diary that her progress would be much greater if she actually did have a secretary to help with the task. Progress on the novel was delayed briefly while Alice and Jenny moved into a new and larger house on East Tenth in Davenport. They decorated it together, painting most of the walls a circumspect gray and hanging in the living room a copy of Cezanne's "Boy with the Red Vest," a gift from Celestine Fejervary. In her study Alice hung the original illustrations that the artists A. B. Frost and Lucius Wolcott Hitchcock had done for her stories. Over the mantel she placed the original of the frontispiece of *The Man of the Hour*, Hitchcock's illustration of young John Winslow being embraced by his intended, Peggy Rutherford. Into the kitchen Alice moved her collection of thirty cookbooks and there directed the preparation of meals as

---

Isles (1907). His renown as a versifier was not established for another ten years when, as "Amy Knish," he and Witter Brynner published "Spectra," their successful satire on Imagist poetry.

[9] But in her speech she supported the club movement for women: "We may truly say of Women's Clubs; they have done a vast deal of work for the world—some of it good work. To name a single instance the work that the Federation of Women's Clubs in Iowa is doing to help the blind by giving them towels to hem, is most praiseworthy." (MS in Newberry Library.)

elegant as those at Clover Bend—roast suckling pig stuffed with prunes, pecans, and apricots, or roast mallard or roast guinea hen stuffed with glazed sweetbreads and mushrooms.

One week after settling in the new house, Alice sent the first two chapters of *The Court of Last Resort* to Bobbs-Merrill; and through the spring of 1907 she continued writing at full speed, in spite of social duties, the meetings of the Tuesday Club, and the Thursday afternoons she now reserved for her French tutor. In May she went to Richmond, Virginia, for the yearly meeting of the Colonial Dames and a tour of Jamestown Island and William Byrd's Westover. From Virginia, she made a quick tour of New York and Boston and returned to Davenport promptly at the end of the month. She had promised Bobbs-Merrill that the novel would be completed by the end of June. She had changed the name from *The Court of Last Resort* to *The Lion's Share*. The first chapters were already appearing in Bobbs-Merrill's *Reader* magazine, and as June ended she was "at *Lion's Share* tooth and nail" to meet the deadline, working all day and through the night of June 20 and sending off the final chapter at 9:00 P.M. the evening of June 21, 1907.

Within the week she began revisions of the novel for its publication in book form. Since proofs were not available, she had started by revising sections as they had appeared in the issues of the *Reader*; and within three days she had reworked the first eighteen chapters, staying at it until late at night in an effort to get the job out of the way early so she could prepare for her sister Fanny's wedding on June 29. But on the day of the wedding Alice was still working on revisions and stopped only briefly to attend the ceremony and see that the reception went off properly before she returned to work on the novel. Then Kermit Roosevelt, Fitzhugh Lee, and Phil Sheridan came to Davenport with the Thirteenth Cavalry and Alice was called upon to act as their hostess during their brief visit, for which she collected a fleet of automobiles from townspeople and took her military guests on a tour of Davenport and Moline, then to a special dinner, and finally to a ball at the golf club.

In November the final chapter of *The Lion's Share* appeared in the *Reader*. A few days later the novel was published in a single volume. Alice thought it was a reputable enough piece of work, although she acknowledged it had "little moral and less manner." She had filled the story with intrigue and violence, kidnapers, industrial moguls, inscrutable Chinese, a railroad president, a farsighted woman, and mountainous improbabilities. The *Outlook*'s reviewer announced that the story was "unconvincingly sensational," [10] while the *Arena* had doctrinal reservations: "The Lion's Share glosses over and condones, not so much directly as by implication, acts on the part of our high financiers which should be unsparingly condemned." [11] The *Bookman* compared the novel to a Christmas bargain counter:

> Everything there that man, woman or child could possibly desire, from the San Francisco earthquake . . . down to the details of an exciting hand at bridge. . . . There are plenty of motor cars of course, no modern story is complete without them, and there is much bridge whist. . . .It reads like some electrical toy, the kind you wind up and then let it go to see what happens. . . . Those who expected something better from Octave Thanet will be disappointed. [12]

The reviewer for *Dial* refused to take the book seriously:

> We do not pretend to understand what the story is about, or just how its episodes and characters are related, but we can testify to its possession of an interest which is continuous if not coherent. The author, who can be a real novelist when she tries, would be the last person in the world to expect us to take this preposterous invention seriously. Its purpose is entertainment of the lightest sort and this it gives in full measure. [13]

A more influential objection came from Sarah Orne Jewett. Alice had written her, sending a copy of the novel and asking for comments. The reply was unhesitating and unsettling:

> I have got to tell you the truth. The Lion may have its share! The great eager reading public may insist upon books of moving pictures and all the swiftness and color and sense of unexpectedness that you can put into such writing—but, dear friend, you can do other things—you must promise me to leave this sort of thing to others who can't write any—thing else.
> Your great heart, your clear discernment of character, your knowledge of values, all belong to work that moves more slowly and is more permanent. You can show the causes of things in your country—leave the surface effects to people who see no deeper. . . . I have a sense of your standing in the middle of a country waiting to be written about, and looking both ways. . . . You know both East and West, and what each lacks

[10] *Outlook*, LXXXVII (November 30, 1907), 745.

[11] Amy C. Rich, *Arena*, XXXVIII (December 1907), 691.

[12] Grace Isabel Colbron, "Twenty-One Books of the Month," *Bookman*, XXVI (January 1908), 532.

[13] William Morton Payne, *Dial*, XLIV (January 16, 1908), 44.

and may find in the other. I call this just a play book (you did, your self!) and I shall let you play at anything else but not play at writing.

Look with new eyes at your winter fields, your Arkansas spring, and the figures against the background. I do long for you to write something now in accordance with the great. . . . Dramatic Unities ! ! and win the Lion's share because you are the Lion. (That is what I'm going to keep and remember about the play book.)

Yours affectionately,

SARAH ORNE JEWETT [14]

But Woodrow Wilson liked it. A month after *The Lion's Share* appeared, Alice was asked to address the Contemporary Club of Indianapolis. For her topic, she suggested an exposé of socialism (she also had one available on syndicalism), but the chairman of the speakers' committee urged her instead to describe her career as a writer, reminding her that the threat of socialism had only recently been the subject of an address to the club by Dr. Woodrow Wilson, "the same president of Princeton who said such nice things about 'The Lion's Share.'" [15]

Alice wrote few short stories now, although in December, 1907, an editor of the *Woman's Home Companion* came to Davenport for tea and to ask for a story and mend fences. Earlier that year at the editor's request Alice had submitted a story for which she expected three hundred dollars. One week later she had received a letter from the editorial offices of the magazine complaining about the story, announcing that it was certainly not what the editors had been led to expect but adding nobly that they would observe their part of the bargain and send her the three hundred dollars. She had immediately replied from her suite in the Mayflower Club, where she was staying while visiting in Boston:

The Companion is not *in the least bound* to take the story if they don't want it. I've a half a dozen places for it. But if they do want it, I shall be quite willing to go over the MSS which my secretary copied in a very great hurry: and see if she has done anything bad. What's the matter with it anyhow?

Alice did not like to be patronized, especially by editors of the *Companion*, but when the story was returned and she was asked to revise it,

[14] Sarah Orne Jewett to Alice French, 1907, quoted in Tucker, "'Octave Thanet,'" p. 142.

[15] Lawrence Chambers to Alice French, November 20, 1907, Newberry Library.

she went to work as soon as she returned to Davenport from her trip, rewriting carefully. A year later it appeared in the *Companion* as "The Real Thing."

For all her traveling, the yearly springtime trips to Colonial Dames meetings, winter visits to the South, and summers in New England, Alice was seldom comfortable except at home. In January, 1908, she reported in her diary that her physician had "examined hernia which after all is not a serious matter." Nonetheless it required her to wear a harnesslike truss that sometimes made her ill-tempered and laggard in her work. Still, she hesitated to have corrective surgery. A friend had died following such an operation, and Alice was perfectly aware that her own great bulk meant a similar operation would be complicated and dangerous.

Now well into her fifties, Alice began to suffer from a new array of ailments. She often had colic and acidosis, both accentuated by her rich and excessive diet. Her body weight continued to increase, and she had difficulty warding off the most common infections. Clusters of boils erupted and healed only slowly. An examination by her physician revealed that she had *diabetes mellitus*. Insulin had not yet been discovered, and in the early 1900's the only treatment for diabetes was strict adherence to a rigid, almost sugarless diet—a regimen requiring supernatural will power from a gourmet of Alice's habits. So even while she planned new recipes (she compiled a "diet for diabetics" in her cookbook in 1908), she continued to overeat and eat the wrong things: to the recipe for Hollandaise sauce listed in her cookbook she added a note to remind her to increase the sugar to improve the taste, and in her list of provisions for the 1908 visit to Clover Bend she included $322 worth of rich delicacies from S. S. Pierce's in Boston.

On her way to Clover Bend in January, 1908, Alice stopped in Indianapolis, and after a day full of visits by reporters and callers, including Booth Tarkington, she made her speech to the Contemporary Club on her development as a writer. She described her storytelling as a child and her make-believe games with Conrad, the paper knight; and she offered her ideas about the requirements for successful writing:

> To write, one must know life—to understand the everlasting exceptional games played by human nature, to be, in fine, a seer. . . . [a writer] must see with clear and keen eyes through no blur of compassion, no distortion of prejudice, moral or intellectual or aesthetic. . . . You can divide novel-

ists into two classes: those who have live creatures in their books; and those who have lay figures. You can also divide critics into two classes; those who ask for life and truth before everything; and those who place the manner of the telling first. . . . yet I shall maintain that the vital thing in art is the truth. . . . I truly believe the mission of the artist is to tell the truth. . . . First truth, then beauty.[16]

When she finished, Alice was applauded by the audience and toasted by her friends from Bobbs-Merrill; and before she resumed her trip to Arkansas, she was asked to speak to the club again the following year.

Alice and Jenny arrived with their maids at Clover Bend to find things in the usual disarray. Thieves had broken into the house and stolen baking pans from the kitchen and tools from the carpentry shop. Restoration took a month of cleaning up with a force of seven to ten workers painting, scraping, and washing, though Alice felt they were so "triflin'" and lazy that they were hardly worth the effort to supervise.

Once everything was repaired, Alice turned to plans for another novel, a "Southern serial" that would mix the melodrama of her adventure novel *Expiation* with the social commentary of *The Man of the Hour*. She sent the outline of her idea to the *Saturday Evening Post, Scribner's, Harper's,* and *Collier's,* planning to accept the offer of the highest bidder. Her letter to *Scribner's* was addressed to Edward L. Burlingame:

MY DEAR MR. BURLINGAME:

I have been thinking that you might like the story which has been in my mind for a long time and which I have just begun to work at.

It is the description of the encounter (the literally hand to hand encounter) with the negro problem by a good New England gentlewoman of abolitionist stock, such a dear highly educated morally nervous, *au fond* sensible woman as one may meet seven days in the week in we will *not* say Pittsfield, Massachusetts.

I know her so well, bless her! She has a comfortable property of her own and a fortune willed to her by a cousin which she regards as a trust. . . .

I haven't got the story quite worked out in my mind but you can see what it may be. The picture of the new Southerner and the unrecognized but really mighty effort which he is making. The domestic side of the

[16] Speech before the Contemporary Club of Indianapolis, January 1908, MS in Newberry Library.

question has not been much treated; it is very funny and not a little tragic. The effect on the Northern mind is nearly invariable. I should treat it with a light hand but let a glimpse now and then appear of what is under the surface. As they say in the East 'Does this appeal to you at all?'

As to terms. I will let you have the serial for 1500 and the book for 10 percent royalty. The serial price to be paid now and the royalties on the book semi-annually. If the sales on my recent books are any clue at all that is a *very* fair offer.[17]

Burlingame's response was noted by Alice in her diary for April 5, 1908: "Letter from Scribner's. Don't want serial. Would like to publish the book on a 10% basis. No money down offered. *Hell!*" A letter from *Harper's* announced that the magazine no longer bid on uncompleted novels. The *Post* was uninterested in her idea for the novel but asked for short stories, as did *Collier's*: "Heard from Collier's—Don't want serial. Want short stories. *Nice? Not!*"

Alice turned to working on a series of articles for *Harper's Bazar*. Elizabeth Jordan, editor of the *Bazar*, had contracted for three essays on men as "Friends," "Lovers," and "Husbands." Alice's lack of direct knowledge was no deterrent. Fifteen years previously she had written "That Man Your Husband" for the *Ladies' Home Journal*, and amid quotations from Chateaubriand and the *Faerie Queene*, she had suggested that the lady readers of the *Journal* keep their husbands satisfied with good meals and a willingness to cook for unexpected guests.

The essays for the *Bazar* were finished in time for Alice's annual trip to Washington for the Colonial Dames meeting in the spring of 1908. After the meeting and another White House dinner, she returned to Davenport to go with her brother George to the Republican Convention in Chicago, where she saw Taft nominated over Roosevelt. The next day she received a letter from Hewitt Hansen Howland at Bobbs-Merrill urging her to write another novel. Alice had not mentioned her idea for a "Southern serial" to Howland. She felt Bobbs-Merrill had not adequately publicized *The Man of the Hour*. But now she sent Howland an outline of the novel, which she had tentatively entitled *The Long Way Out*. Howland replied quickly:

It is a big theme—one to handle in a national not sectional way. One to handle as you handled capital and labor in "The Man of the Hour." It has

[17] Alice French to Edward Burlingame, March 10, 1908, Newberry Library.

not been done, as I see it, with sympathy and a full understanding. Always there has been prejudice or special pleading. My dear friend, we want the book.[18]

At the end of the summer, when Alice was traveling through Chicago on still another trip to Massachusetts, William Conrad Bobbs, president of the publishing company, met her train at the Englewood station on the south side of Chicago; and in twenty minutes while the train traveled to the loop, Bobbs negotiated a contract for the novel, giving Alice three thousand dollars—one thousand on publication and a two-thousand-dollar advance—plus royalties of 10 per cent.

The advance was more than she had expected to get, and it would be useful on her trip. She was still periodically overdrawing her account at the bank, although money was abundant enough now. At the end of the year, the assets she listed on the back page of her diary totaled more than $91,000, and her investments in her brothers' manufacturing plant earned as much as 30 per cent yearly interest, money that made possible her big house and elaborate entertainments. The house was always open to guests who came to her elegant dinners or elaborate afternoon teas. Arthur Ficke came often, and once Alice recorded his dinner conversation about two of Davenport's emerging literary figures, George Cram Cook and Floyd Dell, whom Alice remembered only vaguely in her diary as "the young socialist poet . . . something Dell."

Her wealth had also made winters at Clover Bend possible, although money for that would no longer be needed, since the journey to Arkansas in the winter of 1909 was to be her last. Visits to the plantation had ceased to be a pleasure, and at the prospect of the trip Alice noted in her diary, "Shall have to go to Clover Bend last of month I reckon and I dread it awfully. But it is the last time." When she finally left, she was ill with the grippe, which inspired a poem:

> Oh why left I my home
> Why did I cross the line
> To a country full of grippe
> And with no medicine.[19]

Two days later it was her birthday, doubly depressing now that she was sick: "Dreary day—every way—birthdays are awful after 50."

[18] Hewitt H. Howland to Alice French, February 22, 1909, Newberry Library.
[19] Diary, March 17, 1909.

But Clover Bend did mean peace to work on the novel for Bobbs-Merrill, and she continued to write diligently through the first of May, noting her progress in her diary with observations on the world news and the adventures of her friend, the former President: "Mr. Roosevelt has shot three lions. Oh he is a man and a sport." She was working on a short story at the same time, a mystery, "The Red Hand"; and when it was completed, she sent it to the *Saturday Evening Post*, but the story was rejected. Alice recorded George Horace Lorimer's decision that it was, "'not exactly a Saturday Evening Post Story'... Drat It!" First her outline for a novel had been rejected, now her short stories were being returned, and by the *Saturday Evening Post*, which at one time had begged to see her work and had printed whatever she cared to send.

In the middle of March, 1909, Alice and Jenny closed Thanford for the last time. They paid an extra two months' wages to Steve, the Negro who tended the fires, and to Luke, Dec, Linda, and Augusta, all regular help at Thanford. Then the two women began preparations for their departure. It was lush springtime now in Arkansas, and Alice composed another, more reverent poem to Clover Bend:

> Bathed in the sunshine,
> Blurred by the rain;
> Walled in by forests old,
> Dreaming of pain.
>
> Spaniard and Frenchman passed,
> Left but the name;
> Forgotten settlers died,
> Careless of fame,
>
> Love, death and human hearts
> Played the old game;
> War o'er its smiling fields
> Flung blood and flame.
>
> Still in its darkling brakes,
> So old men tell—
> Ghosts guard the useless hoard
> Hidden too well.
>
> Jeweled with waving grain,
> Gracious with shade
> Lovely and lovely spot
> Where we have played.

Outside the whirling world
Has its wild will.
Here, 'neath the cypress shade,
Time's standing still.[20]

The place had become unmanageable for two women nearing sixty, and it was ever more expensive. Alice listed in her ledger the cost of the visit to Clover Bend in 1909: railroad fare for the two women and their servants had totaled almost three hundred dollars, and during their short stay they spent over two hundred dollars on ice alone.

At home in Davenport, Alice's writing went well enough at first, although *Collier's* became the second magazine to refuse "The Red Hand." Such things had not happened in twenty-five years, and to top it off, the novel for Bobbs-Merrill was growing difficult to write. Work on it had almost ceased when Howland stopped in Davenport on his way to California, "to prod me up," but with such a lack of success that Alice wrote to Bobbs-Merrill the next month and announced that she could not finish the novel and that arrangements for its publication should be canceled.

She was almost sixty, and life's duties kept trespassing on her work. Her niece Grace was getting married, and the wedding took time and energy to organize. Then, in the midst of the preparations, Alice's coachman, Tift, disappeared, no one knew where—a distressing show of servant irresponsibility. Sunday afternoons had been devoted to riding around Davenport, Rock Island, and along the river. With Tift gone, it took Alice and Jenny long practice to learn to control their Northern automobile well enough to re-establish the ritual of the Sunday drive, but soon they were at least adept enough to steer themselves around the roads along the island golf course.

In July, 1909, Howland returned and managed to convince Alice that she should give the novel another try. During July and August both the writing and the driving went well, and toward the end of summer she wrote in her diary: "Worked on story. Motor in evening. Getting used to it now, so that I take it out by myself without hesitation." One month later she finished *The Long Way Out* and sent it to Howland—only twelve days behind schedule. She repeated her usual vacation trip to the East, then went to a Colonial Dames meeting in

[20] "Clover Bend Poke Root," April 11, 1909. The "Poke Root," like the "Perry Street Prowler," was a newsletter that Alice distributed to her family and friends.

Louisville, and finally returned to Davenport in time for a brief trip to Iowa City and a celebration with the university's Octave Thanet Society.

By the time she was home once again, a month had passed since she had submitted the novel to Bobbs-Merrill, and no word had come from Howland. She wrote an inquiry and the reply she received was guarded and delicately phrased, but like the *Saturday Evening Post* and the *Collier's* rejections, it was another rebuff—"not altogether happy over the story." Her reaction was: "Now what T'Hell? Wrote him that politely."

While she waited for Howland's answer, Alice continued to practice driving her electric car, which she had named the "tuberculosis wagon" because it wheezed so realistically. But she really preferred her elegant carriage; her brother Nathaniel had bought a new Pierce Arrow automobile and had given his brougham to Alice, "for I still cling to horses." [21] Nothing was settled about the new novel until the end of autumn, when she passed through Chicago on another trip to the East and met Howland, who presented her with a check from Bobbs-Merrill and a large roll of proofs. The publishers had resolved enough of their doubt about the novel to publish it. The title had been changed to *By Inheritance*.

The money from Bobbs-Merrill disappeared as quickly as other advances; and by the end of December, after all her Christmas shopping was done, she was overdrawn again at the bank, this time for five hundred dollars: "Oh Lord! When I try so hard to keep it down!" Two weeks later, on January 1, 1910, she recorded her New Year's resolution "to pay cash as much as possible and Keep My Temper." But in spite of difficulties with the novel and temporary money worries, it had been a good year. The assets she listed in her ledger at the end of 1909 exceeded $96,000—$5,000 more than the year before; and the 1909 *Gentlewoman* of London placed her on its "Honor Roll" of famous women—a lofty eminence shared with Queen Alexandra, the Countess of Aberdeen, Lady Balfour, and a fellow Andoverian, Elizabeth Stuart Phelps Ward.

As 1910 began, Alice was working hard at the proofs of *By Inheritance*, making extensive revisions suggested by Howland, and on January 15, 1910, she sent off the first eleven revised chapters. She had

[21] Alice French to her sister, Frances French Brothers, December 24, 1909, Newberry Library.

tried to make the novel "a coherent mass instead of its present clumsy chaos. There is too much iteration—the same idea repeated under another form." [22] Howland felt the "chaos" came partly from the epistolary device Alice had adopted: newsy letters a middle-aged spinster named Agatha Danforth wrote to her friend Henrietta in Massachusetts.

Alice noted in her diary the alterations she had made in the novel's structure:

> Have written one entire new chapter for the book. . . . and crammed two or three chapters into [another] . . . I hope it is more intelligible. Howland is so keen against the letters that I have chopped out a lot of them: but I think myself that the trouble, the effect of heaviness comes from the length rather than the frequency of these same letters.
>
> So I have chopped out and chopped out. And spread out and tried to vary. I don't know.

Two days after she mailed the revised first eleven chapters, she came home from an evening of visiting, "took off my glad rags and went to work on my nigger lady"; by the next morning at 3:00 A.M. she had completed *By Inheritance*, although she was still unsure about it: "Is it good or bad—I swear I can't tell. Some chapters . . . seem to be rather tremendous, but—I'm no judge of my own work, alas! . . . I thought a good deal better of it last summer when I finished than now. . . . I'm a poor fumbler and jumbler, I am!"

With revisions out of the way, Alice left with Jenny for Augusta, Georgia, stopping briefly in Indianapolis, where Howland met with Alice to complete arrangements for the publication of *By Inheritance* and then escorted both ladies to see moving pictures of the Johnson-Ketchell fight.

In Augusta, Alice revisited the places she had seen with Nora Scott almost thirty years before. She missed her car: "I wish to God I had my tuberculosis wagon. How I should whizz around these hills." She gave some readings before Augusta audiences—one of her favorite stories, "A Captured Dream," and another she termed "a humorous monologue." Shortly after her sixtieth birthday, while she was still in Augusta, *By Inheritance* was published, and Bobbs-Merrill sent her copies of the book, along with some early reviews and an advertising pamphlet in which the publishers had printed endorsements that the

[22] Diary, January 15, 1910.

novel had received from a variety of worthies: "From a Bishop writing to a friend who had lent him the book; From a Boston Lady; From a New England woman of wide experience in society; From a blind man." Even a Belgian princess praised the book, taking the opportunity in her letter to offer Bobbs-Merrill two sketches of her own. Professional critics immediately compared the novel to *Dred: A Tale of the Great Dismal Swamp*, the story Harriet Beecher Stowe had written in the stone house near the Frenches' home in Andover, more than a half-century before.

The heroine of *By Inheritance* was a wealthy New England spinster who was nearing sixty, drove an electric car, and visited in Arkansas. Her name was Agatha Danforth, and she dreamed of using a portion of her great riches to establish a university for Negroes. The novel was the story of her slow realization that the uncivilized blacks, only one generation from slavery, were not ready for higher education, and efforts to provide it were like labor agitation—misdirected because they were bound to fail.

The principal advocate of a university for Negroes was Sydney Danton, a mulatto who wished to become its president. He had been put through Harvard College and Harvard Law School by Agatha, who believed that education could bridge the gulf between the Negro and the white man. But just when she was about to establish the university, Agatha received word that her young nephew, Giles Danforth, was ill on his plantation in Arkansas. Giles had typhoid, and Agatha rushed from New England to Arkansas to care for him.

As soon as she arrived at her nephew's plantation, Agatha's ideas about the Negro began to change. She came to know the shiftless Tobias, the evil Lafe, and Lily Pearl, a beautiful mulatto whose only moral flaws were revealed in her failure to marry her "husbands." The novel's Negroes were unredeemable children of nature, often performing as minstrel show caricatures, one even making the hoary reply of the thief discovered in the chicken house: "Ain't nobuddy hyar but us chickens, boss!" The white southerners argued that the Negro was happiest as a menial:

"agriculture is the work for the niggro. It has variety. I don't believe they will be any good for the manufactures, cotton or steel. It is too monotonous. They get tired and quit. They like to work three days in the week and loaf four; and they can't compete with people who work six. Same with other trades. The Greeks are running them out of the bootblacking business. When I was down in Little Rock last week a Greek blacked my boots. I didn't like it."

Alice provided the plantation with Gothic properties similar to those she had enjoyed at Clover Bend: a series of "hants," a buried treasure, an unsolved murder, and mysterious doings in the swamp. Agatha's remedy for all ghosts she happened to confront was to fire her revolver over their heads. She likewise was not afraid when, on a picnic in the swamp, she was present at the discovery of the disintegrating corpse of a conjure man. Unfortunately, Danton, whose grandmother happened to live nearby, appeared on the scene in time to help bury the dead conjure man, and (in a chapter entitled "The Taint of His Race") Danton's superstitious Negro blood caused him to shudder in uncontrolled horror at the conjure man's corpse. Danton then explained his feeling to Agatha's nephew, Giles: "How'd you like to belong to that fiend's race and have it rubbed into you all of a sudden? How'd you like to *understand* his kind? I never believed I was a nigger. Now I know how it feels. I never did before."

The whites blamed Danton's superior ways on Agatha and her advanced ideas: "You're forcing their growth. Now that boy—he'd be a heap happier and a heap better if, instead of going to Harvard University, he'd gone into a good private family and learned to wait on table or drive an automobile." Finally Agatha began to believe that for the Negro, happiness was better than enlightenment. Thus, while she lost her faith in the Negro, she began to develop affection for him, and she came to accept Giles' suggestion that instead of a university, she should establish a school to train Negroes as servants. The weakness of Negroes was constitutional, according to Giles:

"You know the brutal scientific facts that the negro skull is open like any white skull until the child reaches a certain age; then it does not, like the white skull, retain a certain elasticity; it becomes ossified, stiff as iron; and that means something; it means the why a negro child up to a certain age is brighter and more precocious than most white children; after that he lags, he falls behind; he has reached his possible, as the French say."

Even Danton finally saw that white men would kill all Negroes before permitting them to take what they deserved, that the only way out was "the long way out," the way of patience, obedience, and subservience; Negroes must win the respect of their employers by being good servants and workers. Such a realization did not mean Danton had lost sight of the fact that it was unjust:

"I know you will have none of us; you will drench the land in our blood first. . . . We are to you like dogs; and we haven't the dog's love for his master. Something like that we had, but you have taken it away. You have thrust all the duties all the responsibilities of freemen upon us whom you will never allow to be truly free; and who can never be anything but dogs in your sight; dogs which once you petted, but now you only beat if they presume. The North thrust our freedom at us, flung the ballot at us, and washed its hands of us. . . . We were better off as slaves who never had known the light."

And Agatha had learned the folly of her earlier views: "It is an awful thing, my friend, to run your theories into facts. Like nothing so much as a motorcar striking a locomotive, I only know the problem is too vast for me."

In 1910, science, sociology, and politics had not converged to show the flaws of the racist theories that Alice French propagated. Fifty years ago the majority of Americans not only assumed that Negroes were inferior, the majority had never heard such assumptions seriously questioned. Out of such certainty had come a progression of stereotypes that began to disappear from the stage and fiction only in the 1940's. They remain in the folk mind: Negroes were immoral, lazy, unaccountable, and unreliable. They were incapable of being educated and of developing self-control, all of which was caused partly by the fact that they possessed a variety of atavistic physical qualities ranging from solid heads and splayed feet on the extremes, to more awesome properties in between.

The plantation ideal had long exerted an influence on Alice, particularly its suggestion of a good patriarchal society. Even so, her novel was more than an ante-bellum romance populated with dashing southrons and wooly-headed Negroes—jolly illiterates plucking banjoes and dispensing folk wisdom. After the Civil War, plantation fiction had turned to examining the disruptions of Reconstruction. Constance Fenimore Woolson had written "King David," also about a well-meaning New Englander who set out to help the blacks and discovered that they were unruly, childish, and laden with problems incapable of being solved by northern idealism and good intentions. And in such novels as *Red Rock* (1898), *Gabriel Tolliver* (1902), and *The Clansman* (1905), writers like Page, Harris, and Dixon had attempted, as Alice had, to present a rational solution to a national problem.

Yet for Alice's purposes, her refractory blacks might just as well have been Polish butchers marching in a May Day parade, for her fundamental aim was not to answer the "Negro Question" as much as to advocate a Platonic doctrine of aristocratic prejudice which she felt provided the solution to the problems of society. As a result, she wrote of Negroes as she had written of laborers, as a means of demonstrating her theories; and she used the plantation as she had used the mill owner's mansion, as a means of displaying the values of an entrenched society that had managed to reconcile American tradition with American experience. Like any institution, her society had developed instincts for self-preservation and could call forth apologists.

By 1910, novels dealing with miscegenation were no longer new. Howells himself had touched on the subject almost twenty years before in *An Imperative Duty* (1892). Nor was the story of the touring northerner who was bent on doing good deeds for the Negroes and who got his comeuppance a particularly new idea, even when Constance Fenimore Woolson wrote "King David," in the 1870's. Alice had taken her plots where she found them, from folk tales, newspaper articles, from conventional ideas that were in the air, and from other writers.

Unrelieved by either lurid details of miscegenation or an expression of true insight into the oppressed, *By Inheritance* had little chance to survive a half-century of changing attitudes, but it brought acclaim in 1910. Thomas Wentworth Higginson wrote to Bobbs-Merrill saying that *By Inheritance* was "the next best book of its kind to 'Uncle Tom's Cabin;' far superior to 'Dred' in a rivalry often vainly attempted by others." [23] The governor of Kentucky endorsed the novel, and southern newspapers urged it upon northerners. The Baltimore *Sun* particularly approved of Alice's anthropological pronouncements: "Miss French does not believe in the higher education of the negro, her conviction being based on scientifically proven differences in racial development between the white and African races and the acknowledged mental limitation of the latter race." The New York *Times* announced "Mrs. Stowe's negroes are whites wrapped in dusky skins. Mr. Dixon's crude and cruel books may well be ruled out of court. Miss French recognizes the unplumbed mystery of race and is reverent before it." [24]

Alice was called the Harriet Beecher Stowe of her generation and *By Inheritance* the best work on the race problem ever written. In

[23] Thomas Wentworth Higginson to Bobbs-Merrill Company, March 30, 1910, Newberry Library.
[24] Baltimore *Sun* and New York *Times* clippings, Newberry Library.

December the *Atlantic* counted her among the few authors blessed with the true art of fiction,[25] and Thomas Wentworth Higginson made a further observation: "I can truly say that Octave Thanet has placed herself at the head of American writers of fiction." [26]

The first advertisement for the novel appeared on Alice's birthday, in the March 19, 1910, issue of *Publisher's Weekly*. Below a picture of an avenue of noble trees leading to a Greek revival mansion, Bobbs-Merrill announced: "A ripe, many-sided, illuminative novel of American life today, dealing with one of the most serious of our national problems. . . . A big book, worthy of the author, worthy of America. . . . Elaborate wrapper $1.50." The next issue of the magazine carried a full-page advertisement of the novel, more space than Bobbs-Merrill devoted to any of its other books, even Mary Roberts Rinehart's *When a Man Marries*, the best-selling book in the nation.

In April, *By Inheritance* was outselling Clarence Mulford's *Hopalong Cassidy* and was tied for fifth place nationally with *The Kingdom of the Slender Swords*. As a consequence, Alice began to receive letters of congratulations and requests for her autograph. She answered each of the letters that followed her from Davenport to Augusta and then to Washington, D.C., where she had gone in the spring of 1910 to attend the yearly Colonial Dames meeting. From Washington she went to New York and then to Boston for what had originally been planned as a lengthy visit; but early in May she became ill, suffering from diarrhea and nausea, and was forced to return to Davenport, where a trained nurse met her at the railroad station with an entourage including Nathaniel's big Pierce Arrow, Alice's own electric car, and the brougham and two horses. Diabetes complicated every illness, and just when she was getting better, she caught cold and her teeth began to ache. She took morphine for the pain until a dentist drilled holes in her teeth and poured formaldehyde on the exposed nerves. In May, 1910, she wrote in her diary:

> Impossible to conceive of an absolute ending—impossible to conceive of continuing. Only a sick whirl of conjecture whichever! And I have lost that irrational inexplicable but annoyingly comfortable confidence of pulling through somehow which once was mine. All at once I seem to know I am old. And it isn't nice.

[25] Margaret Sherwood, "Lying Like Truth," *Atlantic Monthly*, CVI (December 1910), 809.
[26] Tucker, "'Octave Thanet,'" p. 158.

Her disappointment included *By Inheritance*; she felt her publishers were again failing to promote her book as they should. "I wonder how the book is doing. I get many letters about it from lots of people. But the Bobbs-Merrill people do not seem to be pushing it as I think they ought for I believe it has elements of success not transient but permanent." She had expected it to surpass easily the 38,000 copies of *The Man of the Hour* sold, but the sales figures she recorded in her diary were disquieting: "There are but bad reports of By Inheritance. Not 20,000 sold: and me, I think it is purely because the Bobbs-Merrill people don't push it as they should. Have written Howland frankly to that effect and suggested that he come talk it over with me." [27]

Two weeks later Howland came to Davenport and openly told her that Bobbs-Merrill felt it was useless to put more money in the novel. It was not going to be a best seller, and the advertising campaign had failed to make it one. The company would not speculate further with the money of its stockholders.[28] After Howland left, she described the meeting in her diary:

> They don't feel as if they could get back their money in making a big display. *I do*. However, we shall try an . . . appeal to the women's clubs. I'll have most of the work to do—but I think I can do it. The book is the best they ever published and they ought to admit it.

Her efforts to increase sales of *By Inheritance* were briefly delayed by a visit from Theodore Roosevelt, who had just returned from his hunting expedition in Africa and was coming to Davenport on a speaking tour of Indiana, Illinois, and Iowa. Alice was to be his hostess. Her brother George arranged a special railroad car to bring Roosevelt from Chicago to Davenport.

When the former President arrived on the morning of November 4, 1910, Alice gave him a meal of quail, trout, waffles, caviar, fresh mushrooms, black strawberry grapes, and "Avacato Grapefruit a la Teddy de Roos." Conversation ranged over politics and literature, and Roosevelt told his hostess that he had included her *Stories of a Western Town* in the "pigskin library" he had taken on his African safari. Bound in protective pigskin, her short stories had been carried in Roosevelt's saddle bags, sharing a place with works by Darwin,

[27] Diary, July 5 and August 14, 1910.
[28] Among them was Alice, who owned $10,000 in Bobbs-Merrill stock.

Cervantes, Montaigne, Goethe, and Dumas. Then after breakfast, Alice led her guest on a tour of the Mississippi River cities before taking him to the depot, where a train waited to take him to Des Moines, the next stop on his speech-making tour.

Shortly after Roosevelt's visit, Alice heard again from Bobbs-Merrill, but not about *By Inheritance*; instead, the publishers wanted to bring out a new collection of short stories. Payment would be small, less than one thousand dollars, but she wrote in her diary, "sent some stories to Bobbs-Merrill. . . . Might as well pick up a few hundred dollars easy!" The collection became *Stories That End Well*, a compilation of undistinguished tales with happy endings, some of which were over a decade old.

While the short stories were being published, Alice was in the midst of her annual ritual of setting her desk and papers in order. Her study was always crowded with confusing piles of manuscripts, letters and notes, references, opened books and pamphlets—all of them placed in ordered disarray: "A Herculean Task! All day at it and not much done. I must get my papers in order in case I should die either suddenly or as just would be my luck after a long illness."

Among her papers was a request for a story. Toward the end of December, 1910, she had received a letter from Earl Edwin Harriman, editor of Chicago's *Red Book Magazine*:

> Long ago we published a story by you. . . . We'd like some more at your established rate.
>
> What we particularly desire is precisely that sort of stories which you have made your own—that is to say, stories of the ordinary people out here in the middle-west who are doing their share of the world's work, without any reward particularly, save a consciousness on their own part of having done their duty.[29]

In his letter Harriman described her work as "modern, American and optimistic," but that no longer seemed to satisfy the public. On December 31, 1910, she wrote in her diary: "Last day of the year. On the whole not a good one for me. I hoped much from *By Inheritance* and got little not even fame which it surely deserved. Will pick myself up and try again." Alice did not recognize any impoverishment of her mind or art. She felt the age was at fault, and the change in tastes was another aspect of the general weakening of old-time virtue, morality,

[29] Earl Edwin Harriman to Alice French, December 21, 1910, Newberry Library.

and decency. That winter she presented her ideas to an assembly of the student body at the state university in Iowa City and the next day repeated them in a speech to the Chicago Press Club: "Unless a democracy contrive to revive and preserve the cardinal virtues of aristocracy, reverence, loyalty and unsullied honesty, it is as surely doomed as a fire-balloon." [30] Then she wrote to Celestine Fejervary in Hungary:

> I have a pretty stiff courage, but this maelstrom of an age scares me. In my small way . . . I . . . plead for sanity and for caution. This is no time to be shooting off fireworks in the powder magazine. The worst of the prevailing unrest is that it is worldwide. It would seem as if the whole civilized world—and the uncivilized—had taken an emetic. These are evil days for sane and thoughtful men. Why is the beginning of every century such a fighting ground I wonder.[31]

She went up and down the state repeating her speech on "reform" and "socialism." In Des Moines the following November, 1911, she gave her speech again, this time as "The Passing of Sanity":

> Democracy is not a natural gift; it is an acquired virtue. The only safe reform is gradual reform, and the only security for any republic is the individual righteousness of its people. And righteousness cannot be legislated; it must grow. Socialism is another of the symptoms of the prodigious spiritual ferment. . . . With socialism, all kinds of get-rich-quick schemes fill the air; all kinds of alleged reforms of Big Business by destroying it. . . . Now, I am not a special pleader for Big Business; I am not denying its special sins of the past . . . but you can't smash the front wheels of the car and expect the rear wheels to keep on the track. And the American people will not be attracted by a program which ushers in the Golden Age in financial panic.

She was fearful lest a riot of social reform be "costlier than vulgar orgies," and disgusted by "modern" literature, which seemed to imply that "knowing all there is to know about vice and telling all we know will make us grow purer and purer." She offered views on art in a speech, "The Short Story as a Mirror of Our Age," that she gave on various occasions after 1910.

> Futuristic pictures, free verse, free fiction, jazz music and socialist legislation—they are all swept on us by the same wave. . . . Modern life is a very mean and squalid tragedy. . . . The horror of our age is reflected in our

[30] MS of various versions in Newberry Library.
[31] Quoted in Tucker, "'Octave Thanet,'" pp. 166–167.

art, the passionate pilgrims of the garbage can who believe in picking out horror and disregarding any relief or hope or gaiety. They are as dreary as Dostoyevsky. *Dostoyevsky, you may remember was an epileptic.*[32]

To Alice, the growing movement for woman suffrage was another aspect of the same folly. Aggressive females in bloomers had appeared in the West as early as 1851. In 1854, Amelia Bloomer herself, a native Iowan, had delivered lectures on woman suffrage throughout the state, and in 1870 militant females organized the Iowa Woman Suffrage Society. By the early years of the twentieth century, the movement had become conspicuous and powerful, but Alice was opposed. It was too rapid a change. In times of national peril women must be particularly calm and wise—"and there is no question of public policy which so tends to distract, irritate and divide good women as this."[33]

The leaders of the antisuffrage movement were women of exquisite social standing, the wives of generals, senators, and business barons, seldom ladies of the sort given to the entertainment of lasting dissatisfaction with their role in life. Such wealthy women opposed suffrage on the grounds that it worked a hardship on the homemakers, for whom they spoke although they rarely had the drudgery of making a home themselves. The antisuffrage movement derived some of its force from such confusion about the sanctity of motherhood and hearth, but more than that, the antisuffrage movement was a union of disparate groups who found it advantageous to make friends among the enemies of their enemies. Antisuffragism united all who feared the "coming of the people to the front," the rise of Populism, unionism, divorce, and nihilism. Southerners saw in it the threat of the Negro vote, middle westerners saw it as a maneuver by the drys, and Easterners could voice agreement that the coming of the "new woman" would "convert all the now harmonious elements of society into a state of war, and make every home a hell on earth."[34]

Alice began making antisuffrage speeches, pointing out that the vote, like too much knowledge, was dangerous:

> There still clings to my old-fashioned Victorian memory certain lines of Pope's about vice, that monster of hideous mien that to be hated needs but to be seen; but seen too oft, familiar with her face, we first endure, then pity, then embrace.
> It is fair to demand of the women who ask the wider life that at least the

[32] MS in Newberry Library.
[33] MSS in Newberry Library.
[34] Eleanor Flexner, *Century of Struggle* (Cambridge, Mass., 1962), p. 148.

wider life should not make us worse women. For women have in charge the ideals of the race.

To them is committed the divine fire. What they *are*, not what they say will keep the torch aflame.

Agitation of this question and the entrance into political life has increased the nervous strain on women, already too great, has made her intolerant, irritable and blindly partisan.

As she was organizing antisuffrage groups in the spring of 1911, Alice received a letter from the state university announcing that it wished to confer on her a Litt.D. Her appearance in Iowa City that June was an occasion for a celebration by the Octave Thanet Society, thirty members of which greeted her at a reception and shared the cake she brought, decorated in the society's colors—pink and white (a choice that had always disturbed her, thinking of herself as she did, "in more stalwart colors").

Later that summer, Alice began work for Bobbs-Merrill on another novel to be named *Maggie, a Lady*. In September, 1911, Alice wrote to William C. Bobbs in Indianapolis:

> I don't think we shall have any trouble fixing up things. I will undertake, if you send me 1500.00 Oct. 1st 1911 to deliver the finished MSS on Oct. 1912—or repay the money. I trust the money however will all have been repaid before that time. You know I'm square with you at present, and instead of having any royalties to pay . . . you can turn them all in on the $1500.00 until that is paid. *Not?* So we both ought to be contented.
>
> I'm getting Maggie blocked out pretty well and getting acquainted with her.
>
> She's really a very decent sort with a warm heart and a cool head and the saving grace of humor as well as a Celtic passion for beauty. (That's really why she wants to be a lady.)
>
> [I] desire to publish the book anonymously. I believe it will be good business, too. We can arrange if you wish to have it sent your readers under a feigned name (John Eagan) from Lawrenceville, New Jersey. You can get their comments and publish them. Later you can announce that the author is a well known writer. If it succeeds we can try a play out of it. And revive waning interest by letting out the secret.
>
> I hope you are well and I'm glad the new building is so lovely. "Gluck Auf"
>
> Always faithfully your,
ALICE FRENCH [35]

[35] Alice French to William Bobbs, September 26, 1911, Bobbs-Merrill Company, Indianapolis.

She got the fifteen hundred dollars and began working on the novel in spite of intermittent sieges of colic and nausea, an "enemy" that seemed to come whenever she had important things to do and that sometimes lasted for two or three weeks. She continued to accept speaking engagements, giving her "Passing of Sanity" speech to the Iowa Press and Author's Club and repeating it from the pulpit of Davenport's Congregational Church. She had also begun to write another mystery, "The Unterrified Citizen" for the *National Magazine*.

On March 19, 1912, she celebrated her sixty-second birthday. "Aged badly now and feel it too." Later she added in her diary: "'Drag the dull remains of life along the weary road.' My father died only a year older than I. Queer to think isn't it?" She had another bad siege of illness that summer, and finally her physicians convinced her that she should undergo surgery for her hernia. It was done at home in her bedroom, which had been elaborately prepared with sterilized white sheets hung on the walls. Her great size made the operation a complicated procedure that took three surgeons almost an hour and a half to complete; but when it was over, Alice felt better than she had in years and had only minor complaints while recuperating: "These sordid necessities of the flesh are awful tyrants." [36]

More disquieting problems soon arose. Bobbs-Merrill was anxious for her to return to work on *Maggie*. She avoided it, offering her failing eyesight as an excuse, although that did not keep her from accepting other assignments. In the beginning of 1913, she received a letter from Elizabeth Jordan, who until that year had been editor of *Harper's Bazar*. She had a proposition for Alice:

> Nine years ago I wrote a novel. Fifty per cent of it was very bad. It is laid in Algeria and has a love affair between an Arab Pretender and an American woman tourist.
>
> My hero is impossibly good, my heroine not human. The style is very stilted in spots.[37]

She suggested that if Alice rewrote the novel, they could publish it under both names and each could make one or two thousand dollars. It was an attractive offer, for the spectacular success of Robert Hichens' *The Garden of Allah* (it had sold 700,000 copies) had revealed a public appetite for novels of desert passion, an appetite that was not slaked even by 1921 and the publication of *The Sheik*.

[36] Diary, October 8, 1912.
[37] Elizabeth Jordan to Alice French, February 13, 1913, Newberry Library.

While Alice was negotiating with Elizabeth Jordan in 1913, Howland wrote, asking about progress on *Maggie*. Alice, who had appointed herself unofficial aunt to Howland, although she was only thirteen years his senior, replied:

DEAR BOY:—

Excuse pencil—(Gripe Getting well—Everybody's had it). Maggie has two months hard steady work due her before she's anything. I've written you an abstract of her but I know parts of it have to be changed. . . .

Faithfully and affectionately,

AUNT A.[38]

In addition to grippe, Alice had developed skin inflammations; and after having a urinalysis, she was put on another rigid diet, no sweets or starch—"I shall try it this week and then ———!"

During the summer, work on *Maggie* ceased altogether while Alice attended to Colonial Dames business. Howland at Bobbs-Merrill wrote another inquiry about completion of the novel, now almost a year overdue. Alice was slow in answering, so he wrote again. Her reply revealed both her irresolution and her reluctance to acknowledge it.

DEAR BOY:—For a week, every day I have tried to write; but my cook is out of commission with Something Awful (maybe spider sting maybe bruised bone) to her hand; and I've had dinners and buffet suppers and a sewing woman in the house and Molly French, poor dear, has been laid up with torn tendons falling four feet into a cellar window pit; and Grace and I have divided the day with her so maybe, a kind boy will excuse me. . . .

As to Maggie; I've a whole drawer of her; and she is a right human, Celtic-American thing. But licking her and the others into shape is Maddening Work.

I wonder could you run down for the week's end or if not could you meet me in Chicago Saturday? I want most earnestly to see you. If Saturday will not fit; when could you come?

Regards to your sister,

Your aff. Aunt

AF[39]

[38] Alice French to Hewitt H. Howland, April 1913, Bobbs-Merrill Company.
[39] Alice French to Hewitt H. Howland, September 23, 1913, Bobbs-Merrill Company.

Howland came to Chicago, but little was accomplished on the novel. Alice was no longer interested in *Maggie* as either a work of art or a refutation of "modernism" and crudity in the day's literature, especially the kind of naturalism she found objectionable in Stephen Crane's *Maggie*. She needed neither the money nor the entertainment, and at sixty-three, she felt her time was short. In 1911, on January 27, she had written in her diary, in the space for the same date in 1914, three years in the future, "I wonder shall I ever write here?" Now, three years later, she answered: "Yes you will. Le Voila! You not only wrote but went to Dorothy Toney's Party and won the best prize with a score of 2258 in 2 rubbers."

She started work again on *Maggie*, but her efforts were only sporadic, and Howland grew more and more insistent, particularly after her mystery story, "The Unterrified Citizen" (the title had been changed to "The Dalrymple Mystery"), began running in the *National Magazine*. The month after the story first appeared, Howland sent another letter asking about *Maggie*. This time it was not the grippe, the press of social engagements, or a sick cook—but rather the world war that was delaying the novel, now three years overdue.

In the early summer of 1914, Alice had written her friend Celestine Fejervary in Hungary, warning of the social upheavals America faced. Celestine replied in July: "If your social conditions give you cause for the pessimistic descriptions which opened your letter, what shall I say a week after the horrible double murder at Sarajevo."[40] Celestine asked Alice to help dispose of the Fejervary property in Davenport. Alice agreed and also began organizing aid for the Hungarian war wounded by establishing sewing and knitting groups and arranging for shipment of the finished goods to Hungary. It was like her work a half-century before when as a child she had helped pick lint and prepare bandages for the Union soldiers. Through her efforts, the first contributions of money and supplies sent by the Davenport chapter of the American Red Cross to the warring nations went to Hungary, and later she formed a Fejervary Committee to continue a program of aid.

In October, 1914, Alice briefly interrupted her work when the Iowa Press and Author's Club held a "Homecoming of Iowa Authors," a reply to those who suggested that "Iowa acres could turn out hogs, corn and politicians, but could make no contribution in the realm of

[40] Celestine Fejervary to Alice French, July 5, 1914, Newberry Library.

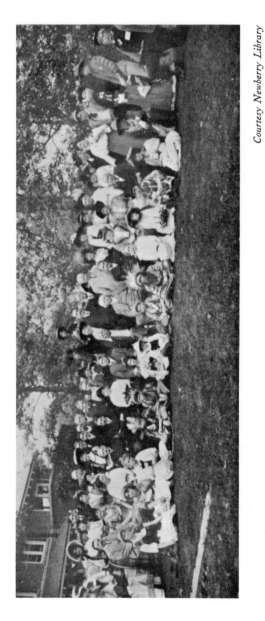

Prominent Iowa authors at the Iowa Authors' Homecoming in 1914. Included in the photograph, seated in the second row from left to right, are: Rupert Hughes, Julia Ellen Rogers, Helen Sherman Griffith, Emerson Hough, Arthur Davison Ficke, Mrs. Randall Parrish, Randall Parrish, S. H. M. Byers, John P. Irish, Hamlin Garland, and Alice French.

the spirit." Invitations had gone out to all authors, journalists, and illustrators who might respond to a call from "Mother Iowa," including Hamlin Garland, Emerson Hough, Rupert Hughes, Edna Ferber, Herbert Quick, Susan Glaspell, Albert Bigelow Paine, and Alice French.

Homecoming activities took place in Des Moines and included tours of the state capitol, speeches, and pageants. On the second day of the homecoming, an "afternoon" was held at the home of the publisher Gardner Cowles, where costumed characters from authors' works appeared in skits and tableaus. That night Alice was chairman of an "authors' evening" given before an audience of 2,500 in the University Place Church, a program that was to include Herbert Quick, Emerson Hough, Edna Ferber, and Rupert Hughes, although at the last minute Herbert Quick and Edna Ferber failed to appear. On the final day of the homecoming, a crowd of four hundred attended a banquet to hear speeches by Hamlin Garland, Randall Parrish, and Alice French. Alice described the beauties of Iowa and its people, calling them a "blend of the Puritan and the Teuton with a happy dash of the Celt." Since that included almost everyone present, she could list some of the Iowan's faults:

> [he] may try to outwit human nature by legislation—which is much like Violet and Lionel in the Nonsense Book churning salt water violently— in hopes that it would turn into butter, which you will remember the Book reports "it seldom if ever did!" So, now and then his legislatures with the best intentions pass laws which have to be patched until there is more patch than original law. But in the end he finds out that salt water is not milk; and discharges the dairyman. . . .
>
> [The cultivated people] generally have the outspoken motto of Safety First; and the Victorian attitude does not seem to them so ridiculous as to the passionate explorers of the garbage can or the lighthearted cutthroats of convention who in Harrison's phrase, "only live to shock grandmother." [41]

She saved the manuscript of her speech and pasted on the back of it a copy of a poem by Hamlin Garland, whom she had sat next to for a group picture of the literary notables and the costumed characters who appeared at the "authors' afternoon." Garland thought the homecoming was an immense success, so much so that he made plans to establish a permanent organization of middle western writers on an

[41] MS in Newberry Library.

even grander scale. In December he wrote Alice asking for her help in setting up the organization:

> I think the time has come to make this most significant movement. It will be the only important author's club in which women are a part of the organization. We are especially anxious that you and Zona Gale should come on its committee from Iowa and Wisconsin. . . . After we get our organization complete, we will make out a list of "Charter Members" and send them an invitation to join. Let me have your consent to serve.[42]

The group became the Society of Midland Authors and operated under the direction of Garland and John Stahl, with Alice as its representative from Iowa.

Shortly after the homecoming of Iowa authors, and while she was corresponding with Garland about the new society of authors, Alice injured her toe again. It healed slowly, a circumstance that she ascribed to old age. On the flyleaf of her diary for 1915 she wrote, "I wonder shall I ever finish this book"; and on New Year's Day she noted: "So many gone and who knows how soon I'll be off myself— if I can finish Maggie and the other and leave all my affairs in good shape I shall not mind much."

Howland wrote again asking, for news of *Maggie*, and Elizabeth Jordan wrote to ask about progress on *Abdullah*, which Alice had agreed to revise. Plans for "Abdullah" had changed after 1914. The novel was no longer merely a North African romance between an Arab and an American gentlewoman. The idea now was to "show the effect of the war on a very modern woman. She is enmeshed in the Suffragists but rights herself starving in prison where she comes to loathe the whole business."[43]

But Alice's work for the Davenport Red Cross and Colonial Dames increased until she had little time for *Abdullah* and none at all for *Maggie*. The war even made domestic life difficult:

> How little time I get: It takes me from half an hour to two hours (depending on my going down to market or not) to keep the house going.
>   Then there are letters to answer (it's a cold morning when I don't have some Colonial Dames business to tackle and accounts etc). . . . Me for a lodge in some vast wilderness.[44]

[42] Hamlin Garland to Alice French, December 12, 1914, Newberry Library.
[43] Diary, January 30, 1915.   [44] Diary, February 15, 1915.

Early in 1915 she wrote to Howland at Bobbs-Merrill in reply to one of his regular pleas for information on *Maggie*:

January 22, 1915

DEAR HEWITT:

    I should have written before but Mrs. Crawford has pneumonia and I am very occupied besides I've nothing but discouragement to write. Mrs. Crawford is better and I hope next week I can write more at length. But—I'm a broken reed, no account at all for domestic fiction and I'm keen to go to Europe and describe the war—from the *shore*.[45]

Six months later Alice was still reporting lack of progress: "Maggie is on tenth lap, running unevenly. Drat her. But I'm doing better and working as many hours a day as my eyes will let me."[46] Eleven months' work had stretched to four years and she still had not finished. Finally she gave it up:

DEAR HEWITT;—

    I'm no good at all and the only chance in the world I have to get away from the continual demands on my time is to hide somewhere. And I'm going to do it. But that will not help you *now*. So cut me out as a miserable sinner. Maggie is Rot. I've burned a lot of her up. So you may imagine I feel pretty bad. I'll write more later.

Yours remorsefully
A. F.[47]

She was collecting another Red Cross shipment for Hungary, where Celestine had turned her mansion into a nursing home for wounded soldiers. Alice was also working on *Abdullah*, although she disliked the title and asked in her diary, "How should Souls Reborn do? Not at all I reckon." Beginning hard work in March, 1915, she completed four chapters by April and sent them to Elizabeth Jordan in New York. Two weeks later she finished three more. "Got off three chapters of Abdullah Tale (Souls Reborn I call it which is a punky title). But still rather a growing thing." Elizabeth Jordan was pleased with the chapters Alice had revised—"thinks we've got punch in them at last"— and she tried to place the novel for serial publication in one of the popular magazines. In June she wrote to "Sister Alice," saying she

[45] Alice French to Hewitt H. Howland, January 22, 1915, Bobbs-Merrill Company.
[46] Alice French to Hewitt H. Howland, July 22, 1915, Bobbs-Merrill Company.
[47] Alice French to Hewitt H. Howland, 1915, Bobbs-Merrill Company.

had placed the novel in the hands of an agent and suggesting that the title be changed to *Olga* instead of *Abdullah*;[48] but even with an agent and a new title, they could not sell the book in 1915.

In the early years of the war, Alice had subscribed to the *Illustrated London News* to read how Britain faced the Hun. Before the toll of dead became too great, the magazine ran a weekly feature picturing Englishmen "Dead on the Field of Honor." Alice read it in every issue, and some of the faces were so young and handsome they made her think of her brother Robert, who had died of typhoid a decade before—"If he only could have led his company into battle and fallen so! He was a born soldier." She felt that civilized men could not afford to be indifferent; the German sinking of the *Lusitania* was an outrage against humanity, and Wilson's reaction was treasonous. "President will doubtless shut himself up with God and the dictionary again and— write another eloquent note. Oh he's the Rotter!"[49]

In May she addressed the Federated Women's Clubs of Iowa, urging intervention in the war because "people never were permitted to have peace unless they were willing to fight for it";[50] and in October an interview published in New York *Times* quoted her attack on Wilson's neutralism and his feminine supporters:

> I believe that neutrality has its limits and I do not accept the platform of the women's peace party. . . . There has grown up among women a blind horror of war, a blind devotion to peace. In time of trouble the innocent peace-loving bystander may prove to be a poor thing for safety. Our historical failures in national preparedness for war, I should class as sins of blind optimism and cowardly indolence.

Alice wanted the nation to have a large army, and she pushed for elimination of both pacifism and pension laws, to toughen the race— "we mustn't neglect decent people to save decadents." She also had strong views on Henry Ford, his peace ship, and the pacifism of Jane Addams: "How long do you think Henry Ford or Jane Adams [*sic*] would stay pacifists were a foreign foe to land on our shores. I give Miss Adams a week; but I don't give Mr. Ford more than 24 hours to become a rabid militarist."[51]

[48] Elizabeth Jordan to Alice French, June 3, 1915, Newberry Library.
[49] Diary, May 29, 1915.
[50] Davenport *Democrat Leader*, May 21, 1915.
[51] MS in Newberry Library.

Early in 1916 she returned to work on *Maggie* for Bobbs-Merrill, putting in full working days on the book but still finding it "a deuce of a chore." Five days after the new year began in 1916, she complained in her diary, "Whole day on Maggie and mighty little accomplished too. There is a plain hoo doo over that book." A major problem was her inability to deal with Frank, the book's radical: "The work on Maggie is mighty slow. Frank doesn't develope as I wish. He should be the best type of socialist but I reckon I am constitutionally unable to do justice to the idealist."

Five years after Alice had begun it, *Maggie* was far from completion, but Alice sent what she had finished to Indianapolis:

DEAR HEWITT;—Sometime this week when they get copied I'll send you a few chapters of Maggie. Grippe and my eyes giving out are why you haven't heard. I've been "mean" myself and the domestics and Mrs. Crawford have been laid low. All better except my eyes on which I'm spending a lot of money. The worst is I'm not allowed night work and I simply *can't* get any other time except at night. So—you can't feel much worse than I do about it. But I'll do the only thing in sight. I am going to Charleston, S.C. the 29th to a quiet house where we are the only boarders and where I can work everyday regularly and I'm going to finish Maggie, refusing to do anything else (except for the Country) until I have it all done. I have tried but I'm clean discouraged. I'll finish Maggie before I die, I reckon. . . .

Your sad but affectionate Aunt
ALICE F——[52]

Letters to Elizabeth Jordan indicate, however, that Alice was devoting more time to *Abdullah* than to *Maggie*, but results there were also disappointing. The same month she wrote to Howland, Alice received word that everyone in New York felt that "Olga (Abdullah) Right of the Strongest—*whatever*, needs recasting in form. The letters and diaries dissipate the interest." The problem of a suitable pen name had been easier to solve. The two authors decided on "David Gault" as sufficient disguise to protect Alice from complaints by Bobbs-Merrill. Thus during her visit to Charleston, Alice tried to work on *Olga* for Elizabeth Jordan as well as *Maggie* for Bobbs-Merrill; and shortly after arriving, she replied to another letter from Howland, who had asked about progress on *Maggie* and questioned some of the novel's dialogue:

[52] Alice French to Hewitt H. Howland, January 21, 1916, Bobbs-Merrill Company.

DEAR HEWITT, What you say is most interesting. And a good deal of it has your uncanny prescience! Yes, sir. You're absolutely right. . . . About the dialect—Lambie, I've been soaking myself for six months in working girl's talk. And it *is* the incongruous mixture of cheap and showy literature, and cheaper slang. Maggie is in the cheap literature stage that's why she "considers" Mother and Mickey: She thinks it an awfully nice word, to be sure. As for Tilly she isn't a simon-pure working girl but a socialist who as a socialist knows a queer mixed crowd who do talk of "bulls" and "frisking." However, I'm not a bit biggity and although the expressions are almost all repeated from life *that* isn't a sure argument for them; the actual isn't always the convincing. And it's the convincing we are after. What you say about my monster is true enough—though I do want him to be repulsive at first—as such a creature would be!

It is easy enough straightening him out one way or the other.

But all of it isn't what I call the "punk" of the stuff. It hasn't "go." Somehow; and I don't know why since I do feel reasonably well acquainted with Tilly and I really know *Maggie*. However, I'll lick it into better shape and see if I can't get a grip into it. I believe in having a grip in the first chapter and a hint. . . .

Your affectionate
AUNT ALICE [53].

Even in Charleston, writing *Maggie* was a great chore. Alice's vision began to fail and caused her much distress. It was one sign of her declining health, a decline accelerated by her obesity. She was sixty-six years old, and her attempts at dieting were only partially successful, although that spring of 1916 she reported hopefully in her diary that the new bathroom scales showed she had lost weight and was down to 217 pounds.

When she returned to Davenport, Alice put *Maggie* aside once again, this time to join in the controversy over the 1916 referendum for woman suffrage in Iowa. The movement to grant the vote to women had gained momentum and Iowa suffragettes had established a headquarters in Davenport. Shortly after returning from Charleston, Alice helped organize headquarters for an Iowa antisuffrage group in offices she rented next door to the prosuffrage headquarters.

Though she seemed to embody the rights of self-assertion that other women wished to express at the polls, Alice opposed suffrage for its taint of radicalism and its reflection of the dangerous philosophies of

[53] Alice French to Hewitt H. Howland, February 23–24, 1916, Bobbs-Merrill Company.

do-goods. She had expressed her views in antisuffrage speeches throughout the state and in the interview, "Dangers Confronting American Peoples from New Movements and Modern Ideas," published in the New York *Times* in 1915, yet the suffrage movement had grown away from its early radicalism and by the second decade of the twentieth century was less a challenge to propriety than Alice thought. National opposition still remained congealed around a number of fears—of the Negro vote in the South and of unionism in the North. In Iowa, as elsewhere in the Middle West, opposition came from brewers and liquor dealers who feared that women would vote in prohibition if they had the chance, a possibility that stimulated secret campaign contributions by Iowa brewers, who announced in 1915, "We are of the opinion that woman's suffrage can be defeated, although we believe that the liquor interests should not be known as the contending force against this campaign." [54]

When the campaign was well under way in Iowa, Alice went to Washington for the year's meeting of the Colonial Dames, and then to New York, once going out to Oyster Bay and Sagamore Hill to visit Teddy Roosevelt. She met Elizabeth Jordan in New York and discussed their novel. Elizabeth Jordan was still hopeful that it could be placed—perhaps a play could be made out of it. Then Alice returned to Davenport in time to address a pre-referendum day rally at the Opera House and warn of the dangers of the ideas lurking behind woman suffrage. Her address climaxed the organization's work of sending speakers throughout the state and writing letters to newspapers and ministers; and on June 7, Alice recorded in her diary that woman suffrage lost in the 1916 referendum by five thousand votes. [55]

During the campaign, Alice's eyesight grew much worse. She had cataracts, which meant the end of work on *Maggie* and little more done on *Olga*. She explained it all to Howland:

DEAR HEWITT;—I wish I could write a more encouraging letter, but I can't. My eyes are not good. I can't use them half an hour without pain. For some years I've had what seemed a light attack of diabetes, but probably wasn't and diet doesn't seem to cure it. And I suppose this growing haziness of vision and pain is caused by it. I'm worried enough not to question the oculist and obey him implicitly. So there I am. And if

[54] Flexner, *Century of Struggle*, pp. 278, 297.

[55] But she failed to record the exposure of widespread vote frauds that had been perpetrated in favor of the antisuffrage forces.

you hear I am doing Anti things and Red Cross things you will understand why. Anyhow you wouldn't like Maggie if you got the girl. She's
too chaotic but the Charleston people are all right anyhow. Excuse this
poor writing. Writing with one's eyes shut most of the time *is* queer. But
anyhow I am your aff.

ALICE FRENCH [56]

Two months later she had given up on *Maggie* again:

11 Sept. 1916

DEAR HEWITT:—Thanks for your letter. There isn't much to tell.
The oculist talks of an operation. *Maybe*—I've some new glasses which
help a little.

I'm trying to learn to write a typewriter without seeing the letters.
That's my best working chance.

Not very good to be sure. I'm truly desperately sorry to disappoint
you.

But you saw for yourself I couldn't really get my teeth into the job.

[James Whitcomb] Rielly's death saddened me. I wish he could know
how universally he is loved and honoured.

Are you still giving Wilson's beautiful phrases 100% rating. He's
defeated already. Watch Maine!

Yours aff.
A. FRENCH. [57]

In 1917 the federal government seized Celestine Fejervary's
Davenport property. The United States had entered the war and
Hungary was now an enemy. Everything the Fejervary family had
not given to the city of Davenport was taken as alien property, a
move that Alice opposed by starting petitions for the return of the
property to its rightful owner who was, after all, an American citizen.
While circulating petitions, Alice continued her work for the Red
Cross and the antisuffrage movement. With the United States' entry
into the war, she was made a commander in the Motor Car Service—
her two brothers gave her money for a car and a larger garage to put
it in—twelve thousand dollars in all. And she became a Four-Minute
Man, giving brief, rousing patriotic speeches at club meetings and on
street corners. She felt America had too few patriots: "Lots of rich
chaps are volunteering. . . . But our nice, soft livered, white-feathered

[56] Alice French to Hewitt H. Howland, July 10, 1916, Bobbs-Merrill Company.
[57] Alice French to Hewitt H. Howland, September 11, 1916, Bobbs-Merrill
Company.

middle class men *they* are neither giving nor doing nor going. Me for compulsory military service."

To fight pacifism and cowards she wrote a novelette, *The Might of the Dead*. It was war propaganda, and when she finished it in the spring of 1917, she wrote from Washington, D.C., to Howland at Bobbs-Merrill, who had agreed to publish the story:

DEAR BOY;—

The story is finished but it needs a little polishing up and copying. I shall hope to send it to you the last of next week or the first of the week after. The Saturday Evening Post wants something from me, and would probably like it. The title is "The Might of the Dead" and the dead grandfather of the hero, a veteran of the Civil War is stronger than the live pacifist mother. It's rather biggish. I really rather like it myself.

If you prefer I can send it to you direct and you can rush it out without waiting for the Saturday Evening Post. Illustrations take such a time. But, of course, there would be a deal of advertising in the publication by the Saturday Evening Post, but you can decide.

I have spent the winter in the South, and go home today. I have been consulting Dr. Wilmer here about my eyes, and may come here again next month for an operation.

Your affectionate Aunt,
ALICE (FRENCH)

P.S. This is a most interesting time here, and I picked up a lot of thrilling inside gossip, which I wish I could tell you. All I can say is an awful lot hinges on the success of Root's mission. I saw the Colonel at Sagamore Hill a week ago Sunday. It is an awful pity they don't let him go to France.[58]

The cataracts that slowly were blinding Alice forced her to begin typing entries in her diary; and one month later, when she returned to Washington for the first of a series of eye operations, she had to dictate all revisions on her patriotic novelette, the title of which she had changed from *The Might of the Dead* to *And the Captain Answered*.

In the middle of May, 1917, she underwent the first operations to remove her cataracts. The result was not a complete success, and for a time, she was completely blind in one eye. On July 31 her niece wrote to Howland about *And the Captain Answered*:

[58] Alice French to Hewitt H. Howland, April 28, 1917, Bobbs-Merrill Company.

DEAR MR. HOWLAND:

My Aunt Miss French is sending you tomorrow, The Might of the Dead. She wanted you to understand it is only a short story, not a book. It has been a tremendous handicap to her having to dictate the corrections. The story shows how a dead patriotic grandfather conquers a live pacifist mother contending for the soul of an average American boy.

She is learning to write touch typewriting and hopes to write you a letter soon. She hopes to see a little sometime out of her bad eye which is under treatment all the time. She has a nurse with her. She expects to go to Washington in October for an operation on the other eye.

However her eyes turn out she says she will not grumble if only her country wins out and her boys come back safe. She sends ever so much love to you and thanks you for the book which Mrs. Crawford is reading to her. . . .

Very sincerely, yours,
GRACE FRENCH EVANS [59]

The book came out November, 1917, the same month Alice had expected to return to Washington for another operation, but her surgeon was busy. On the stationery of her Woman's National Council of Defense for Iowa, Committee on Patriotic Meetings, she wrote to Howland:

I had hoped to be safe on a hospital cot by today; but when your great occulist is a major doing all sorts of wonder witchery with experimental work—you have to take him when you can get him. And after much planning and wiring and writing I have had to give up my first date and be as content as I may with January 8th. . . . Except for being blind in one eye and not able to see out of the other I am right well and fit and you can tell by the paper head what I am doing. What I should love above all things to do is to go into a munition factory. But that doesn't seem at hand just at present. So I go at the thing at hand and I am organized all over the state. Propaganda is our job and we seem to be making right good progress.

Affectionately,
AUNT ALICE [60]

Early in January, while awaiting the operation in a Washington hospital, she tried to type a business letter to Howland:

[59] Grace French Evans to Hewitt H. Howland, July 31, 1917, Bobbs-Merrill Company.
[60] Alice French to Hewitt H. Howland, December 18, 1917, Bobbs-Merrill Company.

(Escaped the censor and after 3 interruptions probably *A Mess*)

MY DEAR HEWETT;—I am sending you by regisxxx resisteredmail the Bibbs Merrill certificate (ten shares if stock) stock and a check for seven hundred and thirty-eight dollars and ninty cents (&738.90 I think the monney will be mire axxept able than the bond . I remember the amount due was — 1737.50 securities for one thousand deducted leaves the ballance of &737.ro adding exchange exchange at the rate of 20 cents a hundred mas oy 738.90. If there is any mistake in ,y ,e ,ory it can easily be remedied and ammount deducted from my small crcdedit. And we can start with aclean slate. I will have this letter registeredtomorrow and itxxwill reach you Monday the 31st. . . .

Affectionately yours

AUNT ALICE[61]

A preliminary operation was completed in January, and one month later, February, 1918, when Alice was sixty-eight, the cataract was successfully removed in a second operation. Teddy Roosevelt, who himself was now blind in one eye, wrote to congratulate her on her novel and added that *And the Captain Answered* was "the kind of book which represents something very real and necessary at this time."[62]

When Alice returned to Davenport, she took up her patriotic duties once more; and by the end of the war, the following November, she was serving a dozen patriotic organizations.[63] She had sometimes lectured immigrants in Davenport upon the occasion of their being granted United States citizenship, and with the end of the war, she continued to appear at the courthouse to address the new Americans, warning them not to expect perfection and above all not to complain if some things were not as good as in the old country. The end of the war also brought restitution to Celestine Fejervary. Alice had helped prepare and submit to Washington a petition with six thousand

---

[61] Alice French to Hewitt H. Howland, January 2, 1918, Bobbs-Merrill Company.

[62] Theodore Roosevelt to Alice French, January 3, 1918, quoted in Tucker, "'Octave Thanet,'" p. 184.

[63] In addition to other organizations she now belonged to the League to Enforce Peace, the State Committee on Public Safety, the National Security League, and the Iowa War Savings Committee; and she was president of the Iowa Author's and Writer's Club. In her diary she also recorded that she was a member of the "Society for Suppression of Ill Manners on Street Cars"— a society whose members were required to step on the feet of those guilty of sitting while old women stood.

signatures, and Celestine was granted ten thousand dollars for the property seized by the federal government.

In 1919, Alice underwent her fourth eye operation (but far from the last—before she was through, she would undergo eight operations, resulting in the loss of one eye and severe damage to the other). To convalesce, she went to Savannah and there met her early critic, William Dean Howells. It was a great pleasure finally to meet the man she had esteemed so highly for so long a time. Later that summer she received a letter from Howells' daughter, Mildred, thanking Alice

> for the second Atlantic with the letters from the Russian Lady in which I read with the blood running cold in my veins, and so took to heart that I have learned how to make myself a shirt-waist in case the Bolshevik should be upon us. [64]

Alice continued to feel that Howells was her mentor, that he embodied the ideals she had honored. She was not put off by his liberalism or his worship of Tolstoy's philosophies—what Howells' critics called his "Russian measles." Howells was genteel and seemed to Alice to stand for the good era that had passed.

The same year as her meeting with Howells, Bobbs-Merrill wrote, asking permission to publish a new edition of *The Lion's Share* in a series of books ten or more years old, and at a royalty of one cent a copy. The payment was low, but the book had never sold well. Sometime before, the remainder of the original printing had been sold to F. W. Woolworth at only four cents a copy.

[64] Mildred Howells to Alice French, July 16, 1919, Newberry Library.

XI. A Sick Old Woman, Shuffling down the Way

In 1920, Alice's brother Nathaniel and sister Fanny died. Their deaths made Alice feel wasted, miserable, and old. To make it worse, her vogue as a writer was clearly past, and only occasional signs of her popularity reappeared. In 1921, S. S. McClure wrote that he was re-establishing his newspaper syndicate and asked permission to reprint two of her stories that had run in *McClure's* twenty-five years before.[1] Alice quickly sent the stories, hopefully adding several others in the same envelope, but McClure returned the extras with apologies for being able to afford only two.[2] For the first six months of 1921, her royalties from Bobbs-Merrill amounted to only forty-five cents— fifteen cents for one copy of *The Lion's Share* and thirty cents for two copies of *The Man of the Hour*.[3] Book dealers had returned more copies of *And the Captain Answered* than they had sold.

Now her friend Jenny Crawford was immobilized much of the time with angina pectoris, which required Alice to keep strychnine pellets and a flask of whiskey constantly on hand. When news came that Nora Scott was ill in New York, Alice recorded in her diary a premonition that the next day would bring word of Nora's death. The following morning a telegram arrived announcing that Nora had died, and Alice was moved by the bad news and her own black mood to set down her depression: "Life is mighty tedious and hard working nowadays. If I only had everything straightened out, how glad I'd be to quit it all

[1] S. S. McClure to Alice French, April 2, 1921, Newberry Library. McClure was interested in "The Merry Thanksgiving of the Burglar and the Plumber" and "The Ladder of Grief," which had been published in *McClure's* in 1895 and 1896. He had sold his interest in *McClure's* and resigned as editor in 1913.

[2] S. S. McClure to Alice French, June 20, 1921, Newberry Library.

[3] Royalties report from Bobbs-Merrill Company, August 1, 1921, Newberry Library.

for 'the dark'—Ah if we knew a little—only a little of this uncharted dark."

Alice had ceased to believe in the ultimate perfectibility of mankind a half-century before, but she was still unprepared for the retrogression she identified around her. Children were disobedient; men were more interested in their pleasures than their duties, and women now had bobbed hair, the right to vote, and the habit of smoking. Alice's ideas had remained firmly fixed in the era just before the United States became a complex, industrialized nation, and she now looked for the society that she thought would always be there and saw only the void into which it had disappeared.

She was an old woman from a good family, and she still drove her electric car, making visits to friends and their children; but more frequently now, in her long dresses and lavender perfume, she remained at home, playing the solitaire of the 1890's, "spread eagle" and "Napoleon," or she sat in Iowa parlors and watched the younger generation with disapproval. When she heard their complaints about the state of the world, she congratulated herself that she had the grace not to answer them out loud, but she spoke her mind in her diary: "'What do you expect you feminists?' No, I sat still, and listened while they puffed their cigarettes sorrowfully."

To add to her other woes, postwar prosperity collapsed dramatically in 1920. Foreign markets disappeared, wages were cut—20 per cent at U.S. Steel—and hardest hit were the farmers and the industries that supplied them. Early in 1922, her brother George warned her not to expect a stock dividend. On January 15 she wrote in her diary:

> To have the ravening little money cares added to the chill and heavy weight on my heart seems about the last straw. Well, I'll get whole heartedly to work and get off two $350 tales for use in the house and try [to] wish our expensive cook on the Wimans, for certainly I can't afford her.

Real frugality had never been necessary before, and it was cruel now, in old age and sickness, although her frugality was less rigorous than she thought. Her concession to thrift was to give up the secretary she had finally hired; but she retained the waitress, the cook, a maid, Jenny's yardman Davis, and the chauffeur, the last an expensive luxury, for the car alone cost twenty dollars a month to run, although Alice later found that was partly because the chauffeur used it at night to drive about Davenport with his inamoratas.

Money still slid through her fingers with exasperating speed. It seemed that no sooner had she added to her bank account than she was notified of an overdraft. Her first attempt at earning $350 was "The Knees of Arabella," a story begun shortly after notice came that her bank account was overdrawn by $380. She sent the story to Robert Bridges at *Scribner's* (Edward Burlingame had retired nine years before) in March, 1923:

Years and years ago I sent you all; and you accepted and paid for an article on The Amana Community of this state. Then along came Spanish American War; and the article was pushed off its advertised moorings by the need of the hour. Somehow it never got published. And I had that two hundred or two hundred and fifty dollars. And I always meant to send you something in its place. What I am considering now is a little portrait gallery of the New Woman. I believe our unspeakable vogue of irredescent Scum is ready to pass. We are fed up on bizarre horror; we are fed up on Sex; we are fed up on Pep and Punch. In short we are tired of having our nerves twitched.

And really you know the new woman is just the old putting on airs because she has new clothes.

At bottom the nice girl is the nice girl if she does smoke and drink and say Damn. She resents a liberty as much as her Victorian grandmother; Hence the Knees of Arabella. I was getting until my eyes went back on me 350 to 400 $ per tale. If you like the Knees of Arabella you can have her for a hundred. And if you think you would like the gallery, I will give you a sketch of the portraits in Trash! The Alley Cat, the Grandmother Bless Her, and The Victim. They all show the same familiar faces in their new guise. . . .

This May I hope to be in New York for a couple of days and won't you run over and have a bite with me at the Colony, then? It would be so nice to talk over old times.

Yours faithfully
ALICE FRENCH [4]

Three weeks later Alice received Bridges' reply:

It has been a pleasure to read your story "The Knees of Arabella." It depicts an amusing character and an interesting situation, but I cannot see a place for it on our very crowded program. Indeed we have on hand in type stories enough for more than a year, and we are adding very few to the number.

[4] Alice French to Robert Bridges, March 22, 1923, Newberry Library.

We had to put off long ago the Amana article and two others in the series because the war changed conditions very rapidly.

I hope you will let me know when you come to town.[5]

The felicity of the rejection did not mislead Alice, and it came just when her needs seemed to be greatest. She protested in her diary: "Damn it all! Life is a ruthless mockery."

After many eye operations, she had to use two pairs of thick spectacles—"near glasses" for the house, "far glasses" for outdoors— yet she had confidence enough in her hand and eye; it was fate and her fellow man that worried her: she slept with an automatic pistol under her pillow and carried it with her wherever she traveled. In 1922, at a Colonial Dames meeting in Des Moines, someone stole her gun from her hotel room and emptied her whiskey flask; and although Alice accused the maid, the embarrassed hotel manager refused to punish her.

As for having the whiskey in the first place, Alice felt that flouting the Volstead Act was the right of free-born people everywhere, regardless of the fugitive ordinances of the federal government. Epicurean habits of a lifetime had made her impatient with Prohibition—an attempt to legislate virtue. The Eighteenth Amendment had emptied her wine cellar—the stock, "so beautiful two years ago," was by January, 1922, on its "last dregs now, despite my personal abstemiousness," and relief was only sporadic, as when five months later she thankfully recorded her appreciation in her diary: "George gave me *a whole case of Gordon Dry Gin.* Bless him! Bless him!"

Prohibition was merely one of many problems besetting her, but she managed to hide her dismay and impress most of her friends with her vigor and bravery, though she was really frightened and angry. One who sensed her unhappiness was Arthur Ficke, the Davenport poet who was now a national literary figure. He had known Alice in her earlier days and knew her family and the stories the town told of her; and he saw what others failed to see. In 1922 he sent a poem titled "My Princess" to *Scribner's.* It was about Alice, though Ficke was wise enough to keep that a secret.

I

I have known but one princess in my day....
I always knew that princesses would wear

[5] Robert Bridges to Alice French, April 11, 1923, Newberry Library.

Alice French, in the garden at Clover Bend plantation

Long strings of pearls wound through their golden hair,—
That they were young and delicate as some fay
Caught in mid-forest, and that smiles must live
Like sunlight in the swift blue of their eyes.
A princess, though a hunted fugitive,
Surely still trails her cloud of mysteries!
But this my princess was distressed and tired,
Her eyes were puffy and her hands were old;
She had forgotten all she once desired;
Eternal grayness held her in its fold:—
A sick old woman, shuffling down the way,
That leads to where the story's end is told.

II

And yet a princess is a princess still,
Though she remembers 40 years behind,
The days when lovers to the Hollow Hill
Came for her sake, and lonely, bitter, blind,
My princess was my princess as she said—
"I will deny while I have living breath,
All that is lonely, bitter, blind," she said:
"I will allege life though I look on death.
All things are nothing. Happiness is a dream.
Yet, now that I am honored with the old
I will contest everything but that gleam
Which makes, a little while, the days of gold.
Spare me your kindness:—For my pennon shall stream,
Down to the place where the story's end is told." [6]

In her seventies, Alice turned her attention ever more to her civic duties, writing letters to the inmates of the Soldiers' Home hospital on Memorial Day and greeting newly naturalized citizens. In June, 1923, she addressed a group in the Davenport courthouse, in ceremonies in which she distributed flowers and led the Orphan's Home band in a salute to the new Americans. But her doubts about immigrants and foreigners were as strong as ever. The Swedes of neighboring Minnesota roused her wrath by sending "that roaring hick Magnus Johnson to the Senate," and on August 24 she recorded in her diary her feelings about the inadequacies of democracy:

[6] Arthur Davison Ficke, "My Princess," *Scribner's Magazine*, LXXII (December 1922), 666.

Sometimes I wonder dully at my unremovable depression which drags like a weight of iron on my heart. Time doesn't do much to cure the weary desolation of my heart and nothing seems to arouse a new interest in the world or my own affairs. I seem a futile failure and the world a muddle of tawdry ambitions. What a squalid failure is democracy! What a sentimental mess!

The postwar reversion to conservatism and nationalism was little satisfaction to her, for while the twenties had brought rejection of the League of Nations, they also brought Harding and his "Ohio Gang," and the clamor over two Italian anarchists Sacco and Vanzetti, scofflaws and immigrants. Other literary people found America wanting— but not as she did. Sinclair Lewis' *Main Street* had appeared in 1920 and was making the people of America's midland look foolish. Only in Europe did Alice see some answer to the disruptions of critics and radicals. By 1922 a new leader in Italy had four million followers; and to Alice, as to many well-meaning Americans, Mussolini was fighting the world's battle against Bolshevism and bringing discipline to a disorderly nation. On Independence Day, 1922, she was moved to note despondently that his achievements might well be copied in the United States, "If the Ku Klux would play the same conservative role.... But they haven't the art."

Little in her early life had prepared her for the America that had emerged from World War I, and in the summer of 1922, when she got a tax bill from the federal government for $230 in unpaid income taxes for 1917, she announced her reaction in her diary: "What I want is to live in a free country! Where the best man wins: and the worst get his neck stretched—and serve him right!"

Fortunately, she still enjoyed traveling, and she made frequent excursions in her Cadillac, driven by Peterson, the chauffeur, although some of the pleasure was diminished by the constant threat of sickness. For weeks at a time Jenny suffered daily attacks of angina pectoris, and Alice was often plagued with a siege of diabetic boils, which made her feel weak and caused her to stumble when she walked. She was taking the new insulin, but an irregular and rich diet made absolute control of the disease impossible. Yet sickness was not as dreadful as before—or at least not dreadful for the same reasons. Her chief concern was the expense of illness, not the suffering. When she learned that another operation on her eyes was necessary, she reported it in her diary and added: "It is not the pain which is nothing or even the boring four days of darkness but it is such an expense! Will cost probably a hundred for nurses and hospital and 300 or more for the operation. It makes me *sick.*"

Alice had also developed a diabetic ulcer on her foot. It healed slowly, only to reappear, and accounted for some, but not all, of her acerbity. She read much and commonly didn't like what she read. *Jurgen* had appeared four years before, and *Ulysses* had just been published. Such things were appalling and indecipherable, incomprehensibly divorced from her ideas and tradition. And short stories had changed by the 1920's. Sarah Jewett, Grace King, Joel Chandler Harris, and James Lane Allen had been replaced by new names: Waldo Frank, Joseph Hergesheimer, F. Scott Fitzgerald, Conrad Aiken, and Sherwood Anderson. All of them were represented in *The Best Short Stories of 1922.* Although the stories now seem mild enough and only Sherwood Anderson's "I'm a Fool" is well remembered, Alice saw them differently: "If these are the 'Best' what are the worst! I felt I had crawled out of a cesspool when I finished. Such a strain for force and for the novel, the grotesque, the bizarre. They are mostly 'over-sexed' in their own loathsome phrase."

In 1922, S. S. McClure sent her twenty-five dollars for reprint rights to another story. The following year, in November, the Allied Arts Association of Chicago gave a dinner to honor her as the writer who "put the midland into midland literature."[7] Then Opie Read included her as one of the characters in his best-selling novel, *The Gold Gauze Veil*; and in 1926, when the Crown Prince of Sweden came to Davenport, Alice was presented to him as one of Davenport's notables.[8]

That same spring Alice and Jenny went to New Orleans, where they were entertained by Grace King and Dorothy Dix, whom Alice had met years before. But in spite of old friends, New Orleans was unpleasant. Both women got the flu and were unhappy and alone in an unfriendly hotel room—although when Dorothy Dix brought them a big bottle of apricot brandy, they were a little comforted. The news from home was bad. Alice was overdrawn again at the bank, for $600, even though the trip had partly been justified as an economy,

[7] See John M. Stahl, *Growing with the West* (New York, 1930), pp. 408, 425, 452. Stahl had been one of the organizers, along with Hamlin Garland, of the Society of Midland Authors.

[8] For the ceremony Alice ordered a "pin head dotted voille" dress from Marshall Field's in Chicago. When the dress was delivered, it turned out to have polka dots "as big as my thumb-nail—Ugly! But it was all cut and ready to try on so there was nothing for it but to take it like a lady." And on the day of the Crown Prince's visit she added in her diary, "I hate polka dots."

for the weekly hotel bill of $139 for the two women and their maid was less than the expense of running the big house in Davenport for one week: "Even at [this] expensive hotel it is cheaper than staying at home. But the damn taxes go on just the same—So do the wages."

To make things worse, Alice had to increase her insulin dosage, changing from weekly to daily injections and keeping her meals down to two a day when she could. But no sooner had she and Jenny returned to Davenport that summer than they began planning to motor east in the fall. Alice bought a new Buick touring car, and a few months later the two women and Peterson began driving to Boston in a car loaded with luggage—Alice carrying her black satin automobile bag, which held her automatic pistol, her whiskey flask, and a purse of silver change.

They passed through Poughkeepsie, and Alice saw Vassar, where she had been a student almost sixty years before. Then to Andover:

> But how changed. More prosperous looking, smarter and smugger! No more the old-fashioned godly New England village where Professor Park's sermons were a week's talk and Miss McKeen ruled the school . . . and the Phillips boys hid in the Female Seminary coal closet.[9]

Alice had begun the trip with a slight infection in her right foot; and by the time she returned to Davenport at the end of the year, the inflammation of her toes had become extensive. The pain and swelling grew, until at the end of March, 1927, a surgeon amputated her right foot to forestall the spread of diabetic gangrene. When she had recuperated, she was fitted with an artificial leg, a clumsy device weighing more than six pounds, with a padded socket for the stump of her right leg and an artificial foot dangling below. But her great size made walking with it impossible, and she was forced to use crutches or a wheel chair. Jenny was now an invalid confined to a stretcher. Her illnesses frightened Alice. In June, 1926, she wrote in her diary:

> I am scared stiff. What would life be without her, the sweetest noblest, truest friend and sister. I don't want to be in any world without her. . . . Ever since Nat died I have felt mutilated and every friend who goes takes a part of my very soul away. How cruelly fast they have gone this year. . . . 'Tis a lonesome job growing old.

No longer able to manage their big house, the two women were moved into a Davenport hotel in 1927 and sadly watched their home

[9] Trip diary, September 23–October 20, 1926, Newberry Library.

sold and most of their possessions dispersed, although Alice kept her sideboard, a drop-leaf table and screen, a wing chair, and her desk and two typewriters.

Jane Crawford died in 1932. By then Alice was eighty-two and had finally learned to walk again. Although partially deaf and almost totally blind, she was not quiescent. Several times she traveled west in the winters to visit her niece in Arizona. On one occasion Alice heard whispers that a rattlesnake had been seen outside on the patio. Somewhere she found a revolver and hobbled out, crutches in one hand, gun in the other, where her hosts found her, intent on dispatching the snake that had long since disappeared.

She continued to write in her eighties, completing an essay about her artificial foot entitled "To Anyone Considering Adopting a Leg," but no magazine wanted it. She also rewrote her old mystery story, "Footsteps of Fear," and sent it to Bobbs-Merrill. They turned it down: "It is the very ingenious quality of the story to which our detective story fans object. Then too, there are a great many details which date the story as belonging to the past." [10] When a Davenport newspaper sent a reporter to interview her, she announced:

> My work is done. This generation does not know and does not understand the days in which I lived. What I have written already must stand for me in literature, as I myself will stand or fall by judgement of the generation in which I lived and for which I wrote. . . . Literature of today is drunk. It is intoxicated with its own vanity, with its appreciation of changes which it doesn't understand. . . . [It] is an amusing conglomeration of fancy and horror—the general impression is that gropers along the literary way are really straining themselves to be horrid in delving into human nature. [11]

The years that brought literary eclipse now brought poverty. The depression of the thirties depleted her capital. Her speculative investments disappeared in the general economic collapse; and when the bank failed in which she had stock, the remainder of her assets were taken to pay her portion of the bank's liabilities. She had become the victim of the kind of economic storm she had once endorsed as an agent of progress and a means of eliminating the feeble and the weak. But there was never any indication that her views on uncontrolled

[10] D. L. Chambers to Alice French, December 7, 1931, Newberry Library.
[11] Davenport *Democrat and Leader*, January 9, 1934.

capitalism changed, though it had taken her money and left her to wait out her last few years in rented rooms in Bettendorf, Iowa, where she was supported by a niece who had to search for the bills Alice hid away to camouflage her poverty.

In the Christmas season of 1933, Alice caught a cold. On January 9, 1934, after two days of unconsciousness, she died. Her newspaper obituary said she was "ready for this last adventure," but little other than her readiness remained—only the residue of her literary reputation and the leavings of wealth. After her death, her will was not probated: nothing remained of her estate.

She had honored her father and her mother and had lived a long life. Perhaps 1934 was a good time for her to die. The world no longer wanted a literature that was heartwarming, fortifying, kind, and civilized.

She had mistaken the shape of a half-century for the form of eternity, but late nineteenth-century middle-class taste no longer governed literature. She had identified the Negro with the irresponsible minstrel blackface, labor and its leaders with "harmful wellwishers," and capitalism with the rights of man; and for that, modern historians called her a "sentimental reactionary." [12] She had seen herself as a realist; critics now called her Victorian. She had outlived almost all the local-color writers of her time: Grace King, Kate Chopin, Mary Noailles Murfree, Sara Jewett, Mary Wilkins Freeman, Joel Chandler Harris, and James Lane Allen had all been born within two years of Alice, and all were dead, as was the local-color movement in literature.

Alice French's novels were antiquated long before the 1920's, and only a few of her short stories were remembered, although some of them had qualities rarely equaled in the stories of her compatriots. Her weaknesses had been those of the other local colorists. She had avoided moral questions; her heroes triumphed and her villains perished through coincidence, good luck, and authorial intrusion. Controversial characters and their thorny problems were killed off to the relief of all. Her fiction seldom concentrated on fundamental human conflicts because she seldom faced them herself, a limitation which was perhaps responsible for her failure with the novel form.

Like Garland and Twain, she wrote of the rural world and of small towns and she used vernacular speech, but she had a different angle of

[12] Oscar Cargill, *The Social Revolt: American Literature from 1888 to 1914* (New York, 1933), p. 123.

vision. She believed that right would triumph, an error that led her to suggest that what triumphed was right and made her writing, like Elizabethan sermons, a vehicle for instruction in obedience to authority. She lacked compassion for men, and in her fiction she erected a moral universe that argued for faith in the rich at a time when men began to believe they knew better and American literature at its best was a demonstration of alienation, dissent, and rebellion.

Had she written of her own group, the emerging middle class, she would have worn better. But perhaps that required too much self-criticism and perception, or it may have been that she lacked faith in the artist's essential calling and was misled by her awesome respect for the merchant powers that controlled her world. She reconnoitered where she might have penetrated, for she was an observer, as were all local colorists.

Alice French's realism was shallow and sentimental. She had too many high-toned heroes, and was a victim of dialect that went out of fashion for more stylish obscurities. The philosophies she warned against have now become literary precepts; and today it is difficult to accept her preaching as ever having been agreeable or inspiring, although that is perhaps because it was directed to a world in which the concept of sin was not old-fashioned, relief was found in prayer and cold baths, and evolution was disgusting in more places than Tennessee.

Maggie was never published. *Olga* or *The Leash* or *The Coming of Abdullah* was never completed. Clover Bend plantation was sold and later taken over by the federal government as a farm resettlement project. Thanford was remodeled as a Georgian colonial mansion and made into project headquarters; the tenant houses were wired for electricity—the Negroes had left years before. In Iowa, the Octave Thanet Society disappeared from the university, while a shrine was built to honor the state's most famous literary work—Dr. Pitt's "The Little Brown Church in the Vale."

Memories of Alice French are faint today. The details of her conquests and her era are preserved only on the crumbling pages of Iowa newspapers and in genteel magazines—along with accounts of the murder of Garfield, ads for electric health belts, and pictures of barouche landaus. It seems a long time ago.

Alice French's Writings

1871

"Hugo's Waiting," *Davenport Gazette*, February 18 (?), 1871. (Signed "Frances Essex".)

1878

"Communists and Capitalists: A Sketch from Life," *Lippincott's Magazine*, XXII (October 1878), 485–93. Reprinted as "A Communist's Wife: A Sketch from Life," *Knitters in the Sun*. Reprinted in *The Social Revolt, American Literature from 1888 to 1914*, ed. Oscar Cargill (New York, 1933).

1879

"One of the Congregation," *Sunday Afternoon*, III (March 1879), 193–204.

"The Tramp in Four Centuries," *Lippincott's Magazine*, XXIII (May 1879), 565–74.

"Daisy Miller: Is She a Caricature or a Portrait?" *Abbot Courant*, V, No. 2 (June 1879), 19–21. (Alice French was one of five contributors to a symposium.)

"Latimer as a Social Reformer," *Sunday Afternoon*, III (September 1879), 838–48.

"Schopenhauer on Lake Pepin: A Study," *Good Company*, IV, No. 2 (1879), 97–107. Reprinted in *Knitters in the Sun*.

1880

"My Lorelei: A Heidelberg Romance—From the Diary of Mrs. Louis Danton Lynde," *Western*, VI, No. 1 (January 1880), 1–22.

"Father Quinnailon's Convert: A Study," *Good Company*, V, No. 1 (1880), 24–35. Reprinted in *Knitters in the Sun*.

"The Canada Thistle," *Good Company*, V (April 1880), 214–25. Reprinted in *Midland Monthly*, I (January 1894), 3–21.

"The English Workingman and the Commercial Crises," *Lippincott's Magazine*, XXV (April and May 1880), 438–51, 586–601.

"The First Xerxes Loan Collection," *Californian*, I (May 1880), 454–62.

"Jails: A Colloquy," *Good Company*, VI (December 1880), 289–99.

1881

"The American Imitation of England," *Californian*, III (January 1881), 5–8.

"Charity: A Colloquy," *Good Company*, VI (February 1881), 498–509.

"Creeds: A Colloquy," *Good Company*, VII (May 1881), 229–39.

"The Indoor Pauper: A Study," *Atlantic Monthly*, XLVII (June 1881), 749–64; XLVIII (August 1881), 241–52.

"A Day in an English Town," *Good Company*, VII (August 1881), 551–58.

1882

"A Neglected Career for Unmarried Women" *Harper's Bazar*, XV (March 4, 1882), 130. (An unsigned editorial.)

"Through Great Britain in a Drag," *Lippincott's Magazine*, N.S. IV, No. 21 (September 1882), 247–59.

"The Decline in Hospitality," *Nation*, XXXV, No. 912 (December 21, 1882), 526. (An unsigned essay.)

1884

"The Bishop's Vagabond," *Atlantic Monthly*, LIII (January 1884), 26–41. Reprinted in *Knitters in the Sun; A Library of American Literature*, ed. Edmund C. Stedman (New York, 1894), X; *Stories by American Authors* (New York, 1900), VII.

"Mrs. Finlay's Elizabethan Chair," *Century Magazine*, XXVII (March 1884), 765–74. Reprinted in *Knitters in the Sun*.

1885

"Planchette's Prescription," *Harper's Weekly*, XXIX (September 19, 1885), 614–15.

"The Ogre of Ha Ha Bay," *Atlantic Monthly*, LVI (October 1885), 505–22. Reprinted in *Knitters in the Sun*.

"General Laurence's Son in the Air," *Harper's Bazar* (December 19, 1885), 826–27.

1886

"Dialect Difficulties," *Atlantic Monthly*, LVII (January 1886), 136–37. (An unsigned contribution to the "Contributor's Club" section.)

"Six Visions of St. Augustine," *Atlantic Monthly*, LVIII (August 1886), 187–95.

1887

"Ma' Bowlin'," *Harper's Weekly*, XXXI (January 15, 1887), 38–39. Reprinted in *Knitters in the Sun*.

"Half a Curse," *Scribner's Magazine*, I (February 1887), 151–60. Reprinted in *Knitters in the Sun*.

"Whitsun Harp, Regulator," *Century Magazine*, XXXIV (May 1887), 111–25. Reprinted in *Knitters in the Sun*.

"The Mortgage on Jeffy," *Scribner's Magazine*, II (October 1887), 473–84. Reprinted in *Otto the Knight*; *American Local-Color Stories*, ed. Harry R. Warfel (New York, 1941).

Knitters in the Sun. New York: Houghton, Mifflin, 1887. Contents: "The Ogre of Ha Ha Bay" (1885), "The Bishop's Vagabond" (1884), "Mrs. Finlay's Elizabethan Chair" (1884), "Father Quinnailon's Convert" (1880), "A Communist's Wife" (1878), "Schopenhauer on Lake Pepin" (1879), "Ma' Bowlin'" (1887), "Half a Curse" (1887), "Whitsun Harp, Regulator" (1887).

1888

"Riding in Arkansas," *Abbot Courant*, XIV, No. 1 (January 1888), 19–21.

"The Governor's Prerogative," *Century Magazine*, XXXV (February 1888), 555–61. Reprinted in *Otto the Knight*.

"The Day of the Cyclone," *Scribner's Magazine*, III (March 1888), 350–60. Reprinted in *Otto the Knight*.

"The Short Story," *Literature: A Weekly Magazine* (June 9, 1888), 28–33. Reprinted in *The Literature of the Louisiana Territory*, ed. Alexander De Menil (St. Louis, 1904).

"Otto the Knight," *Scribner's Magazine*, IV, No. 2 (August 1888), 156–73. Reprinted in *Otto the Knight*.

"The Courtship of Miles Standish," *Book Buyer*, V (December 1888), 451–53. (Book review.)

"The Loaf of Peace," *St. Nicholas*, XVI (November 1888), 48–54. Reprinted in *Otto the Knight*; *American Local-Color Stories*, ed. Harry R. Warfel (New York, 1941).

1889

"In the Headsman's Room," *Cosmopolitan*, VI (March 1889), 446–52.

"The Dilemma of Sir Guy the Neuter," *Scribner's Magazine*, V (May 1889), 586–601. Reprinted in *A Book of True Lovers*.

"'The Land of Nod' on a Plantation," *St. Nicholas*, XVI, No. 7 (May 1889), 529–32.

"Sist' Chaney's Black Silk," *Harper's Bazar*, XXII (May 4, 1889), 330–31. Reprinted in *Otto the Knight*.

A Browning Courtship, dramatized by M. C. Gray. (A play.) Copyright by Mary C. Gray, Watkins, New York, July 5, 1889.

"A Spanish Court Painter and His Times," *Dial*, X (October 1889), 133–35. (Book review.)

"The First Mayor," *Atlantic Monthly*, LXIV (November 1889), 611–27. Reprinted in *Otto the Knight*.

1890

"Expiation," *Scribner's Magazine*, VII (January–April 1890), 55–71, 239–54, 283–302, 443–55. Reprinted as *Expiation* (New York: Charles Scribner's Sons, 1890; London: Frederick Warne & Co., 1890; *Une Expiation* (Tours: A. Mame et fils, 1894).

"Trusty, No. 49," *Century Magazine*, XL (June 1890), 212–25. Reprinted in *Otto the Knight*.

"Under Five Shillings," *Scribner's Magazine*, VIII (July 1890), 68–80.

"The Plumb Idiot," *Scribner's Magazine*, VIII (December 1890), 749–57. Reprinted in *Otto the Knight*.

The Best Letters of Lady Mary Wortley Montagu, ed. Octave Thanet. Chicago: A. C. McClurg & Co., 1890.

Amerikanische Kriminal Erzahlungen, No. 16. Berlin: Verlag der Zehnpfennig Bibliotek, 1890.

1891

"An Irish Gentlewoman in the Famine Time," *Century Magazine*, XLI (January 1891), 338–49.

"A Spectre of Folly," *Scribner's Magazine*, IX (May 1891), 563–68.

"Plantation Life in Arkansas," *Atlantic Monthly*, LXVIII (July 1891), 32–49.

"The Letters of Horace Walpole," *Dial*, XI (July 1891), 66–67. (Book review.)

"Town Life in Arkansas," *Atlantic Monthly*, LXVIII (September 1891), 332–40.

"A Recognition," *Scribner's Magazine*, X (November 1891), 612–19.

"The Return of the Rejected," *Lippincott's Magazine*, XLVIII (November 1891), 593–611.

Otto the Knight and Other Trans-Mississippi Stories. New York: Houghton Mifflin & Co., 1891; London: Cassell & Co., 1891. Contents: "Otto the Knight" (1888), "The Conjured Kitchen" (1891), "The First Mayor" (1889), "Sist' Chaney's Black Silk" (1889), "The Loaf of Peace" (1888), "The Day of the Cyclone" (1888), "Trusty, No. 49" (1890), "The Plumb Idiot" (1890), "The Governor's Prerogative" (1888), "The Mortgage on Jeffy" (1887).

We All. New York: D. Appleton & Co., 1891.

1892

"If It Could Be," *Scribner's Magazine*, XI (February 1892), 178–85.

"Folk Lore in Arkansas," *Journal of American Folklore*, V (April–June 1892), 121–25.

"United States to Russia," *Abbot Courant*, XVIII (June 1892), 24. (Poem) Reprinted in *A Cycle of Abbot Verse* (Andover, Massachusetts, 1929).

"The Besetment of Kurt Lieders," *Scribner's Magazine*, XII (August 1892), 135–47. Reprinted in *Stories of a Western Town*; *The Library of Southern Literature*, ed. Edwin Anderson Alderman (New Orleans, 1909), IV.

"His Father's Own Son," *Romance*, VII (August 1892), 134–51.

"The Face of Failure," *Scribner's Magazine*, XII (September 1892), 346–60. Reprinted in *Stories of a Western Town; Golden Tales of the Prairie States*, ed. Mrs. May Lamberton Baker (New York, 1932).

"Tommy and Thomas," *Scribner's Magazine*, XII (October 1892), 449–62. Reprinted in *Stories of a Western Town.*

"The Rowdy," *Century Magazine*, XLV (November 1892), 67–78.

"Mother Emeritus," *Scribner's Magazine*, XII (November 1892), 628–38. Reprinted in *Stories of a Western Town.*

"An Assisted Providence: A Christmas Story," *Scribner's Magazine*, XII (December 1892), 684–91. Reprinted in *Stories of a Western Town.*

"A Little Classic of the War," *Book Buyer*, IX (December 1892), 496–99. (Review of Thomas Nelson Page's *Marse Chan.*)

1893

"The Court of Last Resort," *New Peterson's Magazine*, I (January 1893), 19–24. Reprinted in *A Book of True Lovers.*

"Harry Lossing," *Scribner's Magazine*, XII (February 1893), 208–23. Reprinted in *Stories of a Western Town.*

"That Man: Your Husband," *Ladies Home Journal*, X (February 1893), 8.

"Town Lot No. 1303," *McClure's*, II (March 1894), 330–39. Reprinted in *Tales from McClure's: The West* (New York, 1897).

"A Shelf Full of Western Books," *New Peterson's Magazine*, I (June, 1893), 631–35; II (July, 1893), 733–35. (Book reviews.)

"The Proud Pynsents," *Scribner's Magazine*, XIV (November 1893), 549–60.

"The Judgement on Mrs. Swift," *New Peterson's Magazine*, II (November 1893), 1107–19. Reprinted in *A Book of True Lovers.*

"Was It the Good Bear?" *McClure's*, II (December 1893), 61–66.

"The Labor Question at Glasscock's," *Northwestern Miller Holiday Number* (December 1893), pp. 12–15. Reprinted in *The Miller's*

Holiday, ed. Randolph Edgar (Minneapolis, 1920); also as "The Strike at Glasscock's" in *A Book of True Lovers*.
"But They Do Marry," *Ladies Home Journal*, X (December 1893), 10.
An Adventure in Photography. New York: Charles Scribner's Sons, 1893.
Stories of a Western Town. New York: Charles Scribner's Sons, 1893.
    Contents: "The Besetment of Kurt Lieders" (1892), "The Face of Failure" (1892), "Tommy and Thomas" (1892), "Mother Emeritus" (1892), "An Assisted Providence" (1892), "Harry Lossing" (1893). Reprinted by Scribner's in 1907.

1894

"Sketches of American Types: The Farmer in the North," *Scribner's Magazine*, XV (March 1894), 323–32.
"Sketches of American Types: The Farmer in the South," *Scribner's Magazine*, XV (April 1894), 399–409.
"Sketches of American Types: The Provincials," *Scribner's Magazine*, XV (May 1894), 565–72.
"The Good Angel," *McClure's*, III (June 1894), 21–29.
"Sketches of American Types: The Working Man," *Scribner's Magazine*, XVI (July 1894), 100–107.
"Sketches of American Types: The People That We Serve," *Scribner's Magazine*, XVI (August 1894), 190–98.
"Sketches of American Types: The People of the Cities," *Scribner's Magazine*, XVI (September 1894), 328–38.
"Miss Maria's Fiftieth," *Ladies Home Journal*, XI (September 1894), 5–6.
"The Contented Masses," *Forum*, XVIII (October 1894), 204–15.
"When Is Woman at Her Best?" *Ladies Home Journal*, XI (November 1894), 3.
"Mr. Ruthven's Black List," *Harper's Bazar*, XXVII (December 15, 1894), 1013–15.

1895

"The Prisoner," *Midland Monthly*, III (January 1895), 3–11.
"The 'Scab,'" *Scribner's Magazine*, XVII (August 1895), 223–34. Reprinted in *The Heart of Toil*.
"The Merry Thanksgiving of the Burglar and the Plumber," *McClure's*, V (November 1895), 515–22. Reprinted in *Tales from McClure's: Humor* (New York, 1897).

1896

"The Missionary Sheriff," *Harper's Monthly*, XCII (April 1896), 773–87. Reprinted in *The Missionary Sheriff; Library of the World's Best*

Literature, Ancient and Modern, ed. Charles Dudley Warner (New York, 1902), XXXVII.

"A Son of the Revolution," *Atlantic Monthly,* LXXVII (April 1896), 471–85.

"The Nightmare Page," *Scribner's Magazine,* XIX (May 1896), 638–43.

"The Cabinet Organ," *Harper's Monthly,* XCIII (July 1896), 238–51. Reprinted in *The Missionary Sheriff.*

"The Old Partisan," *Chap Book,* V (July 15, 1896), 266–80. Reprinted in *Stories from the Chap-Book* (Chicago, 1896); *Short Story Masterpieces (American),* ed. William Patten (New York, 1905), III; *Stories That End Well.*

"A Colonial Dame," *Woman's Home Companion,* XXIII (August 1896), 3–4, 23. Reprinted in *A Slave to Duty and Other Women.*

"The Ladder of Grief," *McClure's,* VII (August 1896), 214–22. Reprinted in *A Book of True Lovers.*

"His Duty," *Harper's Monthly,* XCIII (September 1896), 612–21. Reprinted in *The Missionary Sheriff; The Captured Dream.*

"The Hypnotist," *Harper's Monthly,* XCIII (October 1896), 678–89. Reprinted in *The Missionary Sheriff.*

"The Next Room," *Harper's Monthly,* XCIII (November 1896), 954–59. Reprinted in *The Missionary Sheriff.*

"The Defeat of Amos Wickliff," *Harper's Monthly,* XCIV (December 1896), 86–94. Reprinted in *The Missionary Sheriff.*

1897

"The Stout Miss Hopkins's Bicycle," *Harper's Monthly,* XCIV (February 1897), 409–19. Reprinted in *Different Girls,* ed. William Dean Howells (New York, 1906); *The Captured Dream; Stories That End Well.*

"The Spellbinder," *McClure's,* VII (April 1897), 529–36. Reprinted in *Stories That End Well.*

"The Captured Dream," *Harper's Monthly,* XCIV (May 1897), 920–26. Reprinted in *A Book of True Lovers; The Captured Dream; The Library of Southern Literature,* ed. Edwin Anderson Alderman (New Orleans, 1909), IV; *Prairie Gold by Iowa Authors and Artists* (Chicago, 1917).

"Poor Partner," *Outlook,* LVI (May 1897), 72–78.

"The Non-Combatant," *Scribner's Magazine,* XXI (June 1897), 741–56. Reprinted in *The Heart of Toil.*

"A Pastel," *Woman's Home Companion,* XXIV (July 1897), 6.

"A Jealous Woman," *Independent,* XLIX (July 29, 1897), 961–65. Reprinted in *A Slave to Duty and Other Women.*

"Voice of Nature," *Pocket Magazine,* IV (August 1897), 62–110.

"The Way of an Election," *Scribner's Magazine*, XXII (September 1897), 296–307. Reprinted in *The Heart of Toil; The Library of Southern Literature*, ed. Edwin Anderson Alderman (New Orleans, 1909), IV.

"The Grateful Reporter," *McClure's*, IX (October 1897), 1089–97.

The Missionary Sheriff: Being Incidents in the Life of a Plain Man Who Tried To Do His Duty. New York: Harper & Bros., 1897. Contents: "The Missionary Sheriff" (1896), "The Cabinet Organ" (1896), "His Duty" (1896), "The Hypnotist" (1896), "The Next Room" (1896), "The Defeat of Amos Wickliff" (1896). Reprinted (London: Harper & Bros., 1897).

A Book of True Lovers. Chicago: Way & Williams, 1897. Contents: "The Strike at Glasscock's" (1893), "The Judgement on Mrs. Swift" (1893), "The Dilemma of Sir Guy the Neuter" (1889), "The Court of Last Resort" (1893), "Why Abbylonia Surrendered" (1897?), "The Ladder of Grief" (1896), "The Captured Dream" (1897). Reprinted (New York: Doubleday & McClure Co., 1899).

1898

"A Slave to Duty," *Woman's Home Companion*, XXV (January–March 1898), 1–2, 3–4, 1–2. Reprinted in *A Slave to Duty and Other Women*.

"Two Old Hunters," *National Magazine*, VII (January 1898), 321–27.

"The Blazing Hen-Coop, A True Narrative," *Harper's Monthly*, XCVI (January 1898), 210–21.

"The Moment of Clear Vision," *Scribner's Magazine*, XXIII (March 1898), 311–24. Reprinted in *The Heart of Toil*.

"An Old Grand Army Man," *McClure's*, XI (June 1898), 162–69.

"The Conscience of Alderman McGinnis," *McClure's*, XI (July 1898), 287–96.

"David Nelson Richardson," *Iowa Historical Record*, XV (July 1899), 495. Reprinted from Davenport *Democrat*, July 10, 1898.

"The Miller's Seal," *National Magazine*, VIII (August 1898), 474–81.

"Six Days in a Guardsman's Life," *National Magazine*, VIII (September 1898), 579–82.

"The Conscience of a Business Man," *Scribner's Magazine*, XXIV (September 1898), 310–19. Reprinted in *The Heart of Toil*.

"The Peace Offering," *McClure's*, XI (September 1898), 458–68.

"Johnny's Job," *Scribner's Magazine*, XXIV (October 1898), 439–50. Reprinted in *The Heart of Toil*.

"The Trans-Mississippi Exposition," *Cosmopolitan*, XXV (October 1898), 599–614.

"A Problem of Honor," *Pocket Magazine*, V (February 1898), 1–63. Reprinted in *A Slave to Duty and Other Women; Current Literature*,

XXV (April 1899), 349–51; A. N. De Menil, *The Literature of the Louisiana Territory* (St. Louis, 1904), as "Miss Conway's Horse."

A Slave to Duty and Other Women. New York: Herbert S. Stone, 1898. Contents: "A Slave to Duty" (1898), "A Colonial Dame" (1896), "A Jealous Woman" (1897), "A Problem of Honor" (1898), "On the Blank Side of the Wall" (1898).

The Heart of Toil. New York: Charles Scribner's Sons, 1898. Reprinted (London: Downey & Co., 1899). Contents: "The Non-Combatant" (1897), "The Way of an Election" (1897), "The Moment of Clear Vision" (1898), "Johnny's Job" (1898), "The 'Scab'" (1895), "The Conscience of a Business Man" (1898).

Nicholas Fejervary, In Memoriam. Budapest: Franklin Society, 1898.

1899

"Lost! December 25," *National Magazine*, IX (March 1899), 593–604.

"The Rented House, A Story," *Harper's Monthly*, XCVIII (March 1899), 630–49.

"To Lecture Committees Only," *National Magazine*, X (May 1899), 176–82.

"Mrs. Parkhurst's Interference," *Saturday Evening Post*, CLXXI (May 20, 1899), 748–50.

"Not Legal Testimony," *Saturday Evening Post*, CLXXII (September 9, 1899), 162–64.

"At Dawn: A Tale of the West," *Saturday Evening Post*, CLXXII (November 25, 1899), 428–29.

"Max—Or His Picture," *Scribner's Magazine*, XXVI (December 1899), 739–50. Reprinted in *Stories That End Well*.

"Ned Bruce's Temper," *National Magazine*, XI (December 1899), 297–306.

The Captured Dream and Other Stories. New York and London: Harper & Bros., 1899. Contents: "The Captured Dream" (1897), "His Duty" (1896), "The Stout Miss Hopkins's Bicycle" (1897).

1900

"The Bewildered President: A Monologue Dedicated to Women's Clubs," *Harper's Monthly*, C (January 1900), 326–29.

"Chained to Virtue," *Harper's Bazar*, XXXIII (January 20, 1900), 52–53, 61.

"A Woman's Way," *Woman's Home Companion*, XXVII (February 1900), 1–2, 38.

"The Dress Suit," *National Magazine*, XI (February 1900), 502–7.

"The Revolt of the Elderly," *Churchman*, LXXXI (March 1900), 396.

"His Word as Good as His Oath," *Saturday Evening Post*, CLXXII (January 20, 1900), 632–33.

"The Argument for Doty," *Saturday Evening Post*, CLXXII (February 10, 1900), 708–709.

"A Matter of Rivalry," *Harper's Bazar*, XXXIII (May 12, 1900), 78–87. Reprinted in *Life at High Tide*, ed. William Dean Howells (New York, 1907).

"The Great Boer War at Francis' Store," *Saturday Evening Post*, CLXXIII (August 25, 1900), 3–6.

"The Woman That Understood," *Scribner's Magazine*, XXVIII (December 1900), 729–42.

"My Lady's Chamber," *National Magazine*, XIII (December 1900– February 1901), 137–41, 275–81, 345–58.

1901

"The Power of the Press," *Saturday Evening Post*, CLXXIII (January 12, 1901), 3–5.

"The Object of the Federation," *Scribner's Magazine*, XXX (August 1901), 329–50. Reprinted in *Stories That End Well*.

"Fine Portraits by Miss Jewett," *Book Buyer*, XXIII (October 1901), 227–28. (Review of *The Tory Lover*.)

"The Last Conquest of Mrs. Byrd," *Harper's Bazar*, XXXV (November 1901), 609–20.

"The Portion of Labor," *Book Buyer*, XXIII (December 1901), 379–80. (Book review.)

1902

"What One Man Can Do," *Harper's Monthly*, CIV (January 1902), 205–18.

"Victor," *Harper's Monthly*, CIV (April 1902), 785–96.

"The Right of the Strongest," *Scribner's Magazine*, XXXII (December 1902), 718–30.

1903

"Beyond the Limit," *Cosmopolitan*, XXXIV (February 1903), 451–59.

"Brothers," *Harper's Monthly*, CVI (May 1903), 852–62.

1904

"Cougar Brothers' Waterloo," *Saturday Evening Post*, CLXXVI (April 9, 1904), 4-6, 31-32.

"Not Honorably Discharged," *Collier's*, XXXIII (May 14, 1904), 14–15, 27–28.

"The Apparition," *Cosmopolitan*, XXXVII (June 1904), 165–70.

"By the Terrors of the Law," *Century Magazine*, LXVIII (June 1904), 258–63. Reprinted as "Through the Terrors of the Law" in *Stories That End Well.*

"For All These Thy Saints," *Harper's Bazar*, XXXVIII (November 1904), 1043–53.

"The Angel of His Youth," *Scribner's Magazine*, XXXVI (December 1904), 750–57.

"The Man of the Hour," *Reader Magazine*, V (December 1904–May 1905), 23–37, 189–205, 319–38, 437–48, 576–89, 737–50; VI (June 1905), 69–84.

1905

The Man of the Hour. Indianapolis: Bobbs-Merrill Co., 1905. Partially reprinted in *The Library of Southern Literature*, ed. Edwin Anderson Alderman (New Orleans, 1909), IV. Reprinted (New York: Crosset & Dunlap, 1908).

"Finding of Nicholas," *Saturday Evening Post*, CLXXVII (April 8, 1905), 7–9, 24–25.

"The Greater Courage," *Cosmopolitan*, XXXIX (June 1905), 125–36.

1906

His Duty; copyright, November 22, 1906 [with George R. Morse]. (Play based on "His Duty," 1896.)

1907

"The Lion's Share," *Reader Magazine*, IX (May 1907), 589–602; X (June–November 1907), 17–28, 129–39, 290–300, 401–19, 524–52, 638–52.

The Lion's Share. Indianapolis, Bobbs-Merrill Co., 1907. Reprinted (New York: Crosset & Dunlap, 1909).

"The Accommodaters," *Delineator*, LXX (November 1907), 749–53.

1908

"The Real Thing," *Woman's Home Companion*, XXXV (October 1908), 15–16, 60. Reprinted in *Stories That End Well.*

"Men as Friends," *Harper's Bazar*, XLII (October 1908), 999–1001.

"Men as Lovers," *Harper's Bazar*, XLII (November 1908), 1070–73.

"Men as Husbands," *Harper's Bazar*, XLII (December 1908), 1174–76.

1910

"In Place of Their Own," *Woman's Home Companion*, XXXVII (January 1910), 19–20.

"The Firebug," *Harper's Bazar*, XLIV (August 1910), 492–94.
By Inheritance. Indianapolis: Bobbs-Merrill Co., 1910. Reprinted (New York: Crosset & Dunlap, 1911).

1911

"The By Election at Fairport," [pseudonym J. J. Bell] *Delineator*, LXXVII (March 1911), 174–75.
Stories That End Well. Indianapolis: Bobbs-Merrill Co., 1911. Contents: "An Adventure in Altruria" (1911), "Through the Terrors of the Law" (1904), "The Real Thing" (1908), "The Old Partisan" (1896), "Max—Or His Picture" (1899), "The Stout Miss Hopkins' Bicycle" (1897), "The Spellbinder" (1897), "The Object of the Federation" (1901), "The Little Lonely Girl" (1911), "The Hero of Company G" (1911), "A Miracle Play" (1911). Reprinted (New York: Crosset & Dunlap, 1913).
"A Step on the Stair," New York *Tribune Sunday Magazine*, December 24, 1911, Part III, pp. 5–6, 18–19.

1913

A Step on the Stair. Indianapolis: Bobbs-Merrill Co., 1913.
"The Dalrymple Mystery," *National Magazine*, XXXIX (October 1913–March 1914), 62–76, 297–309, 495–505, 653–63, 824–32, 1004–12.

1914

"Shall We Part with Our Past?" Davenport *Register and Leader*, May 19, 1914.

1915

"The Writers of Iowa," *Iowa Its History and Its Foremost Citizens*, ed. Johnson Brigham (Chicago, 1915), 689–707.

1917

And the Captain Answered. Indianapolis: Bobbs-Merrill Co., 1917.

1919

"Recollections of Arkansas," *Arkansas Gazette*, November 20, 1919.

1920

"The Wild Western Way," *The Miller's Holiday*, ed. Randolph Edgar (Minneapolis, 1920), pp. 35–52.

1926

"Introduction," *Stocking American Mills* (Rock Island, 1926).

UNPUBLISHED AND UNLOCATED WORKS

"The Amana Colony"
"At the Toe of the Stocking"
"A Christmas Gift"
"Corner Counselor"
"Father Quinnailon" (play)
"Footsteps of Fear"
"A Friend of a Dog"
"The Ghost of Carlo"
"A Kansas Honeymoon"
"The Knees of Arabella"
"The Ladies' Chamber"
"The Leash" or "Olga" or "The Coming of Abdullah"
"Maggie"
"A Motor Oasis"
"The Mystery of the Red Hand"
"The Nephew and His Uncle"
"The Patience of Minwell Ogden"
"Poor Eunice"
"Rattlesnake Pete"
"Sister Dora"
"The Sob Story"
"The Student and His Sweetheart"
"A Summer Pest"
"The Swans of Sebastian"
"A Timid Woman"
"To Anyone Considering Adopting a Leg"
"What Men Live By"

Bibliography

I. Archival Sources

Materials for this biography came chiefly from the Alice French Collection in the Newberry Library, Chicago. The Collection includes letters, diaries, manuscripts, commonplace books, ledgers, account books, and memorabilia. In addition to Alice French's personal diaries (which run from January 1, 1905, to December 3, 1931, with some sections missing) and her trip diaries of her coaching tour of England and Scotland with Andrew Carnegie in 1881 and of her visit to Poughkeepsie and Andover in 1926, the Collection contains the French family diary in which various members of the family intermittently recorded their observations and daily adventures between January 1, 1871, and December 25, 1871. In addition, the Newberry Library has a copy of "'Octave Thanet' A Biography of Alice French," a fragmentary and unpublished biography written by Ruth Tucker, who had known Alice French at Clover Bend Plantation, where Ruth Tucker's father, Colonel F. W. Tucker, was manager and part owner. Items with sources not otherwise identified in the text are from the Alice French Collection in the Newberry Library.

A manuscript describing life at Clover Bend, entitled "Clover Bend Reclamation Project of the WPA," is held in the files of the Little Rock *Gazette*, Little Rock, Arkansas. One of Alice French's account books is in the possession of her great-nephew, George Thanet French, Moline, Illinois.

The *Century* Collection of the New York Public Library contains Alice French's correspondence with William Carey, Richard Watson Gilder, and R. W. Johnson of the *Century Magazine*. Alice French's letters to Hannah [?] Davidson, describing negotiations with the *Woman's Home Companion*, are also in the New York Public Library.

Letters from Alice French to William Dean Howells are among the William Dean Howells Papers in the Harvard College Library. Letters from Alice French to Horace Scudder are in the Horace Scudder Papers, also in the Harvard College Library.

The Julia Caroline Ripley Dorr Collection of the Abernethy Library of

American Literature at Middlebury College contains a letter from Alice
French to Julia Dorr.

Alice French's letter to William Ernest Henley is in the Pierpont Morgan
Library in New York. Her correspondence with the Bobbs-Merrill Company,
Indianapolis, and Charles Scribner's Sons, New York, can be found in the
files of those organizations and in the Newberry Library.

The Ida Tarbell Collection in the Allegheny College Library, Meadville,
Pennsylvania, contains Alice French's correspondence with Ida Tarbell.

The Davenport, Iowa, Public Museum holds a copy of Theodore
Roosevelt's letter to William Allen White, dated July 10, 1906, describing
Alice French as "a trump in every way."

Unpublished materials entitled "Literary Societies," History of the State
University of Iowa, Miscellaneous Papers, I, in the library of the State
University of Iowa, contain information on the Octave Thanet Society at
the State University of Iowa.

II. Other Unpublished Sources

LAURENCE, ELWOOD P. "The Immigrant in American Fiction, 1890–1920."
    Unpublished Ph.D. dissertation, Western Reserve University, 1943.

MARTIN, THEODORE K. "The Social Philosophy of Alice French." Un-
    published Master's thesis, Louisiana State University, 1941.

MAYBERRY, GEORGE. "Industrialism and the Industrial Worker in the Ameri-
    can Novel, 1814–1890." Unpublished Ph.D. dissertation, Harvard
    University, 1942.

RHODE, ROBERT. "The Functions of Setting in the American Short Story of
    Local-Color, 1865–1900." Unpublished Ph.D. dissertation, University
    of Texas, 1940.

SCHMALENBECK, HILDEGARDE. "A Study of the Literary Reputation of Alice
    French (1850–1934)." Unpublished Master's thesis, University of
    Texas, 1946.

SEWELL, REBECCA. "Alice French: The Octave Thanet of Literature."
    Unpublished Master's thesis, Southern Methodist University, 1934.

SMITH, HERBERT F. "The Editorial Influence of Richard Watson Gilder."
    Unpublished Ph.D. dissertation, Rutgers University, 1961.

WILSON, WINIFRED. "Octave Thanet as a Writer of Short Stories." Un-
    published Bachelor's thesis, University of Illinois, 1918.

III. Books

ADAMS, GEORGE. *Massachusetts Register for the Year 1853*. Boston, 1853.

ADAMS, JAMES TRUSLOW. *The Founding of New England*. Boston, 1921.
——— . *New England in the Republic*. Boston, 1926.

ALDEN, HENRY MILLS. *Magazine Writing and the New Literature*. New
    York, 1908.

ALDRICH, MRS. T. B. *Crowding Memories*. New York, 1920.

ALLEN, JOHN K. *George Morton of Plymouth and Some of His Descendants.* Chicago, 1908.

ATHERTON, LEWIS. *Main Street on the Middle Border*. Bloomington, 1954.

AURNER, CLARENCE RAY. *History of Education in Iowa*. Iowa City, 1915.

BAILEY, SARAH LORING. *Historical Sketches of Andover*. Boston, 1880.

BANKS, CHARLES EDWARD. *Topographical Dictionary of 2885 English Emigrants to New England, 1620–1650*. Philadelphia, 1937.

BARRETTE, LYDIA M. "Alice French," *A Book of Iowa Authors*, ed. Johnson Brigham. Des Moines, 1930.

BASKERVILLE, WILLIAM M. *Southern Writers, Biographical and Critical Studies*. Nashville, 1897.

BATES, KATHERINE LEE. *American Literature*. New York, 1905.

BEALE, R. C. *Development of the Short Story in the South*. Charlottesville, 1911.

BEER, THOMAS. *The Mauve Decade: American Life at the End of the Nineteenth Century*. New York, 1926.

BENNETT, MARY ANGELA. *Elizabeth Stuart Phelps*. Philadelphia, 1939.

BENTZON, TH. [MARIE THERESE BLANC]. *Les Americaines Chez Elles*. Paris, 1896.

BLAIR, WALTER A. *A Raft Pilot's Log*. Cleveland, 1930.

BLAKENSHIP, RUSSELL. *American Literature as an Expression of the National Mind*. London, 1931.

BLANCHARD, RUFUS. *Handbook of Iowa*. Chicago, 1867.

The Boston Almanac for the Year 1856. Cleveland, 1855.

BOTKIN, B. A. *A Treasury of Mississippi River Folklore*. New York, 1955.

BOYLE, REGIS LOUISE. *Mrs. E. D. E. N. Southworth, Novelist*. Washington, 1939.

BRANCH, EDWARD DOUGLAS. *The Sentimental Years, 1836–1860*. New York, 1934.

BRIGHAM, JOHNSON. *Iowa, Its History and Foremost Citizens*. Chicago, 1915.

BUNN, ALFRED. *Old England and New England*. London, 1853.

BURLINGAME, ROGER. *Of Making Many Books: A Hundred Years of Reading, Writing and Publishing*. New York, 1946.

BURROWS, J. M. D. *Fifty Years in Davenport*. Davenport, 1888.

CANBY, HENRY S. *A Study of the Short Story*. New York, 1913.

CARNEGIE, ANDREW. *An American Four-in-hand in Britain*. New York, 1883.

———. *Autobiography*. Boston, 1920.

CARTER, EVERETT. *Howells and the Age of Realism*. Philadelphia, 1950.

The Cathedral and College at Davenport. Davenport, 1879.

COLE, CYRENUS. *A History of the People of Iowa*. Cedar Rapids, 1921.

———. *Iowa Through the Years*. Iowa City, 1940.

Colonial and Revolutionary Lineages of America. New York, 1940.

COOK, GEORGE CRAM. *The Chasm.* New York, 1911.

COURTNEY, W. L. *The Feminine Note in Fiction.* London, 1904.

CURTI, MERLE. *American Philanthropy Abroad.* New Brunswick, N.J., 1963.

DEEGAN, D. Y. *The Stereotype of the Single Woman in American Novels.* New York, 1951.

DELAND, MARGARET. *Golden Yesterdays.* New York, 1941.

DELL, FLOYD. *Homecoming.* New York, 1933.

DE MENIL, A. N. *The Literature of the Louisiana Territory.* St. Louis, 1904.

DE VOTO, BERNARD. *Mark Twain's America.* Boston, 1932.

DILLON, ANNA PRICE. *Memoir and Memorials.* New York, 1900.

DORSEY, FLORENCE L. *Master of the Mississippi.* Boston, 1941.

DOUGLAS, TRUMAN O. *The Pilgrims of Iowa.* Boston, 1911.

DOWNER, HARRY E. *A History of Davenport and Scott County, Iowa.* Chicago, 1910.

ELLSWORTH, WILLIAM WEBSTER. *A Golden Age of Authors: A Publisher's Recollection.* Boston, 1937.

FEDERAL WRITERS' PROJECT. *Arkansas: A Guide to the State.* New York, 1941.

———. *Iowa: A Guide to the Hawkeye State.* New York, 1938.

———. *Massachusetts: A Guide to Its Places and People.* Boston, 1937.

FERBER, EDNA. *A Peculiar Treasure.* New York, 1939.

FETZER, JOHN CLARK. *A Study in City Building.* Ames, Iowa, 1945.

FISKE, HORACE SPENCER. *Provincial Types in American Fiction.* Chautauqua, 1903.

FLORY, CLAUDE R. *Economic Criticism in American Fiction, 1792 to 1900.* Philadelphia, 1936.

FONER, PHILIP S. *History of the Labor Movement in the United States.* New York, 1947.

FOSTER, EDWARD. *Mary E. Wilkins Freeman.* New York, 1956.

FULTON, M. G. *Southern Life in Southern Literature.* Boston, 1917.

GALLAHER, RUTH. *Legal and Political Status of Women in Iowa.* Iowa City, 1918.

GARLAND, HAMLIN. *Companions on the Trail.* New York, 1931.

———. *Crumbling Idols.* Chicago, 1894.

———. *Roadside Meetings.* New York, 1932.

GLASPELL, SUSAN. *The Road to the Temple.* New York, 1927.

GOULD, E. W. *Fifty Years on the Mississippi.* St. Louis, 1859.

HALSEY, F. W. *Women Authors of Our Day in Their Homes.* New York, 1901.

———. *American Authors and Their Homes.* New York, 1901.

HARKINS, E. F., and C. H. L. JOHNSTON. *Little Pilgrimages Among the Women Who Have Written Famous Books.* Boston, 1902.

HARLAN, EDGAR R. *The People of Iowa,* Vol. III. New York, 1931.

HARPER, CLIO. "Alice French," *Library of Southern Literature*, ed. E. A. Anderson. Vol. IV, 1713–17. New Orleans, 1909.

HARPER, J. HENRY. *The House of Harper*. New York, 1912.

HAVIGHURST, WALTER. *Upper Mississippi*. New York, 1937.

HAY, JOHN. *The Breadwinners*. New York, 1884.

HAYWARD, JOHN. *Gazetteer of Massachusetts*. Boston, 1847.

HERRON, IMA HONAKER. *The Small Town in American Literature*. Durham, 1939.

HICKS, GRANVILLE. *The Great Tradition: An Interpretation of American Literature since the Civil War*. New York, 1933.

History of Scott County, Iowa. Chicago, 1882.

The History of the First National Bank in the United States. Chicago, 1913.

HOFSTADTER, RICHARD. *Social Darwinism in American Thought*. Boston, 1944.

HOWE, M. A. DEWOLFE. *The Atlantic Monthly and Its Makers*. Boston, 1919.

———. *Memories of a Hostess*. Boston, 1922.

HOWELLS, WILLIAM DEAN. *Criticism and Fiction*. New York, 1892.

———. *Heroines of Fiction*. Vol. II. New York, 1901.

———. *Literary Friends and Acquaintances*. New York, 1901.

HUBBEL, JAY. *The South in American Literature, 1607–1900*. Durham, 1957.

Iowa State Gazetteer, ed. James T. Hair. Chicago, 1865.

JORDAN, ELIZABETH. *Three Rousing Cheers*. New York, 1938.

KERN, JOHN DWIGHT. *Constance Fenimore Woolson*. Philadelphia, 1934.

KING, GRACE. *Memories of a Southern Woman of Letters*. New York, 1932.

KRAMER, STANLEY. *A History of Stone and Kimball and Herbert S. Stone and Co.* Chicago, 1940.

A Library of American Literature, ed. Edmund C. Stedman and Ellen M. Hutchinson, Vol. XI. New York, 1894.

Library of the World's Best Literature, Ancient and Modern, ed. Charles Dudley Warner, Vol. XXXVII. New York, 1902.

LIEBERMAN, E. *The American Short Story: A Study of the Influence of Locality in Its Development*. Ridgewood, N. J., 1912.

LYNCH, DENIS TILDEN. *The Wild Seventies*. New York, 1941.

MAASS, JOHN. *The Gingerbread Age*. New York, 1957.

MACBRIDE, THOMAS HUSTON. *In Cabins and Sod Houses*. Iowa City, 1928.

MACCRACKEN, HENRY NOBLE. *The Hickory Limb*. New York, 1950.

MARPLE, ALICE. *Iowa Authors and Their Works*. Des Moines, 1918.

MATTHIESSEN, F. O. *Sarah Orne Jewett*. Boston, 1929.

———. *The American Renaissance*. London, 1941.

MCILWAINE, SHIELDS. *The Southern Poor-White from Lubberland to Tobacco Road*. Norman, 1939.

MCKEEN, PHILENA and PHEBE. *Annals of Fifty Years: A History of Abbot Academy, Andover, Massachusetts, 1829–1879*. Andover, 1880.

MILLER, PERRY. *The New England Mind.* New York, 1939.

MORISON, SAMUEL ELIOT. *Builders of the Bay Colony.* Boston, 1930.

MORTON, NATHANIEL. *New England's Memoriall,* ed. Howard J. Hall. New York, 1937.

MOTT, FRANK LUTHER. *Golden Multitudes.* New York, 1947.

————. *A History of American Magazines.* Vol. IV. New York, 1930–57.

Mourt's Relation or Journal of the Plantation at Plymouth, ed. Henry Martyn Dexter. Boston, 1865.

MUMFORD, LEWIS. *The Brown Decades, 1865–1895.* New York, 1931.

Municipal History of Essex County, ed. Benjamin F. Arrington. Vol. I. New York, n.d.

NEVINS, ALLAN. *The Emergence of Modern America.* New York, 1928.

NOEL, MARY. *Villains Galore.* New York, 1954.

ODUM, HOWARD, and HARRY E. MOORE. *American Regionalism: A Cultural Historical Approach to National Integration.* New York, 1938.

ORGAIN, KATE. *Southern Authors in Poetry and Prose.* New York, 1908.

PAPASHVILY, HELEN WAITE. *All the Happy Endings.* New York, 1956.

PARKER, NATHAN HOWE. *The Iowa Handbook for 1856.* Boston, 1856.

————. *Iowa as It Is in 1855.* Chicago, 1855.

PARKS, EDD WINFIELD. *Charles Egbert Craddock.* Chapel Hill, 1941.

PATTEE, FRED LEWIS. *A History of American Literature since 1870.* New York, 1915.

————. *The Development of the American Short Story.* New York, 1923.

————. *The New American Literature.* New York, 1930.

PATTEN, WILLIAM. *Short Story Classics (American).* New York, 1905. III, 965.

PERRY, BLISS. *Park Street Papers.* New York, 1908.

PETERSON, THEODORE. *Magazines in the Twentieth Century.* Urbana, 1956.

PETERSON, WILLIAM J. *Steamboating on the Upper Mississippi.* Iowa City, 1937.

PLUM, DOROTHY A. *The Great Experiment: A Chronicle of Vassar College.* Poughkeepsie, 1961.

————. *The Story of Iowa, the Progress of an American State.* New York, 1952.

PORTER, KIRK HAROLD. *History of Suffrage in the United States.* Chicago, 1918.

POWER, JOHN C. *Davenport City Directory.* Davenport, 1863.

Proceedings at the Celebration of the Two Hundred and Fiftieth Anniversary of the Incorporation of the Town. Andover, Mass., 1897.

RANKIN, MRS. RUSSELL L. *Lineage Record of the Members of the Society of Mayflower Descendants in the State of Iowa.* 1933.

READ, OPIE. *The Gold Gauze Veil.* Chicago, 1927.

RICHARDS, L. E. *Stepping Westward.* New York, 1931.

RICHMAN, IRVING B. *Ioway to Iowa.* Iowa City, 1931.

RICHTER, AUGUST P. *History of the City of Davenport*. Chicago, 1917.

RIDEOUT, WALTER B. *The Radical Novel in the United States, 1900–1954.* Cambridge, Mass., 1956.

ROGERS, AGNES. *Vassar Women, an Informal Study*. New York, 1940.

ROOSEVELT, THEODORE. *African Game Trails*. New York, 1909.

———. *The Autobiography of Theodore Roosevelt*, ed. Wayne Andrews. New York, 1958.

———. *Letters of Theodore Roosevelt*, ed. E. E. Morison, Vol. VIII. Cambridge, 1951–54.

ROURKE, CONSTANCE. *American Humor*. New York, 1931.

———. *The Literature of the Middle Western Frontier*. New York, 1925.

RUSSELL, CHARLES EDWARD. *A-Rafting on the Mississip'*. New York, 1928.

RUTHERFORD, MILDRED L. *The South in History and Literature*. Athens, Ga., 1906.

SAVAGE, JAMES. *A Genealogical Dictionary of the First Settlers of New England*, Vol. II. Boston, 1860.

SCHICK, JOSEPH S. *The Early Theater in Iowa*. Chicago, 1939.

Scott County History, Iowa Writers' Program of the Works Projects Administration in the State of Iowa (1942).

SEDGWICK, ELLERY. *The Happy Profession*. Boston, 1946.

The Social Revolt: American Literature from 1888 to 1914, ed. Oscar Cargill. New York, 1933.

SPENCER, J. W., and J. M. D. BURROWS. *The Early Days of Rock Island and Davenport*, ed. Milo Milton Quaife. Chicago, 1942.

STAHL, JOHN. *Growing with the West*. New York, 1930.

STEVENS, GEORGE. *Best Sellers*. London, 1939.

Strength out of Weakness, Massachusetts Historical Society Collection, 3d Series, IV, 149–96.

SWISHER, JACOB A. *Iowa in Times of War*. Iowa City, 1934.

The Times' Davenport and Scott County Directory. Davenport, 1900.

TOOKER, L. FRANK. *The Joys and Tribulations of an Editor*. New York, 1924.

TRENT, W. P. *Southern Writers*. New York, 1910.

VEDDER, HENRY. *American Writers of Today*. New York, 1895.

WARD, ELIZABETH STUART PHELPS. *Chapters from a Life*. Boston, 1896.

WARE, E. F. *The Lyon Campaign in Missouri*. Topeka, 1907.

WARFEL, HARRY R., and G. H. ORIANS. *American Local-Color Stories*. New York, 1941.

WATERLOO, STANLEY, and JOHN HANSON. *Famous American Men and Women*. Chicago, 1896.

WHITE, WILLIAM ALLEN. *Autobiography of William Allen White*. New York, 1946.

WILKIE, FRANC B. *Davenport Past and Present*. Davenport, 1858.

WILSON, FORREST. *Crusader in Crinoline*. New York, 1941.
WRIGHT, LUELLA M. *Peter Melendy*. Iowa City, 1943.

IV. Magazine Articles

"Alice French," *Reader Magazine*, IV (October 1904), 586–88.
"Alice French," *Reader Magazine*, VIII (August 1906), 274.
ATHERTON, GERTRUDE. "Geographical Fiction," *Lippincott's Magazine*, I (July 1892), 112–14.
BARRETTE, LYDIA M. "Alice French (Octave Thanet)," *Midland Schools*, XXXXI (November 1926), 83–85.
BENTZON, TH. [MARIE THERESE BLANC]. "Dans l'Arkansas: A Propos des Romans d' Octave Thanet," *Revue des Deux Mondes*, CXXXIII (February 1, 1896), 542–72. Trans. by Evelyn S. Schaeffer, "In Arkansas Apropos of Octave Thanet's Romances," *Midland Monthly*, VI (July and August 1896), 37–47, 136–45; reprinted in condensed form in *Book Buyer*, XIII (June 1896), 293–94.
BEYER, MARY QUEAL. "Brief History of the French Family," *Annals of Iowa*, IX (July–October 1910), 493–514.
BISHOP, FERMAN. "Sarah Orne Jewett's Ideas of Race," *New England Quarterly*, XXX (June 1957), 243–49.
BRAWLEY, BENJAMIN. "The Negro in American Literature," *Bookman*, LVI (October 1922), 137, 141.
CHRISTIANSEN, THOMAS P. "An Industrial History of Scott County, Iowa," *Annals of Iowa*, XXII (October 1939), 87–127; (April 1940), 259–311; (July 1940), 345–91.
COLEMAN, CHARLES W. "The Recent Movement in Southern Literature," *Harper's Monthly*, LXXIV (May 1887), 837–55.
COOPER, FREDERICK TABER. "The Purpose Novel and Some Recent Books," *Bookman*, XXII (October 1905), 131–35.
COPELAND, C. T. "The Short Story," *Atlantic Monthly*, LXIX (February 1892), 261–70.
DAVIDSON, DONALD. "Regionalism and Nationalism in American Literature," *American Review*, V (April 1935), 48–61.
DOUGHERTY, C. T. "Novels of the Middle Border," *Historical Bulletin*, XXV, No. 4 (May 1947), 77–78, 85–88.
"Editorial Department" (Homecoming of Iowa Authors), *Annals of Iowa*, XI (October 1914), 556.
FREDERICK, J. T. "The Writer's Iowa," *Palimpsest*, XI (February 1930), 57–60.
FRENCH, JOHN M. "Lieut. William French and His Descendants," *New England Historical and Genealogical Register*, XLIV (October 1890), 367–72.

GALLAHER, RUTH. "From Connecticut to Iowa," *Palimpsest*, XXII (March 1941), 65–78.

———. "The Iowa Band," *Palimpsest*, XI (August 1930), 355–66.

"George W. French" (obituary), *Annals of Iowa*, XIX (April 1935), 634.

HAWLEY, CHARLES ARTHUR. "Some Aspects of Congregationalism in Relation to the Early Cultural Development of Iowa," *Iowa Journal of History and Politics*, XXXV, No. 2 (April 1937), 181–285.

HERBST, JOSEPHINE. "Iowa Takes to Literature," *American Mercury*, VII (April 1926), 466–70.

HIGGINSON, THOMAS W. "The Local Short Story," *Independent*, XLIV (November 3, 1892), 1544–45.

HOELTJE, HUBERT H. "Ralph Waldo Emerson in Iowa," *Iowa Journal of History and Politics*, XXV (April 1927), 237–76.

———. "Some Iowa Lectures and Conversations of Amos Bronson Alcott," *Iowa Journal of History and Politics*, XXIX (July 1931), 375–401.

HOWELLS, WILLIAM DEAN. "Editor's Study," *Harper's Magazine*, LXXVI (January 1888), 321–22; (March 1888), 643–44.

"In the World of Letters" (biographical sketch of Alice French), *Book News Monthly*, XXXIV (September 1905), 22–23.

JAMES, W. P. "On the Theory and Practice of Local Color," *Living Age*, CCXIII (June 12, 1897), 743–48.

JOHNSON, HILDEGARDE BINDER. "German Forty-Eighters in Davenport," *Iowa Journal of History and Politics*, XLIV (January 1946), 3–60.

JUDD, REV. FRANCIS E. "Establishment of the Diocese of Iowa, Protestant Episcopal Church of America," *Annals of Iowa*, XI (January 1914), 291–303.

LEVY, BABETTE. "Mutations in New England Local Color," *New England Quarterly*, XIX (September 1946), 338–58.

MABIE, HAMILTON WRIGHT. "Mr. Mabie Answers Some Questions," *Ladies' Home Journal*, XXIII (March 1906), 20.

McCLEOD, WALTER E. "Early Lawrence County History," *Arkansas Historical Quarterly*, III, No. 1 (Spring 1944), 123–34.

McGUIRE, LETHA PEARL. "A Study of the Public Library Movement in Iowa," *Iowa Journal of History and Politics*, XXXV (January 1937), 22–72.

MEYER, MARIE. "River Towns," *Palimpsest*, VII (December 1926), 381–89.

MORSE, JAMES HERBERT. "The Native Elements in American Fiction, since the War," *Century Magazine*, XXVI (July 1883), 362–75.

MOSS, MARY. "Representative American Story Tellers," *Bookman*, XXIV (September 1906), 21–29.

"Nathaniel French" (obituary), *Annals of Iowa*, XII (October 1920), 475–76.

NOBLE, WILLIAM. "The Four Mortons," *Law Society Journal*, VI (November 1934), 353–59.

ORR, A. E. "Is It Sectional or National?" *Century Magazine*, XXXII (October 1886), 961–62.

PARISH, JOHN C. "The First Mississippi Bridge," *Palimpsest*, III, No. 5 (May 1922), 133–41.

PARKMAN, FRANCIS. "The Woman Question," *North American Review*, CCLXXV (October 1879), 303–32.

PELZER, LOUIS. "The History of Political Parties in Iowa, from 1857 to 1860," *Iowa Journal of History and Politics*, VII (April 1909), 179–229.

PORTOR, LAURA S. "In Search of Local Color," *Harper's Magazine*, CXLV (August–September 1922), 281–94, 451–66.

REID, MARY J. "Four Women Writers of the West," *Overland*, XXIV (August 1894), 138–44.

——. "Octave Thanet at Home," *Midland Monthly*, III (January 1895), 36–42. Digested in *Review of Reviews*, XI (February 1895), 192.

——. "Octave Thanet in Her Davenport Home," *Book Buyer*, XII (February 1895), 24–25.

——. "The Theories of Octave Thanet and Other Western Realists," *Midland Monthly*, IX (February 1898), 99–108.

——. "To Octave Thanet," *Midland Monthly*, VI (July 1896), 36.

"Robert T. French" (obituary), *Annals of Iowa*, III (January 1898), 316.

SCHAEFFER, EVELYN SCHUYLER. "American Authoress of the Hour," *Harper's Bazar*, XXXIII (January 13, 1900), 31.

——. "A Novelist of Tomorrow," *National Magazine*, XXXIX (October 1913), 123–31.

——. "Octave Thanet," *Current Literature*, XXV (April 1899), 307–308.

SCUDDER, HORACE E. "A Few Story-Tellers Old and New," *Atlantic Monthly*, LXXII (November 1893), 693–99.

SEWELL, REBECCA. "Clover Bend Plantation," *Southwest Review*, XXI (April 1936), 312–18.

SHERWOOD, MARGARET. "Lying Like Truth," *Atlantic Monthly*, CVI (December 1910), 806–17.

SHINN, JOSIAH H. "Miss Alice French of Clover Bend," *Publications* of the Arkansas Historical Association, II (1906), 344–51.

SMITH, CHARLES FORSTER. "Southern Dialect in Life and Literature," *Southern Bivouac*, IV (November 1885), 343–51.

STEGNER, WALLACE. "The Trail of the Hawkeye," *Saturday Review of Literature*, XVIII (July 30, 1938), 3–4, 16.

SUCKOW, RUTH. "Iowa," *American Mercury*, IX (September 1926), 39–45.

TEMPLE, SETH J. "Camp McClellan During the Civil War," *Annals of Iowa*, XXI (July 1937), 17–55.

TILLINGHAST, B. F. "A Far Reaching Charity," *Midland Monthly*, I (April and May 1894), 325–28, 409–26. Reprinted in *Palimpsest*, XXVI (February 1945), 47–53.

"To Margaret Cary Rutherford, of *The Man of the Hour*," *Reader Magazine*, VIII (August 1906), 274–76.

WELCH, M. H., "Choice of Her Pseudonym," *Harper's Bazar*, XXXIII (November 3, 1900), 1917.

WILSON, BEN HUR. "Abandoned Railroads of Iowa," *Iowa Journal of History and Politics*, XXVI (January 1928), 3–64.

WRIGHT, LUELLA M. "Culture Through Lectures," *Iowa Journal of History and Politics*, XXXVIII (April 1940), 123–62.

———. "The Midland Monthly," *Iowa Journal of History and Politics*, XLV (January 1947), 3–61.

V. Newspapers

Arkansas Gazette, December 2, 1923; January 21, 1934.

Chicago *Tribune*, January 10, 1934.

Davenport *Democrat and Leader*, July 10, 1938.

Davenport *Democrat-Gazette*, October 14, 1888.

Davenport *Register and Leader*, December 26, 1909; March 10, 17, 24, 31, and April 7, 14, 21, 1929.

Des Moines *Register*, June 12, 1927.

New York *Times*, January 10, 1934.

Acknowledgments

In writing this book, I have been helped by a number of people, whom I wish to thank here. I am indebted to Harrison Hayford, Wallace Douglas, and Edward Hungerford, of Northwestern University, for numerous helpful suggestions and judicious commands. I am also grateful to Amy Wood Nyholm, of the Newberry Library in Chicago, for first introducing me to the possibility of writing a biography of Alice French and for helping during the task. Mrs. Gertrude L. Woodward, other members of the Newberry Library staff, and many other people and institutions have given freely of their time and energy. I have a special indebtedness to Miss Luella M. Wright, of the State University of Iowa, who permitted me to use material which she had collected on Alice French. I should also like to express my gratitude to Robert Thanet French for his kind hospitality and the information he gave me on his great-aunt. The Bobbs-Merrill Company and Charles Scribner's Sons permitted me to use material in their files on Alice French. I am also under obligation to other sources, most of which are acknowledged in the text or in the notes.

And I am further indebted to my wife and to William Maxwell.

247

Index